# POCKET WORLD ATLAS

IN ASSOCIATION WITH
THE ROYAL GEOGRAPHICAL SOCIETY
WITH THE INSTITUTE OF BRITISH GEOGRAPHERS

# CONTENTS



## WORLD MAPS



## EUROPE



## ASIA




Published in Great Britain in 2012 by Philip's,
a division of Octopus Publishing Group Limited
(www.octopusbooks.co.uk)
Endeavour House, 189 Shaftesbury Avenue,
London WC2H 8JY
An Hachette UK Company (www.hachette.co.uk)





Cartography by Philip's

ISBN 978–1–84907–242–7

A CIP catalogue record for this book is available from the British Library.





Printed in Singapore


Details of other Philip's titles and services can be found on our website at: **www.philips-maps.co.uk**

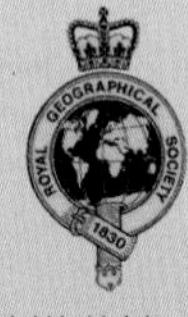

Philip's World Atlases are published in association with The Royal Geographical Society (with The Institute of British Geographers).

The Society was founded in 1830 and given a Royal Charter in 1859 for 'the advancement of geographical science'. Today it is a leading world centre for geographical learning – supporting education, teaching, research and expeditions, and promoting public understanding of the subject.

Further information about the Society and how to join may be found on its website at: **www.rgs.org**

# FLIGHT PATHS

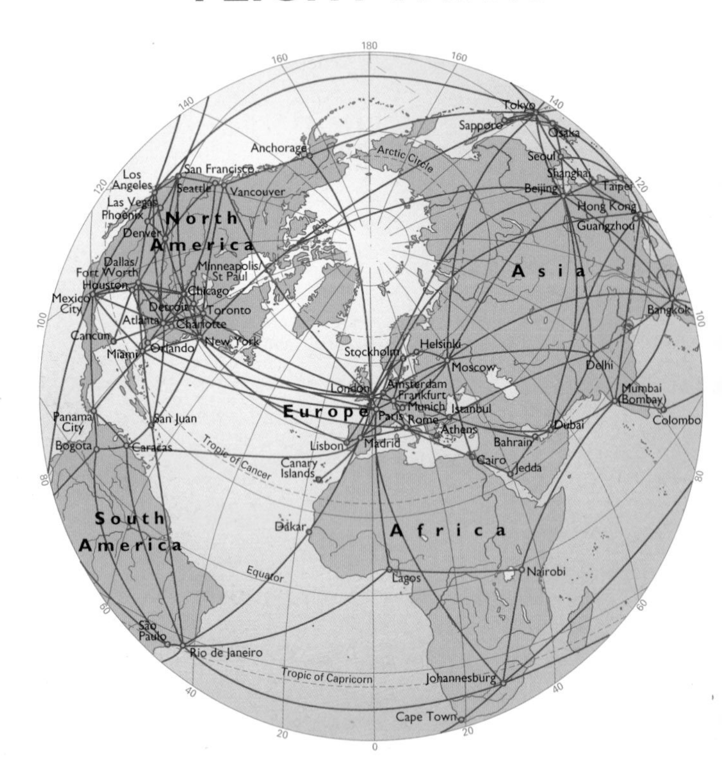


The flight paths shown on the maps above usually follow the shortest, most direct route from A to B, known as the ***great-circle route***. A great circle is any circle that divides the globe into equal halves. Aircraft do not always fly along great-circle routes, however. Lack of search and rescue and emergency landing provisions, together with limits on fuel consumption and minimum flying altitudes, mean that commercial aircraft do not usually fly across Antarctica.

## WORLD'S BUSIEST AIRPORTS

TOTAL NUMBER OF PASSENGERS IN MILLIONS (2011)

| | |
|---|---|
| ATLANTA HARTSFIELD INTL. (ATL) | 92.4 |
| BEIJING CAPITAL INTL. (PEK) | 77.4 |
| LONDON HEATHROW (LHR) | 69.4 |
| CHICAGO O'HARE INTL. (ORD) | 66.5 |
| TOKYO HANEDA (HND) | 62.2 |
| LOS ANGELES INTL. (LAX) | 61.8 |
| PARIS CHARLES DE GAULLE (CDG) | 60.9 |
| DALLAS FORT WORTH INTL. (DFW) | 57.8 |
| FRANKFURT INTL. (FRA) | 56.4 |

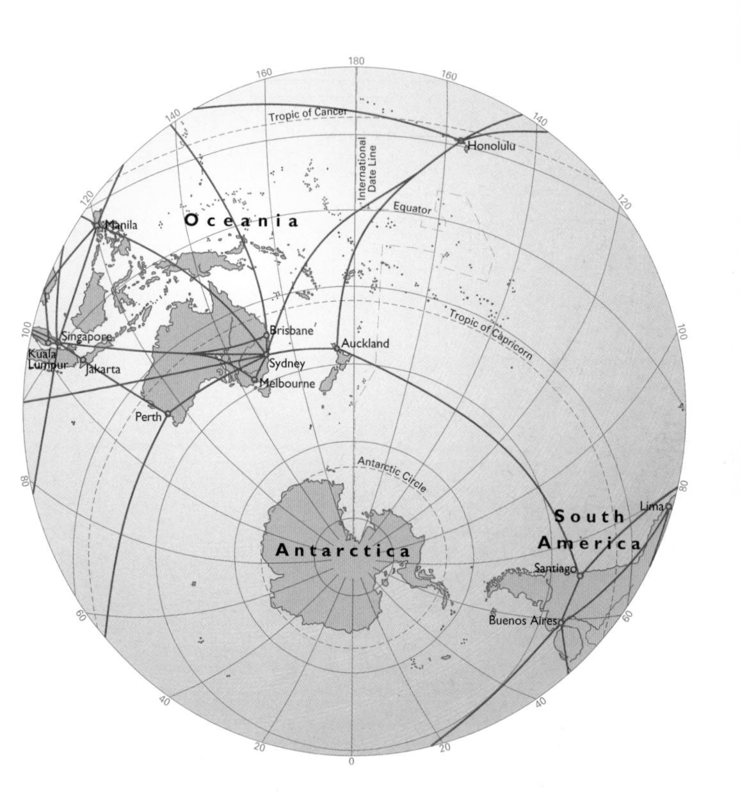


**FLIGHT TIMES FROM LONDON**

| | | |
|---|---|---|
| ATHENS | *4hrs* | *05mins* |
| AUCKLAND | *24hrs* | *20mins* |
| BANGKOK | *14hrs* | *30mins* |
| BUENOS AIRES | *14hrs* | *20mins* |
| HONG KONG | *14hrs* | *10mins* |
| LOS ANGELES | *12hrs* | *00mins* |
| MOSCOW | *3hrs* | *50mins* |
| MUMBAI (BOMBAY) | *11hrs* | *15mins* |
| NEW YORK | *6hrs* | *50mins* |

**FLIGHT TIMES FROM NEW YORK**

| | | |
|---|---|---|
| FRANKFURT | *8hrs* | *35mins* |
| JOHANNESBURG | *17hrs* | *45mins* |
| MEXICO CITY | *5hrs* | *45mins* |
| PARIS | *8hrs* | *15mins* |
| ROME | *9hrs* | *35mins* |
| SANTIAGO | *12hrs* | *55mins* |
| SINGAPORE | *23hrs* | *10mins* |
| TOKYO | *14hrs* | *35mins* |
| VANCOUVER | *7hrs* | *25mins* |

# INTERNATIONAL ORGANIZATIONS

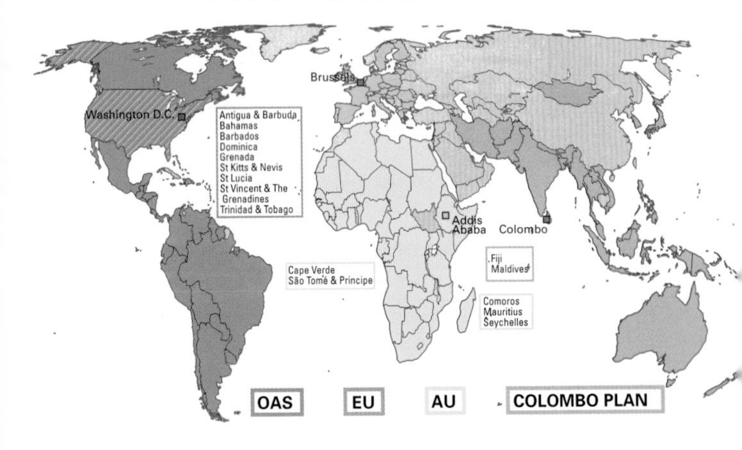


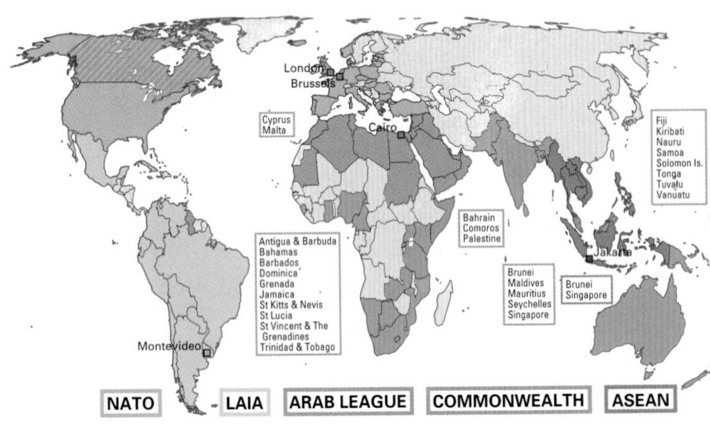


**GLOSSARY OF ACRONYMS**

**ACP** African-Caribbean-Pacific
**APEC** Asia-Pacific Economic Co-operation
**ASEAN** Association of South-east Asian Nations
**AU** African Union
**EU** European Union
**G8** Group of 'Eight'
**LAIA** Latin American Integration Association
**NATO** North Atlantic Treaty Organizatio
**OAS** Organization of American States
**OECD** Organization for Economic Co-operation and Developmer
**OPEC** Oganization for Petroleum Exporting Countries

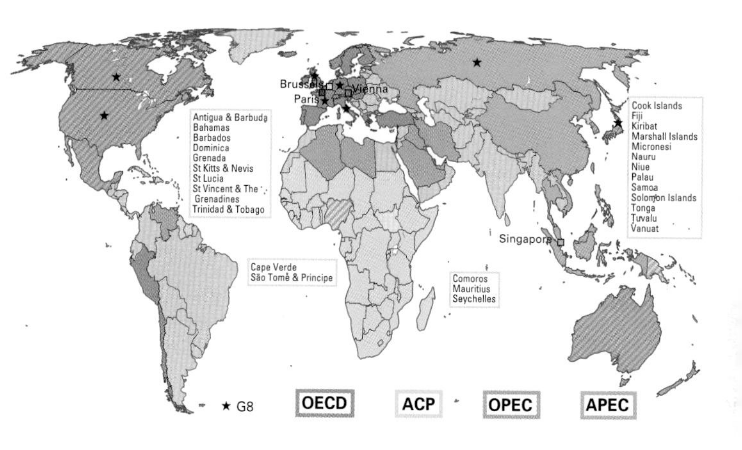


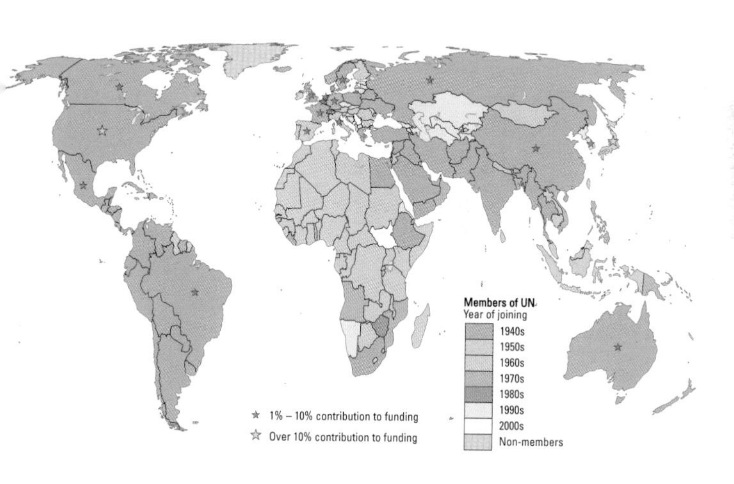


## HE UNITED NATIONS

eated in 1945 to promote peace and co-eration and based in New York, the UN is e world's largest international organization. e UN budget for 2011–12 was nearly S$5.2 billion. Contributions are assessed by e members' ability to pay, with the maximum % of the total (the USA's share), and the minimum 0.001%. The 27-member European Union pays 40% of the budget. From the original 51, membership of the UN has now grown to 193. Recent additions include East Timor, Switzerland and South Sudan. There are only two independent states which are not members – Taiwan and the Vatican City.

# GAZETTEER OF NATIONS

Listed below are the principal countries and territories of the world. The area figures give the total area of land, inland water and ice. The population figures are 2011 estimates where available. The annual income is th Gross Domestic Product per capita in US dollar The figures are the latest available, usually 201 estimates.

### AFGHANISTAN

**AREA** 652,090 sq km [251,772 sq mi]
**POPULATION** 29,835,000
**CAPITAL** Kabul
**GOVERNMENT** Islamic republic
**ANNUAL INCOME** US$1,000
**CURRENCY** Afghani = 100 puls

### ALBANIA

**AREA** 28,748 sq km [11,100 sq mi]
**POPULATION** 2,995,000
**CAPITAL** Tirana
**GOVERNMENT** Multiparty republic
**ANNUAL INCOME** US$7,800
**CURRENCY** Lek = 100 qindars

### ALGERIA

**AREA** 2,381,741 sq km [919,590 sq mi]
**POPULATION** 34,995,000
**CAPITAL** Algiers
**GOVERNMENT** Socialist republic
**ANNUAL INCOME** US$7,200
**CURRENCY** Algerian dinar = 100 centimes

### ANDORRA

**AREA** 468 sq km [181 sq mi]
**POPULATION** 85,000
**CAPITAL** Andorra La Vella
**GOVERNMENT** Parliamentary co-princedom
**ANNUAL INCOME** US$37,200
**CURRENCY** Euro = 100 cents

### ANGOLA

**AREA** 1,246,700 sq km [481,351 sq mi]
**POPULATION** 13,339,000
**CAPITAL** Luanda
**GOVERNMENT** Multiparty republic
**ANNUAL INCOME** US$5,900
**CURRENCY** Kwanza = 100 lwei

### ANTIGUA & BARBUDA

**AREA** 442 sq km [171 sq mi]
**POPULATION** 88,000
**CAPITAL** St John's
**GOVERNMENT** Constitutional monarchy
**ANNUAL INCOME** US$22,100
**CURRENCY** East Caribbean dollar = 100 cents

### ARGENTINA

**AREA** 2,780,400 sq km [1,073,512 sq mi]
**POPULATION** 41,770,000
**CAPITAL** Buenos Aires
**GOVERNMENT** Federal republic
**ANNUAL INCOME** US$17,400
**CURRENCY** Argentine peso = 10,000 australs

### ARMENIA

**AREA** 29,800 sq km [11,506 sq mi]
**POPULATION** 2,968,000
**CAPITAL** Yerevan
**GOVERNMENT** Multiparty republic
**ANNUAL INCOME** US$5,400
**CURRENCY** Dram = 100 couma

### AUSTRALIA

**AREA** 7,741,220 sq km [2,988,885 sq mi]
**POPULATION** 21,767,000
**CAPITAL** Canberra
**GOVERNMENT** Federal constitutional monarchy
**ANNUAL INCOME** US$40,800
**CURRENCY** Australian dollar = 100 cents

### AUSTRIA

**AREA** 83,859 sq km [32,378 sq mi]
**POPULATION** 8,217,000
**CAPITAL** Vienna
**GOVERNMENT** Federal republic
**ANNUAL INCOME** US$41,700
**CURRENCY** Euro = 100 cents

## AZERBAIJAN

**AREA** 86,600 sq km [33,436 sq mi]
**POPULATION** 8,372,000
**CAPITAL** Baku
**GOVERNMENT** Federal multiparty republic
**ANNUAL INCOME** US$10,200
**CURRENCY** Azerbaijani manat = 100 gopik

## BAHAMAS

**AREA** 13,878 sq km [5,358 sq mi]
**POPULATION** 313,000 **CAPITAL** Nassau
**GOVERNMENT** Constitutional parliamentary democracy
**ANNUAL INCOME** US$30,900
**CURRENCY** Bahamian dollar = 100 cents

## BAHRAIN

**AREA** 694 sq km [268 sq mi]
**POPULATION** 1,215,000 **CAPITAL** Manama
**GOVERNMENT** Monarchy (emirate) with a cabinet appointed by the Emir
**ANNUAL INCOME** US$27,300
**CURRENCY** Bahrain dinar = 1,000 fils

## BANGLADESH

**AREA** 143,998 sq km [55,598 sq mi]
**POPULATION** 158,571,000
**CAPITAL** Dhaka
**GOVERNMENT** Multiparty republic
**ANNUAL INCOME** US$1,700
**CURRENCY** Taka = 100 paisas

## BARBADOS

**AREA** 430 sq km [166 sq mi]
**POPULATION** 287,000
**CAPITAL** Bridgetown
**GOVERNMENT** Parliamentary democracy
**ANNUAL INCOME** US$23,600
**CURRENCY** Barbados dollar = 100 cents

## BELARUS

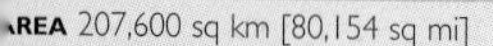

**AREA** 207,600 sq km [80,154 sq mi]
**POPULATION** 9,578,000
**CAPITAL** Minsk
**GOVERNMENT** Multiparty republic
**ANNUAL INCOME** US$14,900
**CURRENCY** Belarusian rouble = 100 kopecks

## BELGIUM

**AREA** 30,528 sq km [11,787 sq mi]
**POPULATION** 10,431,000
**CAPITAL** Brussels
**GOVERNMENT** Federal constitutional monarchy
**ANNUAL INCOME** US$37,600
**CURRENCY** Euro = 100 cents

## BELIZE

**AREA** 22,966 sq km [8,867 sq mi]
**POPULATION** 321,000
**CAPITAL** Belmopan
**GOVERNMENT** Constitutional monarchy
**ANNUAL INCOME** US$8,300
**CURRENCY** Belizean dollar = 100 cents

## BENIN

**AREA** 112,622 sq km [43,483 sq mi]
**POPULATION** 9,325,000
**CAPITAL** Porto-Novo
**GOVERNMENT** Multiparty republic
**ANNUAL INCOME** US$1,500
**CURRENCY** CFA franc = 100 centimes

## BHUTAN

**AREA** 47,000 sq km [18,147 sq mi]
**POPULATION** 708,000
**CAPITAL** Thimphu
**GOVERNMENT** Constitutional monarchy
**ANNUAL INCOME** US$6,000
**CURRENCY** Ngultrum = 100 chetrum

## BOLIVIA

**AREA** 1,098,581 sq km [424,162 sq mi]
**POPULATION** 10,119,000 **CAPITAL** La Paz (seat of government); Sucre (legal capital/seat of judiciary)
**GOVERNMENT** Multiparty republic
**ANNUAL INCOME** US$4,800
**CURRENCY** Boliviano = 100 centavos

## BOSNIA-HERZEGOVINA

**AREA** 51,197 sq km [19,767 sq mi]
**POPULATION** 4,622,000 **CAPITAL** Sarajevo
**GOVERNMENT** Federal republic
**ANNUAL INCOME** US$8,200
**CURRENCY** Convertible marka = 100 convertible pfenniga

## BOTSWANA

**AREA** 581,730 sq km [224,606 sq mi]
**POPULATION** 2,065,000
**CAPITAL** Gaborone
**GOVERNMENT** Multiparty republic
**ANNUAL INCOME** US$16,300
**CURRENCY** Pula = 100 thebe

## BRAZIL

**AREA** 8,514,215 sq km [3,287,338 sq mi]
**POPULATION** 203,430,000
**CAPITAL** Brasília
**GOVERNMENT** Federal republic
**ANNUAL INCOME** US$11,600
**CURRENCY** Real = 100 centavos

## BRUNEI

**AREA** 5,765 sq km [2,226 sq mi]
**POPULATION** 395,000
**CAPITAL** Bandar Seri Begawan
**GOVERNMENT** Constitutional sultanate
**ANNUAL INCOME** US$49,400
**CURRENCY** Bruneian dollar = 100 cents

## BULGARIA

**AREA** 110,912 sq km [42,823 sq mi]
**POPULATION** 7,149,000
**CAPITAL** Sofia
**GOVERNMENT** Multiparty republic
**ANNUAL INCOME** US$13,500
**CURRENCY** Lev = 100 stotinki

## BURKINA FASO

**AREA** 274,000 sq km [105,791 sq mi]
**POPULATION** 16,751,000
**CAPITAL** Ouagadougou
**GOVERNMENT** Multiparty republic
**ANNUAL INCOME** US$1,500
**CURRENCY** CFA franc = 100 centimes

## BURMA (MYANMAR)

**AREA** 676,578 sq km [261,227 sq mi]
**POPULATION** 53,414,000 **CAPITAL** Rangoon (Yangon); Naypyidaw (administrative capital)
**GOVERNMENT** Military regime
**ANNUAL INCOME** US$1,300
**CURRENCY** Kyat = 100 pyas

## BURUNDI

**AREA** 27,834 sq km [10,747 sq mi]
**POPULATION** 10,216,000
**CAPITAL** Bujumbura
**GOVERNMENT** Republic
**ANNUAL INCOME** US$400
**CURRENCY** Burundi franc = 100 centimes

## CAMBODIA

**AREA** 181,035 sq km [69,898 sq mi]
**POPULATION** 14,702,000
**CAPITAL** Phnom Penh
**GOVERNMENT** Constitutional monarchy
**ANNUAL INCOME** US$2,300
**CURRENCY** Riel = 100 sen

## CAMEROON

**AREA** 475,442 sq km [183,568 sq mi]
**POPULATION** 19,711,000
**CAPITAL** Yaoundé
**GOVERNMENT** Multiparty republic
**ANNUAL INCOME** US$2,300
**CURRENCY** CFA franc = 100 centimes

## CANADA

**AREA** 9,970,610 sq km [3,849,653 sq mi]
**POPULATION** 34,031,000 **CAPITAL** Ottawa
**GOVERNMENT** Federal multiparty constitutional monarchy
**ANNUAL INCOME** US$40,300
**CURRENCY** Canadian dollar = 100 cents

## CAPE VERDE

**AREA** 4,033 sq km [1,557 sq mi]
**POPULATION** 516,000
**CAPITAL** Praia
**GOVERNMENT** Multiparty republic
**ANNUAL INCOME** US$4,000
**CURRENCY** Cape Verde escudo = 100 centavo

## CENTRAL AFRICAN REPUBLIC

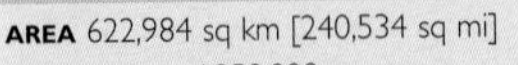

**AREA** 622,984 sq km [240,534 sq mi]
**POPULATION** 4,950,000
**CAPITAL** Bangui
**GOVERNMENT** Multiparty republic
**ANNUAL INCOME** US$800
**CURRENCY** CFA franc = 100 centimes

## CHAD

**AREA** 1,284,000 sq km [495,752 sq mi]
**POPULATION** 10,759,000
**CAPITAL** Ndjamena
**GOVERNMENT** Multiparty republic
**ANNUAL INCOME** US$1,900
**CURRENCY** CFA franc = 100 centimes

## CHILE

**AREA** 756,626 sq km [292,133 sq mi]
**POPULATION** 16,889,000
**CAPITAL** Santiago
**GOVERNMENT** Multiparty republic
**ANNUAL INCOME** US$16,100
**CURRENCY** Chilean peso = 100 centavos

## CHINA

**AREA** 9,596,961 sq km [3,705,387 sq mi]
**POPULATION** 1,336,718,000
**CAPITAL** Beijing
**GOVERNMENT** Single-party Communist republic
**ANNUAL INCOME** US$8,400
**CURRENCY** Renminbi yuan = 10 jiao = 100 fen

## COLOMBIA

**AREA** 1,138,914 sq km [439,735 sq mi]
**POPULATION** 44,726,000
**CAPITAL** Bogotá
**GOVERNMENT** Multiparty republic
**ANNUAL INCOME** US$10,100
**CURRENCY** Colombian peso = 100 centavos

## COMOROS

**AREA** 2,235 sq km [863 sq mi]
**POPULATION** 795,000
**CAPITAL** Moroni
**GOVERNMENT** Multiparty republic
**ANNUAL INCOME** US$1,200
**CURRENCY** CFA franc = 100 centimes

## CONGO

**AREA** 342,000 sq km [132,046 sq mi]
**POPULATION** 4,244,000
**CAPITAL** Brazzaville
**GOVERNMENT** Republic
**ANNUAL INCOME** US$4,600
**CURRENCY** CFA franc = 100 centimes

## CONGO (DEM. REP. OF THE)

**AREA** 2,344,858 sq km [905,350 sq mi]
**POPULATION** 71,713,000
**CAPITAL** Kinshasa
**GOVERNMENT** Single-party republic
**ANNUAL INCOME** US$300
**CURRENCY** Congolese franc = 100 centimes

## COSTA RICA

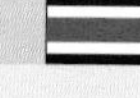

**AREA** 51,100 sq km [19,730 sq mi]
**POPULATION** 4,577,000
**CAPITAL** San José
**GOVERNMENT** Multiparty republic
**ANNUAL INCOME** US$11,500
**CURRENCY** Costa Rican colón = 100 céntimos

## CROATIA

**AREA** 56,538 sq km [21,829 sq mi]
**POPULATION** 4,484,000
**CAPITAL** Zagreb
**GOVERNMENT** Multiparty republic
**ANNUAL INCOME** US$18,300
**CURRENCY** Kuna = 100 lipas

## CUBA

**AREA** 110,861 sq km [42,803 sq mi]
**POPULATION** 11,087,000
**CAPITAL** Havana
**GOVERNMENT** Socialist republic
**ANNUAL INCOME** US$9,900
**CURRENCY** Cuban peso = 100 centavos

## CYPRUS

**AREA** 9,251 sq km [3,572 sq mi]
**POPULATION** 1,120,000
**CAPITAL** Nicosia
**GOVERNMENT** Multiparty republic
**ANNUAL INCOME** US$29,100
**CURRENCY** Euro = 100 cents

## CZECH REPUBLIC

**AREA** 78,866 sq km [30,450 sq mi]
**POPULATION** 10,190,000
**CAPITAL** Prague
**GOVERNMENT** Multiparty republic
**ANNUAL INCOME** US$25,900
**CURRENCY** Czech koruna = 100 haler

## DENMARK

**AREA** 43,094 sq km [16,639 sq mi]
**POPULATION** 5,530,000
**CAPITAL** Copenhagen
**GOVERNMENT** Parliamentary monarchy
**ANNUAL INCOME** US$40,200
**CURRENCY** Danish krone = 100 øre

## DJIBOUTI

**AREA** 23,200 sq km [8,958 sq mi]
**POPULATION** 757,000
**CAPITAL** Djibouti
**GOVERNMENT** Multiparty republic
**ANNUAL INCOME** US$2,600
**CURRENCY** Djiboutian franc = 100 centimes

## DOMINICA

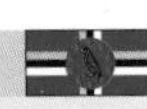

**AREA** 751 sq km [290 sq mi]
**POPULATION** 73,000
**CAPITAL** Roseau
**GOVERNMENT** Parliamentary democracy
**ANNUAL INCOME** US$13,600
**CURRENCY** East Caribbean dollar = 100 cents

## DOMINICAN REPUBLIC

**AREA** 48,511 sq km [18,730 sq mi]
**POPULATION** 9,957,000
**CAPITAL** Santo Domingo
**GOVERNMENT** Multiparty republic
**ANNUAL INCOME** US$9,300
**CURRENCY** Dominican peso = 100 centavos

## EAST TIMOR

**AREA** 14,874 sq km [5,743 sq mi]
**POPULATION** 1,178,000
**CAPITAL** Dili
**GOVERNMENT** Republic
**ANNUAL INCOME** US$3,100
**CURRENCY** US dollar = 100 cents

## ECUADOR

**AREA** 283,561 sq km [109,483 sq mi]
**POPULATION** 15,007,000
**CAPITAL** Quito
**GOVERNMENT** Multiparty republic
**ANNUAL INCOME** US$8,300
**CURRENCY** US dollar = 100 cents

## EGYPT

**AREA** 1,001,449 sq km [386,659 sq mi]
**POPULATION** 82,080,000
**CAPITAL** Cairo
**GOVERNMENT** Republic
**ANNUAL INCOME** US$6,500
**CURRENCY** Egyptian pound = 100 piastres

## EL SALVADOR

**AREA** 21,041 sq km [8,124 sq mi]
**POPULATION** 6,072,000
**CAPITAL** San Salvador
**GOVERNMENT** Republic
**ANNUAL INCOME** US$7,600
**CURRENCY** US dollar = 100 cents

## EQUATORIAL GUINEA

**AREA** 28,051 sq km [10,830 sq mi]
**POPULATION** 668,000
**CAPITAL** Malabo
**GOVERNMENT** Multiparty republic (transitional)
**ANNUAL INCOME** US$19,300
**CURRENCY** CFA franc = 100 centimes

## ERITREA

**AREA** 117,600 sq km [45,405 sq mi]
**POPULATION** 5,939,000
**CAPITAL** Asmara
**GOVERNMENT** Transitional government
**ANNUAL INCOME** US$700
**CURRENCY** Nakfa = 100 cents

## ESTONIA

**AREA** 45,100 sq km [17,413 sq mi]
**POPULATION** 1,283,000
**CAPITAL** Tallinn
**GOVERNMENT** Multiparty republic
**ANNUAL INCOME** US$20,200
**CURRENCY** Euro = 100 cents

## ETHIOPIA

**AREA** 1,104,300 sq km [426,370 sq mi]
**POPULATION** 90,874,000
**CAPITAL** Addis Ababa
**GOVERNMENT** Federation of nine provinces
**ANNUAL INCOME** US$1,100
**CURRENCY** Birr = 100 cents

## FIJI

**AREA** 18,274 sq km [7,056 sq mi]
**POPULATION** 883,000
**CAPITAL** Suva
**GOVERNMENT** Transitional
**ANNUAL INCOME** US$4,600
**CURRENCY** Fijian dollar = 100 cents

## FINLAND

**AREA** 338,145 sq km [130,558 sq mi]
**POPULATION** 5,259,000
**CAPITAL** Helsinki
**GOVERNMENT** Multiparty republic
**ANNUAL INCOME** US$38,300
**CURRENCY** Euro = 100 cents

## FRANCE

**AREA** 551,500 sq km [212,934 sq mi]
**POPULATION** 65,312,000
**CAPITAL** Paris
**GOVERNMENT** Multiparty republic
**ANNUAL INCOME** US$35,000
**CURRENCY** Euro = 100 cents

## FRENCH GUIANA

**AREA** 90,000 sq km [34,749 sq mi]
**POPULATION** 229,000
**CAPITAL** Cayenne
**GOVERNMENT** Overseas department of France
**ANNUAL INCOME** US$8,300
**CURRENCY** Euro = 100 cents

## FRENCH POLYNESIA

**AREA** 4,000 sq km [1,544 sq mi]
**POPULATION** 295,000
**CAPITAL** Papeete
**GOVERNMENT** French overseas territory
**ANNUAL INCOME** US$18,000
**CURRENCY** French Pacific franc = 100 cents

## GABON

**AREA** 267,668 sq km [103,347 sq mi]
**POPULATION** 1,577,000
**CAPITAL** Libreville
**GOVERNMENT** Multiparty republic
**ANNUAL INCOME** US$16,000
**CURRENCY** CFA franc = 100 centimes

## GAMBIA, THE

**AREA** 11,295 sq km [4,361 sq mi]
**POPULATION** 1,798,000
**CAPITAL** Banjul
**GOVERNMENT** Republic
**ANNUAL INCOME** US$2,100
**CURRENCY** Dalasi = 100 butut

## GEORGIA

**AREA** 69,700 sq km [26,911 sq mi]
**POPULATION** 4,586,000
**CAPITAL** Tbilisi
**GOVERNMENT** Multiparty republic
**ANNUAL INCOME** US$5,400
**CURRENCY** Lari = 100 tetri

## GERMANY

**AREA** 357,022 sq km [137,846 sq mi]
**POPULATION** 81,472,000
**CAPITAL** Berlin
**GOVERNMENT** Federal multiparty republic
**ANNUAL INCOME** US$37,900
**CURRENCY** Euro = 100 cents

## GHANA

**AREA** 238,533 sq km [92,098 sq mi]
**POPULATION** 24,791,000
**CAPITAL** Accra
**GOVERNMENT** Republic
**ANNUAL INCOME** US$3,100
**CURRENCY** Cedi = 100 pesewas

## GREECE

**AREA** 131,957 sq km [50,949 sq mi]
**POPULATION** 10,760,000
**CAPITAL** Athens
**GOVERNMENT** Multiparty republic
**ANNUAL INCOME** US$27,600
**CURRENCY** Euro = 100 cents

## GREENLAND

**AREA** 2,175,600 sq km [838,999 sq mi]
**POPULATION** 58,000 **CAPITAL** Nuuk
**GOVERNMENT** Self-governing overseas administrative division of Denmark
**ANNUAL INCOME** US$37,400
**CURRENCY** Danish krone = 100 øre

## GRENADA

**AREA** 344 sq km [133 sq mi]
**POPULATION** 108,000
**CAPITAL** St George's
**GOVERNMENT** Constitutional monarchy
**ANNUAL INCOME** US$13,300
**CURRENCY** East Caribbean dollar = 100 cents

## GUADELOUPE

**AREA** 1,705 sq km [658 sq mi]
**POPULATION** 452,000
**CAPITAL** Basse-Terre
**GOVERNMENT** French overseas territory
**ANNUAL INCOME** US$7,900
**CURRENCY** Euro = 100 cents

## GUATEMALA

**AREA** 108,889 sq km [42,042 sq mi]
**POPULATION** 13,824,000
**CAPITAL** Guatemala City
**GOVERNMENT** Republic
**ANNUAL INCOME** US$5,000
**CURRENCY** US dollar; Quetzal = 100 centavos

## GUINEA

**AREA** 245,857 sq km [94,925 sq mi]
**POPULATION** 10,601,000
**CAPITAL** Conakry
**GOVERNMENT** Multiparty republic
**ANNUAL INCOME** US$1,100
**CURRENCY** Guinean franc = 100 cauris

## GUINEA-BISSAU

**AREA** 36,125 sq km [13,948 sq mi]
**POPULATION** 1,597,000
**CAPITAL** Bissau
**GOVERNMENT** 'Interim' government
**ANNUAL INCOME** US$1,100
**CURRENCY** CFA franc = 100 centimes

## GUYANA

**AREA** 214,969 sq km [83,000 sq mi]
**POPULATION** 775,000
**CAPITAL** Georgetown
**GOVERNMENT** Multiparty republic
**ANNUAL INCOME** US$7,500
**CURRENCY** Guyanese dollar = 100 cents

## HAITI

**AREA** 27,750 sq km [10,714 sq mi]
**POPULATION** 9,720,000
**CAPITAL** Port-au-Prince
**GOVERNMENT** Multiparty republic
**ANNUAL INCOME** US$1,200
**CURRENCY** Gourde = 100 centimes

## HONDURAS

**AREA** 112,088 sq km [43,277 sq mi]
**POPULATION** 8,144,000
**CAPITAL** Tegucigalpa
**GOVERNMENT** Republic
**ANNUAL INCOME** US$4,300
**CURRENCY** Honduran lempira = 100 centavos

## HUNGARY

**AREA** 93,032 sq km [35,920 sq mi]
**POPULATION** 9,976,000
**CAPITAL** Budapest
**GOVERNMENT** Multiparty republic
**ANNUAL INCOME** US$19,600
**CURRENCY** Forint = 100 fillér

## ICELAND

**AREA** 103,000 sq km [39,768 sq mi]
**POPULATION** 311,000
**CAPITAL** Reykjavik
**GOVERNMENT** Multiparty republic
**ANNUAL INCOME** US$38,000
**CURRENCY** Icelandic króna = 100 aurar

## INDIA

**AREA** 3,287,263 sq km [1,269,212 sq mi]
**POPULATION** 1,189,173,000
**CAPITAL** New Delhi
**GOVERNMENT** Multiparty federal republic
**ANNUAL INCOME** US$3,700
**CURRENCY** Indian rupee = 100 paisa

## INDONESIA

**AREA** 1,904,569 sq km [735,354 sq mi]
**POPULATION** 245,613,000
**CAPITAL** Jakarta
**GOVERNMENT** Multiparty republic
**ANNUAL INCOME** US$4,700
**CURRENCY** Indonesian rupiah = 100 sen

## IRAN

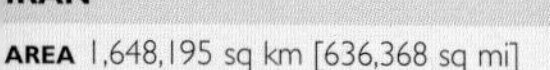

**AREA** 1,648,195 sq km [636,368 sq mi]
**POPULATION** 77,891,000
**CAPITAL** Tehran
**GOVERNMENT** Islamic republic
**ANNUAL INCOME** US$12,200
**CURRENCY** Iranian rial = 100 dinars

## IRAQ

**AREA** 438,317 sq km [169,235 sq mi]
**POPULATION** 30,400,000
**CAPITAL** Baghdad
**GOVERNMENT** Parliamentary democracy
**ANNUAL INCOME** US$3,900
**CURRENCY** New Iraqi dinar

## IRELAND

**AREA** 70,273 sq km [27,132 sq mi]
**POPULATION** 4,671,000
**CAPITAL** Dublin
**GOVERNMENT** Multiparty republic
**ANNUAL INCOME** US$39,500
**CURRENCY** Euro = 100 cents

## ISRAEL

**AREA** 20,600 sq km [7,954 sq mi]
**POPULATION** 7,473,000
**CAPITAL** Jerusalem
**GOVERNMENT** Multiparty republic
**ANNUAL INCOME** US$31,000
**CURRENCY** New Israeli shekel = 100 agorat

## ITALY

**AREA** 301,318 sq km [116,339 sq mi]
**POPULATION** 61,017,000
**CAPITAL** Rome
**GOVERNMENT** Multiparty republic
**ANNUAL INCOME** US$30,100
**CURRENCY** Euro = 100 cents

## IVORY COAST (CÔTE D'IVOIRE)

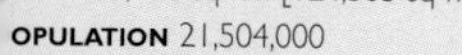

**AREA** 322,463 sq km [124,503 sq mi]
**POPULATION** 21,504,000
**CAPITAL** Yamoussoukro
**GOVERNMENT** Multiparty republic
**ANNUAL INCOME** US$1,600
**CURRENCY** CFA franc = 100 centimes

## JAMAICA

**AREA** 10,991 sq km [4,244 sq mi]
**POPULATION** 2,868,000
**CAPITAL** Kingston
**GOVERNMENT** Constitutional monarchy
**ANNUAL INCOME** US$9,000
**CURRENCY** Jamaican dollar = 100 cents

## JAPAN

**AREA** 377,829 sq km [145,880 sq mi]
**POPULATION** 126,476,000
**CAPITAL** Tokyo
**GOVERNMENT** Constitutional monarchy
**ANNUAL INCOME** US$34,300
**CURRENCY** Yen = 100 sen

## JORDAN

**AREA** 89,342 sq km [34,495 sq mi]
**POPULATION** 6,508,000
**CAPITAL** Amman
**GOVERNMENT** Constitutional monarchy
**ANNUAL INCOME** US$5,900
**CURRENCY** Jordanian dinar = 1,000 fils

## KAZAKHSTAN

**AREA** 2,724,900 sq km [1,052,084 sq mi]
**POPULATION** 15,522,000
**CAPITAL** Astana
**GOVERNMENT** Multiparty republic
**ANNUAL INCOME** US$13,000
**CURRENCY** Tenge = 100 tiyn

## KENYA

**AREA** 580,367 sq km [224,080 sq mi]
**POPULATION** 41,071,000
**CAPITAL** Nairobi
**GOVERNMENT** Multiparty republic
**ANNUAL INCOME** US$1,700
**CURRENCY** Kenyan shilling = 100 cents

## KIRIBATI

**AREA** 726 sq km [280 sq mi]
**POPULATION** 101,000
**CAPITAL** Tarawa
**GOVERNMENT** Republic
**ANNUAL INCOME** US$6,200
**CURRENCY** Australian dollar = 100 cents

## KOREA, NORTH

**AREA** 120,538 sq km [46,540 sq mi]
**POPULATION** 24,457,000
**CAPITAL** Pyŏngyang
**GOVERNMENT** Single-party people's republic
**ANNUAL INCOME** US$1,800
**CURRENCY** North Korean won = 100 chon

## KOREA, SOUTH

**AREA** 99,268 sq km [38,327 sq mi]
**POPULATION** 48,755,000
**CAPITAL** Seoul
**GOVERNMENT** Multiparty republic
**ANNUAL INCOME** US$31,700
**CURRENCY** South Korean won = 100 chon

## KOSOVO

**AREA** 10,887 sq km [4,203 sq mi]
**POPULATION** 1,826,000
**CAPITAL** Pristina
**GOVERNMENT** Republic
**ANNUAL INCOME** US$6,500
**CURRENCY** Euro = 100 cents

## KUWAIT

**AREA** 17,818 sq km [6,880 sq mi]
**POPULATION** 2,596,000
**CAPITAL** Kuwait City
**GOVERNMENT** Constitutional monarchy
**ANNUAL INCOME** US$40,700
**CURRENCY** Kuwaiti dinar = 1,000 fils

## KYRGYZSTAN

**AREA** 199,900 sq km [77,181 sq mi]
**POPULATION** 5,587,000
**CAPITAL** Bishkek
**GOVERNMENT** Multiparty republic
**ANNUAL INCOME** US$2,400
**CURRENCY** Kyrgyzstani som = 100 tyiyn

## LAOS

**AREA** 236,800 sq km [91,428 sq mi]
**POPULATION** 6,477,000
**CAPITAL** Vientiane
**GOVERNMENT** Single-party republic
**ANNUAL INCOME** US$2,700
**CURRENCY** Kip = 100 at

## LATVIA

**AREA** 64,600 sq km [24,942 sq mi]
**POPULATION** 2,205,000
**CAPITAL** Riga
**GOVERNMENT** Multiparty republic
**ANNUAL INCOME** US$15,400
**CURRENCY** Latvian lat = 10 santimi

## LEBANON

**AREA** 10,400 sq km [4,015 sq mi]
**POPULATION** 4,143,000
**CAPITAL** Beirut
**GOVERNMENT** Multiparty republic
**ANNUAL INCOME** US$15,600
**CURRENCY** Lebanese pound = 100 piastres

## LESOTHO

**AREA** 30,355 sq km [11,720 sq mi]
**POPULATION** 1,925,000
**CAPITAL** Maseru
**GOVERNMENT** Constitutional monarchy
**ANNUAL INCOME** US$1,400
**CURRENCY** Loti = 100 lisente

## LIBERIA

**AREA** 111,369 sq km [43,000 sq mi]
**POPULATION** 3,787,000
**CAPITAL** Monrovia
**GOVERNMENT** Multiparty republic
**ANNUAL INCOME** US$400
**CURRENCY** Liberian dollar = 100 cents

## LIBYA

**AREA** 1,759,540 sq km [679,358 sq mi]
**POPULATION** 6,598,000
**CAPITAL** Tripoli
**GOVERNMENT** Transitional
**ANNUAL INCOME** US$14,100
**CURRENCY** Libyan dinar = 1,000 dirhams

## LIECHTENSTEIN

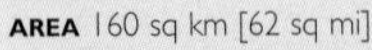

**AREA** 160 sq km [62 sq mi]
**POPULATION** 35,000 **CAPITAL** Vaduz
**GOVERNMENT** Hereditary constitutional monarchy
**ANNUAL INCOME** US$141,100
**CURRENCY** Swiss franc = 100 centimes

## LITHUANIA

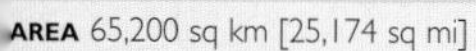

**AREA** 65,200 sq km [25,174 sq mi]
**POPULATION** 3,536,000
**CAPITAL** Vilnius
**GOVERNMENT** Multiparty republic
**ANNUAL INCOME** US$18,700
**CURRENCY** Litas = 100 centai

## LUXEMBOURG

**AREA** 2,586 sq km [998 sq mi]
**POPULATION** 503,000 **CAPITAL** Luxembourg
**GOVERNMENT** Constitutional monarchy (Grand Duchy)
**ANNUAL INCOME** US$84,700
**CURRENCY** Euro = 100 cents

## MACEDONIA (FYROM)

**AREA** 25,713 sq km [9,928 sq mi]
**POPULATION** 2,077,000
**CAPITAL** Skopje
**GOVERNMENT** Multiparty republic
**ANNUAL INCOME** US$10,400
**CURRENCY** Macedonian denar = 100 paras

## MADAGASCAR

**AREA** 587,041 sq km [226,657 sq mi]
**POPULATION** 21,926,000
**CAPITAL** Antananarivo
**GOVERNMENT** Republic
**ANNUAL INCOME** US$900
**CURRENCY** Malagasy franc = 100 centimes

## MALAWI

**AREA** 118,484 sq km [45,747 sq mi]
**POPULATION** 15,879,000
**CAPITAL** Lilongwe
**GOVERNMENT** Multiparty republic
**ANNUAL INCOME** US$900
**CURRENCY** Malawian kwacha = 100 tambala

## MALAYSIA

**AREA** 329,758 sq km [127,320 sq mi]
**POPULATION** 28,729,000 **CAPITAL** Kuala Lumpur; Putrajaya (administrative capital awaiting completion)
**GOVERNMENT** Federal constitutional monarchy
**ANNUAL INCOME** US$15,600
**CURRENCY** Ringgit = 100 cents

## MALDIVES

**AREA** 298 sq km [115 sq mi]
**POPULATION** 395,000
**CAPITAL** Malé
**GOVERNMENT** Republic
**ANNUAL INCOME** US$8,400
**CURRENCY** Rufiyaa = 100 laari

## MALI

**AREA** 1,240,192 sq km [478,838 sq mi]
**POPULATION** 14,160,000
**CAPITAL** Bamako
**GOVERNMENT** Multiparty republic
**ANNUAL INCOME** US$1,300
**CURRENCY** CFA franc = 100 centimes

## MALTA

**AREA** 316 sq km [122 sq mi]
**POPULATION** 408,000
**CAPITAL** Valletta
**GOVERNMENT** Multiparty republic
**ANNUAL INCOME** US$25,700
**CURRENCY** Euro = 100 cents

## MARSHALL ISLANDS

**AREA** 181 sq km [70 sq mi]
**POPULATION** 67,000 **CAPITAL** Majuro
**GOVERNMENT** Constitutional government in free association with the US
**ANNUAL INCOME** US$2,500
**CURRENCY** US dollar = 100 cents

## MARTINIQUE

**AREA** 1,102 sq km [425 sq mi]
**POPULATION** 397,000
**CAPITAL** Fort-de-France
**GOVERNMENT** Overseas department of France
**ANNUAL INCOME** US$14,400
**CURRENCY** Euro = 100 cents

## MAURITANIA

**AREA** 1,025,520 sq km [395,953 sq mi]
**POPULATION** 3,282,000
**CAPITAL** Nouakchott
**GOVERNMENT** Multiparty Islamic republic
**ANNUAL INCOME** US$2,200
**CURRENCY** Ouguiya = 5 khoums

## MAURITIUS

**AREA** 2,040 sq km [788 sq mi]
**POPULATION** 1,304,000
**CAPITAL** Port Louis
**GOVERNMENT** Multiparty democracy
**ANNUAL INCOME** US$15,000
**CURRENCY** Mauritian rupee = 100 cents

## MEXICO

**AREA** 1,958,201 sq km [756,061 sq mi]
**POPULATION** 113,714,000
**CAPITAL** Mexico City
**GOVERNMENT** Federal republic
**ANNUAL INCOME** US$15,100
**CURRENCY** Mexican peso = 100 centavos

## MICRONESIA, FED. STATES OF

**AREA** 702 sq km [271 sq mi]
**POPULATION** 107,000 **CAPITAL** Palikir
**GOVERNMENT** Constitutional government in free association with the US
**ANNUAL INCOME** US$2,200
**CURRENCY** US dollar = 100 cents

## MOLDOVA

**AREA** 33,851 sq km [13,070 sq mi]
**POPULATION** 4,314,000
**CAPITAL** Kishinev
**GOVERNMENT** Multiparty republic
**ANNUAL INCOME** US$3,400
**CURRENCY** Moldovan leu = 100 bani

## MONACO

**AREA** 1 sq km [0.4 sq mi]
**POPULATION** 31,000
**CAPITAL** Monaco
**GOVERNMENT** Constitutional monarchy
**ANNUAL INCOME** US$63,400
**CURRENCY** Euro = 100 cents

## MONGOLIA

**AREA** 1,566,500 sq km [604,826 sq mi]
**POPULATION** 3,133,000
**CAPITAL** Ulan Bator
**GOVERNMENT** Multiparty republic
**ANNUAL INCOME** US$4,500
**CURRENCY** Tugrik = 100 möngös

## MONTENEGRO

**AREA** 14,026 sq km [5,415 sq mi]
**POPULATION** 662,000
**CAPITAL** Podgorica
**GOVERNMENT** Republic
**ANNUAL INCOME** US$11,200
**CURRENCY** Euro = 100 cents

## MOROCCO

**AREA** 446,550 sq km [172,413 sq mi]
**POPULATION** 31,968,000
**CAPITAL** Rabat
**GOVERNMENT** Constitutional monarchy
**ANNUAL INCOME** US$5,100
**CURRENCY** Moroccan dirham = 100 centimes

## MOZAMBIQUE

**AREA** 801,590 sq km [309,494 sq mi]
**POPULATION** 22,949,000
**CAPITAL** Maputo
**GOVERNMENT** Multiparty republic
**ANNUAL INCOME** US$1,100
**CURRENCY** Metical = 100 centavos

## NAMIBIA

**AREA** 824,292 sq km [318,259 sq mi]
**POPULATION** 2,148,000
**CAPITAL** Windhoek
**GOVERNMENT** Multiparty republic
**ANNUAL INCOME** US$7,300
**CURRENCY** Namibian dollar = 100 cents

## NAURU

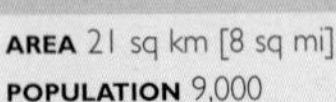

**AREA** 21 sq km [8 sq mi]
**POPULATION** 9,000
**CAPITAL** Yaren
**GOVERNMENT** Republic
**ANNUAL INCOME** US$5,000
**CURRENCY** Australian dollar = 100 cents

## NEPAL

**AREA** 147,181 sq km [56,827 sq mi]
**POPULATION** 29,392,000
**CAPITAL** Katmandu
**GOVERNMENT** Multiparty republic
**ANNUAL INCOME** US$1,300
**CURRENCY** Nepalese rupee = 100 paisa

## NETHERLANDS

**AREA** 41,526 sq km [16,033 sq mi]
**POPULATION** 16,847,000 **CAPITAL** Amsterdam; The Hague (seat of government)
**GOVERNMENT** Constitutional monarchy
**ANNUAL INCOME** US$42,300
**CURRENCY** Euro = 100 cents

## NEW CALEDONIA

**AREA** 18,575 sq km [7,172 sq mi]
**POPULATION** 256,000
**CAPITAL** Nouméa
**GOVERNMENT** French overseas territory
**ANNUAL INCOME** US$15,000
**CURRENCY** French Pacific franc = 100 cents

## NEW ZEALAND

**AREA** 270,534 sq km [104,453 sq mi]
**POPULATION** 4,290,000
**CAPITAL** Wellington
**GOVERNMENT** Constitutional monarchy
**ANNUAL INCOME** US$27,900
**CURRENCY** New Zealand dollar = 100 cents

## NICARAGUA

**AREA** 130,000 sq km [50,193 sq mi]
**POPULATION** 5,666,000 **CAPITAL** Managua
**GOVERNMENT** Multiparty republic
**ANNUAL INCOME** US$3,200
**CURRENCY** Córdoba oro (gold córdoba) = 100 centavos

## NIGER

**AREA** 1,267,000 sq km [489,189 sq mi]
**POPULATION** 16,469,000
**CAPITAL** Niamey
**GOVERNMENT** Multiparty republic
**ANNUAL INCOME** US$800
**CURRENCY** CFA franc = 100 centimes

## NIGERIA

**AREA** 923,768 sq km [356,667 sq mi]
**POPULATION** 155,216,000
**CAPITAL** Abuja
**GOVERNMENT** Federal multiparty republic
**ANNUAL INCOME** US$2,600
**CURRENCY** Naira = 100 kobo

## NORWAY

**AREA** 323,877 sq km [125,049 sq mi]
**POPULATION** 4,692,000
**CAPITAL** Oslo
**GOVERNMENT** Constitutional monarchy
**ANNUAL INCOME** US$53,300
**CURRENCY** Norwegian krone = 100 ore

## OMAN

**AREA** 309,500 sq km [119,498 sq mi]
**POPULATION** 3,028,000 **CAPITAL** Muscat
**GOVERNMENT** Monarchy with consultative council
**ANNUAL INCOME** US$26,200
**CURRENCY** Omani rial = 100 baizas

## PAKISTAN

**AREA** 796,095 sq km [307,372 sq mi]
**POPULATION** 187,343,000
**CAPITAL** Islamabad
**GOVERNMENT** Federal republic
**ANNUAL INCOME** US$2,800
**CURRENCY** Pakistani rupee = 100 paisa

## PANAMA

**AREA** 75,517 sq km [29,157 sq mi]
**POPULATION** 3,460,000
**CAPITAL** Panamá
**GOVERNMENT** Multiparty republic
**ANNUAL INCOME** US$13,600
**CURRENCY** US dollar; Balboa = 100 centésimos

## PAPUA NEW GUINEA

**AREA** 462,840 sq km [178,703 sq mi]
**POPULATION** 6,188,000
**CAPITAL** Port Moresby
**GOVERNMENT** Constitutional monarchy
**ANNUAL INCOME** US$2,500
**CURRENCY** Kina = 100 toea

## PARAGUAY

**AREA** 406,752 sq km [157,047 sq mi]
**POPULATION** 6,459,000
**CAPITAL** Asunción
**GOVERNMENT** Multiparty republic
**ANNUAL INCOME** US$5,500
**CURRENCY** Guaraní = 100 céntimos

## PERU

**AREA** 1,285,216 sq km [496,222 sq mi]
**POPULATION** 29,249,000
**CAPITAL** Lima
**GOVERNMENT** Constitutional republic
**ANNUAL INCOME** US$10,000
**CURRENCY** New sol = 100 centavos

## PHILIPPINES

**AREA** 300,000 sq km [115,830 sq mi]
**POPULATION** 101,834,000
**CAPITAL** Manila
**GOVERNMENT** Multiparty republic
**ANNUAL INCOME** US$4,100
**CURRENCY** Philippine peso = 100 centavos

## POLAND

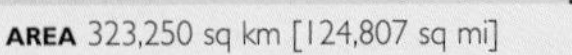

**AREA** 323,250 sq km [124,807 sq mi]
**POPULATION** 38,442,000
**CAPITAL** Warsaw
**GOVERNMENT** Multiparty republic
**ANNUAL INCOME** US$20,100
**CURRENCY** Zloty = 100 groszy

## PORTUGAL

**AREA** 88,797 sq km [34,285 sq mi]
**POPULATION** 10,760,000
**CAPITAL** Lisbon
**GOVERNMENT** Multiparty republic
**ANNUAL INCOME** US$23,200
**CURRENCY** Euro = 100 cents

## PUERTO RICO

**AREA** 8,875 sq km [3,427 sq mi]
**POPULATION** 3,989,000
**CAPITAL** San Juan
**GOVERNMENT** Commonwealth of the US
**ANNUAL INCOME** US$16,300
**CURRENCY** US dollar = 100 cents

## QATAR

**AREA** 11,000 sq km [4,247 sq mi]
**POPULATION** 848,000
**CAPITAL** Doha
**GOVERNMENT** Constitutional absolute monarchy
**ANNUAL INCOME** US$102,700
**CURRENCY** Qatari riyal = 100 dirhams

## RÉUNION

**AREA** 2,510 sq km [969 sq mi]
**POPULATION** 839,000
**CAPITAL** St-Denis
**GOVERNMENT** Overseas department of France
**ANNUAL INCOME** US$6,200
**CURRENCY** Euro = 100 cents

## ROMANIA

**AREA** 238,391 sq km [92,043 sq mi]
**POPULATION** 21,905,000
**CAPITAL** Bucharest
**GOVERNMENT** Multiparty republic
**ANNUAL INCOME** US$12,300
**CURRENCY** Leu = 100 bani

## RUSSIA

**AREA** 17,075,400 sq km [6,592,812 sq mi]
**POPULATION** 138,740,000
**CAPITAL** Moscow
**GOVERNMENT** Federal multiparty republic
**ANNUAL INCOME** US$16,700
**CURRENCY** Russian ruble = 100 kopeks

## RWANDA

**AREA** 26,338 sq km [10,169 sq mi]
**POPULATION** 11,370,000
**CAPITAL** Kigali
**GOVERNMENT** Republic
**ANNUAL INCOME** US$1,300
**CURRENCY** Rwandan franc = 100 centimes

## ST KITTS & NEVIS

**AREA** 261 sq km [101 sq mi]
**POPULATION** 50,000
**CAPITAL** Basseterre
**GOVERNMENT** Constitutional monarchy
**ANNUAL INCOME** US$16,400
**CURRENCY** East Caribbean dollar = 100 cents

## ST LUCIA

**AREA** 539 sq km [208 sq mi]
**POPULATION** 162,000
**CAPITAL** Castries
**GOVERNMENT** Parliamentary democracy
**ANNUAL INCOME** US$12,900
**CURRENCY** East Caribbean dollar = 100 cents

## ST VINCENT & THE GRENADINES

**AREA** 388 sq km [150 sq mi]
**POPULATION** 104,000
**CAPITAL** Kingstown
**GOVERNMENT** Parliamentary democracy
**ANNUAL INCOME** US$11,700
**CURRENCY** East Caribbean dollar = 100 cents

## SAMOA

**AREA** 2,831 sq km [1,093 sq mi]
**POPULATION** 193,000
**CAPITAL** Apia
**GOVERNMENT** Parliamentary democracy
**ANNUAL INCOME** US$6,000
**CURRENCY** Samoan dollar = 100 sene

## SAN MARINO

**AREA** 61 sq km [24 sq mi]
**POPULATION** 32,000
**CAPITAL** San Marino
**GOVERNMENT** Independent republic
**ANNUAL INCOME** US$36,200
**CURRENCY** Euro = 100 cents

## SÃO TOMÉ & PRÍNCIPE

**AREA** 964 sq km [372 sq mi]
**POPULATION** 180,000
**CAPITAL** São Tomé
**GOVERNMENT** Republic
**ANNUAL INCOME** US$2,000
**CURRENCY** Dobra = 100 cêntimos

## SAUDI ARABIA

**AREA** 2,149,690 sq km [829,995 sq mi]
**POPULATION** 26,132,000 **CAPITAL** Riyadh
**GOVERNMENT** Absolute monarchy with consultative assembly
**ANNUAL INCOME** US$24,000
**CURRENCY** Saudi riyal = 100 halalas

## SENEGAL

**AREA** 196,722 sq km [75,954 sq mi]
**POPULATION** 12,644,000
**CAPITAL** Dakar
**GOVERNMENT** Multiparty republic
**ANNUAL INCOME** US$1,900
**CURRENCY** CFA franc = 100 centimes

## SERBIA

**AREA** 77,474 sq km [29,913 sq mi]
**POPULATION** 7,311,000
**CAPITAL** Belgrade
**GOVERNMENT** Republic
**ANNUAL INCOME** US$10,700
**CURRENCY** New dinar = 100 paras

## SEYCHELLES

**AREA** 455 sq km [176 sq mi]
**POPULATION** 89,000
**CAPITAL** Victoria
**GOVERNMENT** Multiparty republic
**ANNUAL INCOME** US$24,700
**CURRENCY** Seychelles rupee = 100 cents

## SIERRA LEONE

**AREA** 71,740 sq km [27,699 sq mi]
**POPULATION** 5,364,000
**CAPITAL** Freetown
**GOVERNMENT** Single-party republic
**ANNUAL INCOME** US$800
**CURRENCY** Leone = 100 cents

## SINGAPORE

**AREA** 683 sq km [264 sq mi]
**POPULATION** 4,741,000
**CAPITAL** Singapore City
**GOVERNMENT** Multiparty republic
**ANNUAL INCOME** US$59,900
**CURRENCY** Singapore dollar = 100 cents

## SLOVAK REPUBLIC

**AREA** 49,012 sq km [18,924 sq mi]
**POPULATION** 5,477,000
**CAPITAL** Bratislava
**GOVERNMENT** Multiparty republic
**ANNUAL INCOME** US$23,400
**CURRENCY** Euro = 100 cents

## SLOVENIA

**AREA** 20,256 sq km [7,821 sq mi]
**POPULATION** 2,003,000
**CAPITAL** Ljubljana
**GOVERNMENT** Multiparty republic
**ANNUAL INCOME** US$29,100
**CURRENCY** Euro = 100 cents

## SOLOMON ISLANDS

**AREA** 28,896 sq km [11,157 sq mi]
**POPULATION** 572,000
**CAPITAL** Honiara
**GOVERNMENT** Parliamentary democracy
**ANNUAL INCOME** US$3,300
**CURRENCY** Solomon Islands dollar = 100 cents

## SOMALIA

**AREA** 637,657 sq km [246,199 sq mi]
**POPULATION** 9,926,000 **CAPITAL** Mogadishu
**GOVERNMENT** Single-party republic, military dominated
**ANNUAL INCOME** US$600
**CURRENCY** Somali shilling = 100 cents

## SOUTH AFRICA

**AREA** 1,221,037 sq km [471,442 sq mi]
**POPULATION** 49,004,000 **CAPITAL** Cape Town (legislative); Pretoria/Tshwane (administrative); Bloemfontein (judiciary) **GOVERNMENT** Multiparty republic **ANNUAL INCOME** US$11,000
**CURRENCY** Rand = 100 cents

## SPAIN

**AREA** 497,548 sq km [192,103 sq mi]
**POPULATION** 46,755,000
**CAPITAL** Madrid
**GOVERNMENT** Constitutional monarchy
**ANNUAL INCOME** US$30,600
**CURRENCY** Euro = 100 cents

## SRI LANKA

**AREA** 65,610 sq km [25,332 sq mi]
**POPULATION** 21,284,000
**CAPITAL** Colombo
**GOVERNMENT** Multiparty republic
**ANNUAL INCOME** US$5,600
**CURRENCY** Sri Lankan rupee = 100 cents

## SUDAN

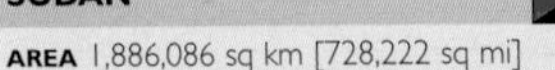

**AREA** 1,886,086 sq km [728,222 sq mi]
**POPULATION** 35,680,000 **CAPITAL** Khartoum
**GOVERNMENT** Federal presidential democratic republic
**ANNUAL INCOME** US$3,000
**CURRENCY** Sudanese pound

## SUDAN, SOUTH

**AREA** 619,745 sq km [239,285 sq mi]
**POPULATION** 8,260,000
**CAPITAL** Juba
**GOVERNMENT** Transitional
**ANNUAL INCOME** US$1,500
**CURRENCY** Sudanese pound

## SURINAME

**AREA** 163,265 sq km [63,037 sq mi]
**POPULATION** 492,000
**CAPITAL** Paramaribo
**GOVERNMENT** Multiparty republic
**ANNUAL INCOME** US$9,500
**CURRENCY** Surinamese dollar = 100 cents

## SWAZILAND

**AREA** 17,364 sq km [6,704 sq mi]
**POPULATION** 1,370,000
**CAPITAL** Mbabane
**GOVERNMENT** Monarchy
**ANNUAL INCOME** US$5,200
**CURRENCY** Lilangeni = 100 cents

## SWEDEN

**AREA** 449,964 sq km [173,731 sq mi]
**POPULATION** 9,089,000
**CAPITAL** Stockholm
**GOVERNMENT** Constitutional monarchy
**ANNUAL INCOME** US$40,600
**CURRENCY** Swedish krona = 100 öre

## SWITZERLAND

**AREA** 41,284 sq km [15,940 sq mi]
**POPULATION** 7,640,000
**CAPITAL** Bern
**GOVERNMENT** Federal republic
**ANNUAL INCOME** US$43,400
**CURRENCY** Swiss franc = 100 centimes

## SYRIA

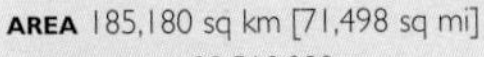

**AREA** 185,180 sq km [71,498 sq mi]
**POPULATION** 22,518,000
**CAPITAL** Damascus
**GOVERNMENT** Multiparty republic
**ANNUAL INCOME** US$5,100
**CURRENCY** Syrian pound = 100 piastres

## TAIWAN

**AREA** 36,000 sq km [13,900 sq mi]
**POPULATION** 23,072,000
**CAPITAL** Taipei
**GOVERNMENT** Unitary multiparty republic
**ANNUAL INCOME** US$37,900
**CURRENCY** New Taiwan dollar = 100 cents

## TAJIKISTAN

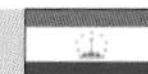

**AREA** 143,100 sq km [55,521 sq mi]
**POPULATION** 7,627,000
**CAPITAL** Dushanbe
**GOVERNMENT** Transitional democracy
**ANNUAL INCOME** US$2,000
**CURRENCY** Somoni = 100 dirams

## TANZANIA

**AREA** 945,090 sq km [364,899 sq mi]
**POPULATION** 42,747,000
**CAPITAL** Dodoma
**GOVERNMENT** Multiparty republic
**ANNUAL INCOME** US$1,500
**CURRENCY** Tanzanian shilling = 100 cents

## THAILAND

**AREA** 513,115 sq km [198,114 sq mi]
**POPULATION** 66,720,000
**CAPITAL** Bangkok
**GOVERNMENT** Constitutional monarchy
**ANNUAL INCOME** US$9,700
**CURRENCY** Baht = 100 satang

## TOGO

**AREA** 56,785 sq km [21,925 sq mi]
**POPULATION** 6,772,000
**CAPITAL** Lomé
**GOVERNMENT** Multiparty republic
**ANNUAL INCOME** US$900
**CURRENCY** CFA franc = 100 centimes

## TONGA

**AREA** 650 sq km [251 sq mi]
**POPULATION** 106,000
**CAPITAL** Nuku'alofa
**GOVERNMENT** Hereditary constitutional monarchy
**ANNUAL INCOME** US$7,500
**CURRENCY** Pa'anga = 100 seniti

## TRINIDAD & TOBAGO

**AREA** 5,130 sq km [1,981 sq mi]
**POPULATION** 1,228,000
**CAPITAL** Port of Spain
**GOVERNMENT** Parliamentary democracy
**ANNUAL INCOME** US$20,300
**CURRENCY** Trinidad & Tobago dollar = 100 cents

## TUNISIA

**AREA** 163,610 sq km [63,170 sq mi]
**POPULATION** 10,629,000
**CAPITAL** Tunis
**GOVERNMENT** Multiparty republic
**ANNUAL INCOME** US$9,500
**CURRENCY** Tunisian dinar = 1,000 millimes

## TURKEY

**AREA** 774,815 sq km [299,156 sq mi]
**POPULATION** 78,786,000
**CAPITAL** Ankara
**GOVERNMENT** Multiparty republic
**ANNUAL INCOME** US$14,600
**CURRENCY** New Turkish lira = 100 kurus

## TURKMENISTAN

**AREA** 488,100 sq km [188,455 sq mi]
**POPULATION** 4,998,000
**CAPITAL** Ashkhabad
**GOVERNMENT** Single-party republic
**ANNUAL INCOME** US$7,500
**CURRENCY** Turkmen manat = 100 tenesi

## TUVALU

**AREA** 26 sq km [10 sq mi]
**POPULATION** 11,000 **CAPITAL** Fongafale
**GOVERNMENT** Constitutional monarchy with parliamentary democracy
**ANNUAL INCOME** US$3,400
**CURRENCY** Australian dollar; Tuvaluan dollar

## UGANDA

**AREA** 241,038 sq km [93,065 sq mi]
**POPULATION** 34,612,000
**CAPITAL** Kampala
**GOVERNMENT** Republic
**ANNUAL INCOME** US$1,300
**CURRENCY** Ugandan shilling = 100 cents

## UKRAINE

**AREA** 603,700 sq km [233,089 sq mi]
**POPULATION** 45,135,000
**CAPITAL** Kiev
**GOVERNMENT** Multiparty republic
**ANNUAL INCOME** US$7,200
**CURRENCY** Hryvnia = 100 kopiykas

## UNITED ARAB EMIRATES

**AREA** 83,600 sq km [32,278 sq mi]
**POPULATION** 5,149,000 **CAPITAL** Abu Dhabi
**GOVERNMENT** Federation of seven emirates, each with its own government
**ANNUAL INCOME** US$48,500
**CURRENCY** Dirham = 100 fils

## UNITED KINGDOM

**AREA** 241,857 sq km [93,381 sq mi]
**POPULATION** 62,698,000
**CAPITAL** London
**GOVERNMENT** Constitutional monarchy
**ANNUAL INCOME** US$35,900
**CURRENCY** Pound sterling = 100 pence

## UNITED STATES OF AMERICA

**AREA** 9,629,091 sq km [3,717,792 sq mi]
**POPULATION** 313,232,000
**CAPITAL** Washington, DC
**GOVERNMENT** Federal republic
**ANNUAL INCOME** US$48,100
**CURRENCY** US dollar = 100 cents

## URUGUAY

**AREA** 175,016 sq km [67,574 sq mi]
**POPULATION** 3,309,000
**CAPITAL** Montevideo
**GOVERNMENT** Multiparty republic
**ANNUAL INCOME** US$15,400
**CURRENCY** Uruguayan peso = 100 centésimos

## UZBEKISTAN

**AREA** 447,400 sq km [172,741 sq mi]
**POPULATION** 28,129,000
**CAPITAL** Tashkent
**GOVERNMENT** Socialist republic
**ANNUAL INCOME** US$3,300
**CURRENCY** Uzbekistani sum = 100 tiyin

## VANUATU

**AREA** 12,189 sq km [4,706 sq mi]
**POPULATION** 225,000
**CAPITAL** Port-Vila
**GOVERNMENT** Parliamentary republic
**ANNUAL INCOME** US$4,900
**CURRENCY** Vatu

## VENEZUELA

**AREA** 912,050 sq km [352,143 sq mi]
**POPULATION** 27,636,000
**CAPITAL** Caracas
**GOVERNMENT** Federal republic
**ANNUAL INCOME** US$12,400
**CURRENCY** Bolívar = 100 céntimos

## VIETNAM

**AREA** 331,689 sq km [128,065 sq mi]
**POPULATION** 90,549,000
**CAPITAL** Hanoi
**GOVERNMENT** Socialist republic
**ANNUAL INCOME** US$3,300
**CURRENCY** Dong = 10 hao = 100 xu

## YEMEN

**AREA** 527,968 sq km [203,848 sq mi]
**POPULATION** 24,133,000
**CAPITAL** Sana'
**GOVERNMENT** Multiparty republic
**ANNUAL INCOME** US$2,500
**CURRENCY** Yemeni rial = 100 fils

## ZAMBIA

**AREA** 752,618 sq km [290,586 sq mi]
**POPULATION** 13,881,000
**CAPITAL** Lusaka
**GOVERNMENT** Multiparty republic
**ANNUAL INCOME** US$1,600
**CURRENCY** Zambian kwacha = 100 ngwee

## ZIMBABWE

**AREA** 390,757 sq km [150,871 sq mi]
**POPULATION** 12,084,000 **CAPITAL** Harare
**GOVERNMENT** Multiparty republic
**ANNUAL INCOME** US$500
**CURRENCY** Zimbabwean new dollar [suspende in 2009]

# ORLD MAPS – GENERAL REFERENCE

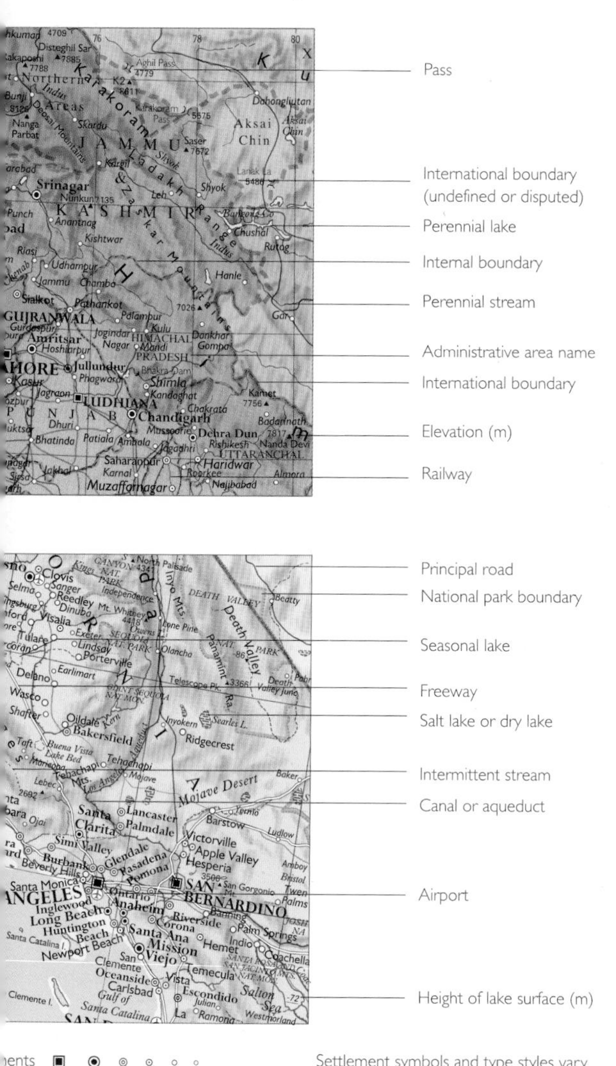


ients

Capital cities have red infills

Settlement symbols and type styles vary according to the scale of each map and indicate the importance of towns rather than specific population figures.

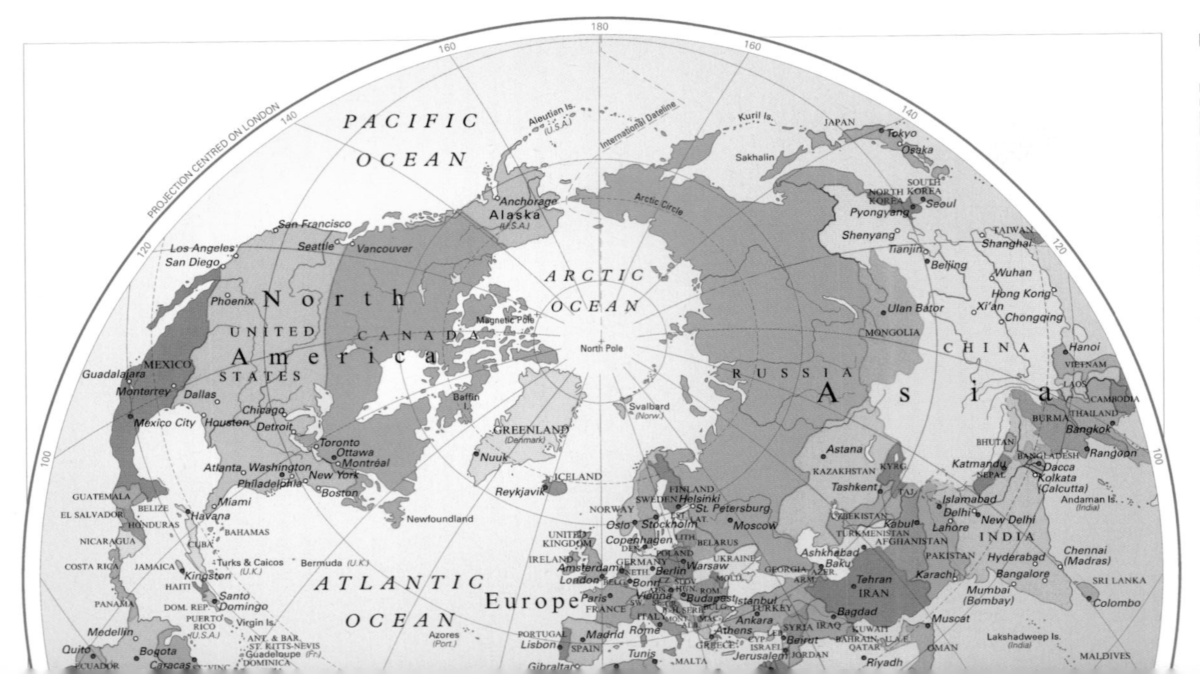
PACIFIC OCEAN
ARCTIC OCEAN
ATLANTIC OCEAN
North America
Europe
Asia
North Pole
Magnetic Pole
Arctic Circle
International Dateline
PROJECTION CENTRED ON LONDON
180
160
140
120
100
CANADA
UNITED STATES
MEXICO
RUSSIA
CHINA
INDIA
MONGOLIA
KAZAKHSTAN
GREENLAND (Denmark)
ICELAND
JAPAN
Alaska (U.S.A.)
Aleutian Is. (U.S.A.)
Anchorage
Kuril Is.
Sakhalin
Svalbard (Norw.)
Baffin I.
Newfoundland
Azores (Port.)
Bermuda (U.K.)
Turks & Caicos (U.K.)
BAHAMAS
CUBA
HAITI
DOM. REP.
PUERTO RICO (U.S.A.)
JAMAICA
BELIZE
HONDURAS
GUATEMALA
EL SALVADOR
NICARAGUA
COSTA RICA
PANAMA
ECUADOR
Virgin Is.
ANT. & BAR.
ST. KITTS-NEVIS
Guadeloupe (Fr.)
DOMINICA
Los Angeles
San Diego
San Francisco
Seattle
Vancouver
Phoenix
Dallas
Houston
Chicago
Detroit
Toronto
Ottawa
Montréal
New York
Boston
Philadelphia
Washington
Atlanta
Miami
Havana
Kingston
Santo Domingo
Mexico City
Monterrey
Guadalajara
Bogota
Caracas
Medellin
Quito
Nuuk
Reykjavik
NORWAY
SWEDEN
FINLAND
UNITED KINGDOM
IRELAND
FRANCE
SPAIN
PORTUGAL
GERMANY
POLAND
BELARUS
UKRAINE
ITALY
GREECE
TURKEY
MALTA
Oslo
Stockholm
Helsinki
St. Petersburg
Moscow
Copenhagen
Amsterdam
London
Paris
Berlin
Warsaw
Vienna
Budapest
Bonn
Rome
Madrid
Lisbon
Gibraltar
Tunis
Athens
Istanbul
Ankara
Beirut
Jerusalem
SYRIA
IRAQ
ISRAEL
JORDAN
KUWAIT
BAHRAIN
QATAR
U.A.E.
OMAN
IRAN
GEORGIA
AZER.
ARM.
TURKMENISTAN
UZBEKISTAN
AFGHANISTAN
PAKISTAN
KYRG.
TAJ.
Bagdad
Tehran
Riyadh
Muscat
Baku
Ashkhabad
Tashkent
Astana
Kabul
Islamabad
Lahore
Karachi
Delhi
New Delhi
Katmandu
NEPAL
BHUTAN
BANGLADESH
Dacca
Kolkata (Calcutta)
Mumbai (Bombay)
Hyderabad
Bangalore
Chennai (Madras)
Colombo
SRI LANKA
MALDIVES
Lakshadweep Is. (India)
Andaman Is. (India)
BURMA
THAILAND
LAOS
VIETNAM
CAMBODIA
Rangoon
Bangkok
Hanoi
Ulan Bator
Beijing
Tianjin
Shenyang
Pyongyang
Seoul
NORTH KOREA
SOUTH KOREA
Tokyo
Osaka
Shanghai
TAIWAN
Wuhan
Hong Kong
Chongqing
Xi'an

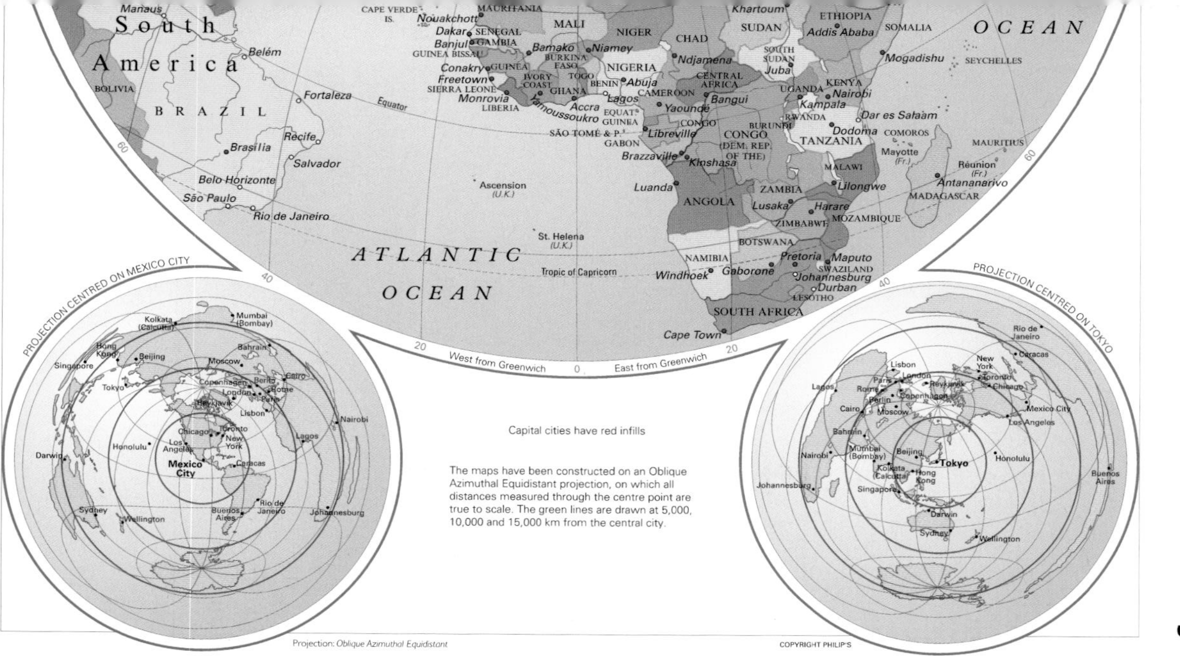


Capital cities have red infills

The maps have been constructed on an Oblique Azimuthal Equidistant projection, on which all distances measured through the centre point are true to scale. The green lines are drawn at 5,000, 10,000 and 15,000 km from the central city.

Projection: *Oblique Azimuthal Equidistant*

East from Greenwich
180
West from Greenwich
160
140
120
100
PROJECTION CENTRED ON THE ANTIPODES OF LONDON
International Dateline
Midway I. (U.S.A.)
Tropic of Cancer
Bonin Is. (Japan)
Wake I. (U.S.A.)
Honolulu
Hawaiian Is. (U.S.A.)
Northern Marianas (U.S.A.)
MARSHALL IS.
PACIFIC
Guam (U.S.A.)
FED. STATES OF MICRONESIA
Equator
PHILIPPINES
PALAU
Oceania
TUVALU
KIRIBATI
Manila
SOLOMON IS.
OCEAN
PAPUA NEW GUINEA
SAMOA
Port Moresby
FIJI
VIETNAM
VANUATU
Marquesas Is. (Fr.)
BRUNEI
TONGA
Cook Is. (N.Z.)
Ho Chi Minh City
Tahiti (Fr.)
Makassar
EAST TIMOR
New Caledonia (Fr.)
FRENCH POLYNESIA
Tuamotu Arch. (Fr.)
Borneo
MALAYSIA
INDONESIA
Brisbane
Kermadec Is. (N.Z.)
SINGAPORE
Auckland
Tropic of Capricorn
Kuala Lumpur
AUSTRALIA
Sydney
NEW ZEALAND
Jakarta
Canberra
Wellington
Pitcairn I. (U.K.)
Adelaide
Melbourne
Chatham Is. (N.Z.)
Tasmania
Auckland Is. (N.Z.)
Antipodes Is. (N.Z.)
Galapagos Is. (Ecuador)
Perth
Easter I. (Chile)
Cocos Is. (Austral.)
Macquarie I. (Austral.)
SOUTHERN OCEAN
INDIAN

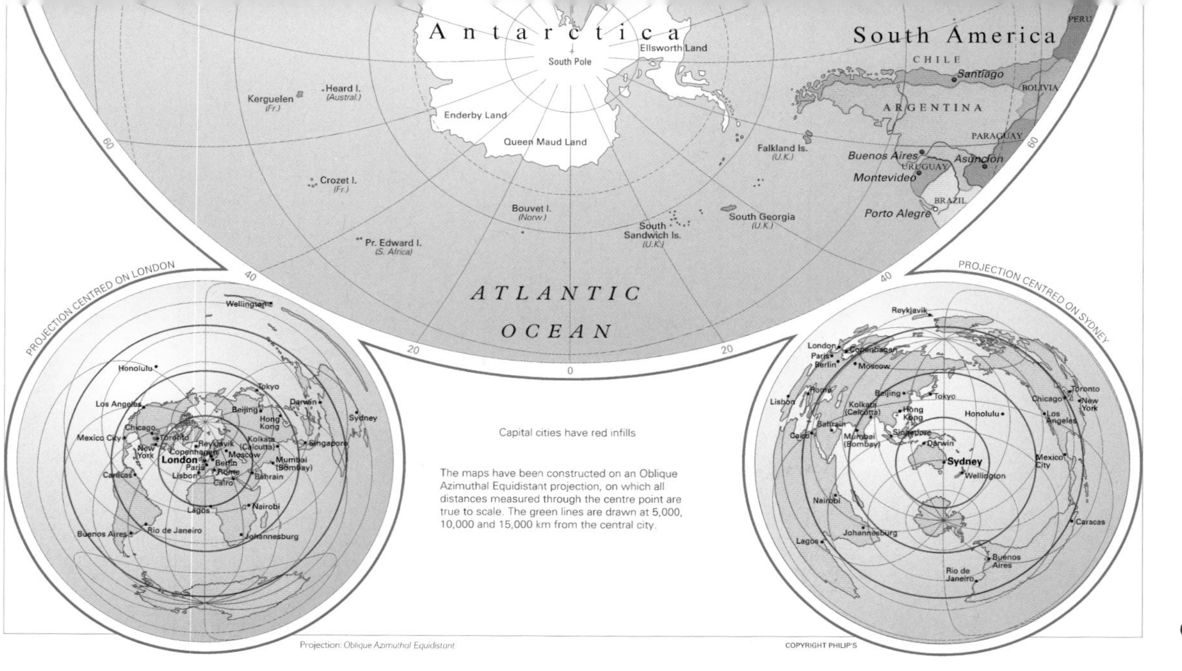


Capital cities have red infills

The maps have been constructed on an Oblique Azimuthal Equidistant projection, on which all distances measured through the centre point are true to scale. The green lines are drawn at 5,000, 10,000 and 15,000 km from the central city.

Projection: *Oblique Azimuthal Equidistant*

# EUROPE

Arctic Circle
ICELAND
Reykjavik
Norwegian Sea
Faroe Is. (Den.)
Shetland Is.
Orkney Is.
SWEDEN
NORWAY
Trondheim
Bergen
Oslo
Stavanger
Uppsala
Örebro
Vänern
Vättern
Jönköping
Gothenburg
Skagerrak
Kattegat
DENMARK
Aalborg
Aarhus
Copenhagen
Malmö
ATLANTIC OCEAN
UNITED KINGDOM
Hebrides
SCOTLAND
Aberdeen
Dundee
Glasgow
Edinburgh
N. IRELAND
Belfast
IRELAND
Dublin
Cork
Newcastle-upon-Tyne
Manchester
Leeds
Liverpool
Sheffield
North Sea
WALES
ENGLAND
Birmingham
Cardiff
Bristol
LONDON
Plymouth
Southampton
English Channel
Channel Is. (U.K.)
Le Havre
Brest
Rouen
Seine
PARIS
Amsterdam
The Hague
Rotterdam
NETHERLANDS
Antwerp
BELGIUM
Brussels
Lille
Meuse
LUX.
Luxembourg
Kiel
Hamburg
Bremen
Hannover
Elbe
Berlin
Magdeburg
GERMANY
Essen
Dortmund
Cologne
Bonn
Halle
Leipzig
Chemnitz
Dresden
Frankfurt am Main
Nuremberg
Stuttgart
Munich
Rhine
Strasbourg
Baltic
Gdańsk
Szczecin
Bydgoszcz
Oder
POLAND
Poznań
Wrocław
Katowice
Prague
CZECH REP.
Ostrava
Vienna
Linz
Salzburg
AUSTRIA
Innsbruck
Graz
Budapest
FRANCE
Nantes
Loire
Dijon
Bay of Biscay
Gironde
Limoges
Lyons
St-Étienne
Bordeaux
Garonne
Toulouse
Rhône
Grenoble
Zürich
Bern
LIECH.
Vaduz
SWITZERLAND
Geneva
SLOVENIA
Ljubljana
Zagreb
CROATIA
Trieste
Milan
Venice
Turin
Genoa
Bologna
Nice
MONACO
Marseilles
Toulon
ANDORRA
Andorra-la-Vella
La Coruña
Vigo
Porto
Douro
Bilbao
PORTUGAL
Lisbon
Tagus
Valladolid
Ebro
Zaragoza
Madrid
SPAIN
Barcelona
Guadiana
Valencia
Seville
Córdoba
Guadalquivir
Murcia
Alicante
Cádiz
Granada
Málaga
Gibraltar (U.K.)
Str. of Gibraltar
Tangier
Ceuta (Sp.)
Melilla (Sp.)
Balearic Is.
Minorca
Palma
Majorca
Ibiza
Corsica
Ajaccio
Sardinia
Cagliari
Florence
SAN MARINO
ITALY
Tiber
Rome
Adriatic Sea
BOSNIA-HERZEGOVINA
Split
MONTENEGRO
Podgorica
Naples
Bari
Taranto
Tyrrhenian Sea
Mediterranean Sea
Palermo
Messina
Sicily
Catania
Ionian
Algiers
Annaba
ALGERIA
Constantine
Tunis
TUNISIA
Pantelleria (Italy)
MALTA
Valletta
MOROCCO
Africa

| m | ft |
|---|---|
| 0 | |
| 200 | 600 |
| 1000 | 3000 |
| 2000 | 6000 |
| 4000 | 12 000 |

Projection: Bonne    West from Greenwich    East from Greenwich

■ LONDON Capital Cities

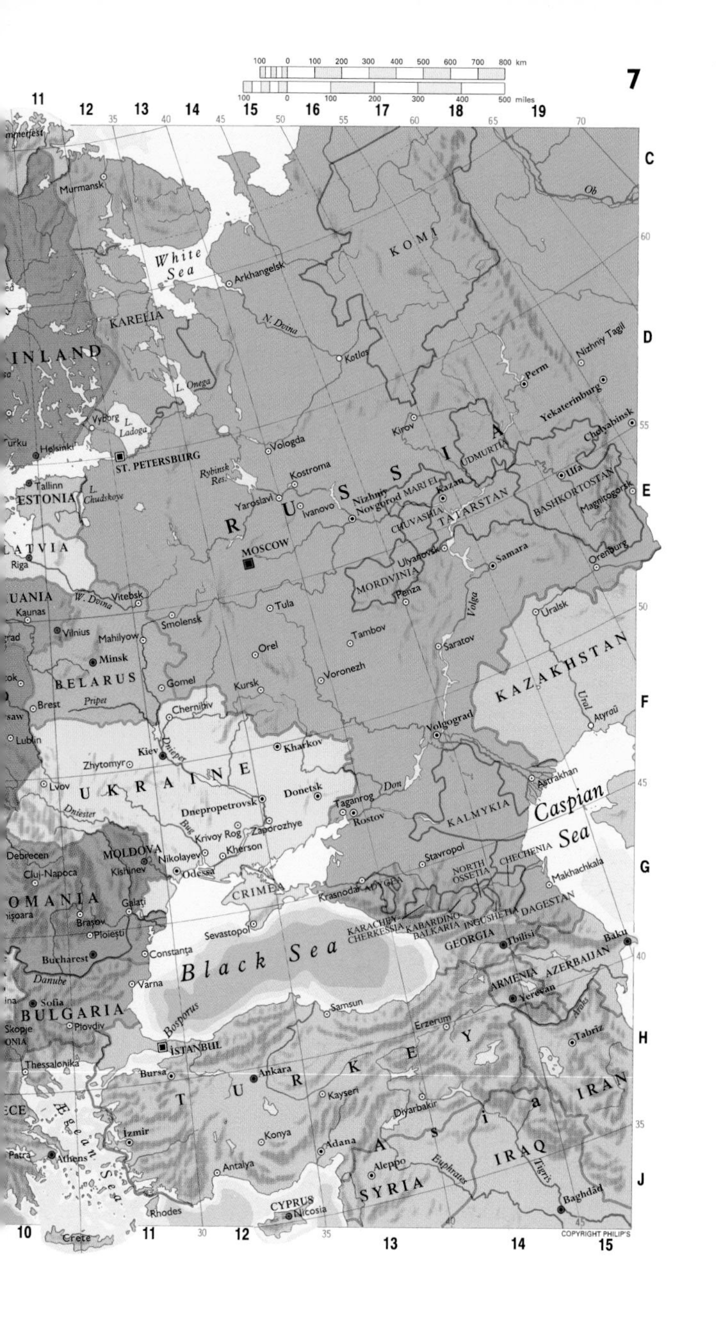

Murmansk
White Sea
Arkhangelsk
KARELIA
N. Dvina
Kotlas
KOMI
Ob
FINLAND
L. Onega
Vyborg
L. Ladoga
Helsinki
ST. PETERSBURG
Rybinsk Res.
Vologda
Kostroma
Kirov
Perm
Nizhniy Tagil
Yekaterinburg
Chelyabinsk
UDMURTIA
Tallinn
ESTONIA
L. Chudskoye
Yaroslavl
Ivanovo
Nizhniy Novgorod
MARI EL
Kazan
CHUVASHIA
TATARSTAN
BASHKORTOSTAN
Ufa
Magnitogorsk
RUSSIA
LATVIA
Riga
MOSCOW
Ulyanovsk
Samara
Orenburg
MORDVINIA
Penza
W. Dvina
Vitebsk
Kaunas
Vilnius
Smolensk
Tula
Volga
Uralsk
Mahilyow
Minsk
Orel
Tambov
Saratov
KAZAKHSTAN
BELARUS
Gomel
Kursk
Voronezh
Ural
Brest
Pripet
Chernihiv
Lublin
Volgograd
Atyraū
Kiev
Dnieper
Kharkov
Zhytomyr
UKRAINE
Lvov
Donetsk
Don
Astrakhan
Dniester
Dnepropetrovsk
Taganrog
Rostov
KALMYKIA
Caspian Sea
Bug
Krivoy Rog
Zaporozhye
Debrecen
MOLDOVA
Nikolayev
Kherson
Stavropol
CHECHENIA
Cluj-Napoca
Kishinev
Odessa
NORTH OSSETIA
Makhachkala
CRIMEA
Krasnodar
ADYGEA
ROMANIA
Galati
Brașov
Ploiești
Sevastopol
KARACHEY-CHERKESSIA
KABARDINO-BALKARIA
INGUSHETIA
DAGESTAN
GEORGIA
Tbilisi
Baku
Constanța
Bucharest
Black Sea
AZERBAIJAN
ARMENIA
Yerevan
Danube
Varna
Sofia
BULGARIA
Plovdiv
Samsun
Araks
Skopje
Bosporus
Erzurum
Tabriz
ISTANBUL
Thessaloniki
Bursa
Ankara
TURKEY
IRAN
Kayseri
Diyarbakir
Asia
Izmir
Konya
Adana
Athens
Aegean Sea
IRAQ
Tigris
Antalya
Aleppo
Euphrates
SYRIA
Patra
CYPRUS
Nicosia
Baghdad
Rhodes
Crete
COPYRIGHT PHILIP'S

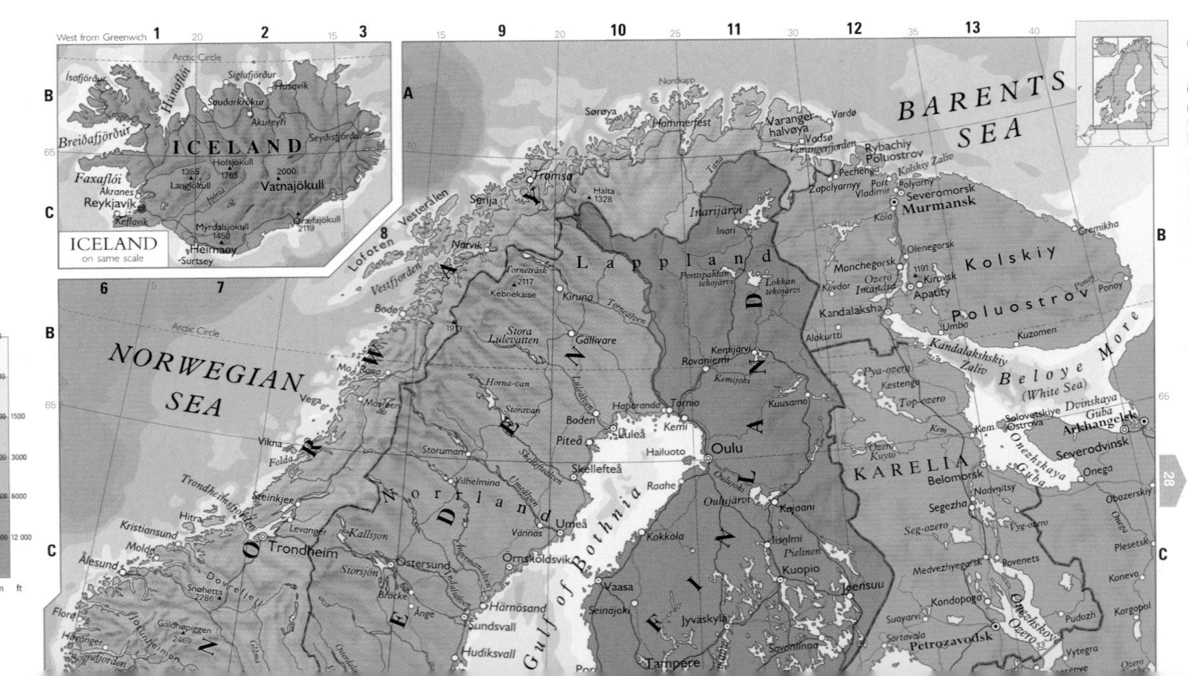
28
BARENTS SEA
NORWEGIAN SEA
Beloye More (White Sea)
Kolskiy Poluostrov
KARELIA
Lappland
Norrland
Gulf of Bothnia
ICELAND
ICELAND on same scale
Reykjavík
Vatnajökull
Murmansk
Arkhangelsk
Petrozavodsk
Oulu
Tromsø
Trondheim
Hammerfest
Narvik
Kiruna
Umeå
Vaasa
Kuopio
Jyväskylä
Tampere
Joensuu
Kemi
Tornio
Luleå
Skellefteå
Östersund
Sundsvall
Härnösand
Bodø
Ålesund
Kristiansund
Lofoten
Vesterålen
Arctic Circle
West from Greenwich

BALTIC SEA
Gulf of Finland
Gulf of Riga
Skagerrak
Kattegat
DENMARK
ESTONIA
LATVIA
LITHUANIA
BELARUS
RUSSIA
POLAND
GERMANY
CZECH REP.
UKRAINE
Götaland
Jylland
STOCKHOLM
KØBENHAVN (Copenhagen)
Tallinn
Rīga
Vilnius
MINSK
WARSZAWA (Warsaw)
BERLIN
PRAHA (Prague)
KYYIV (Kiev)
MOSKVA (Moscow)
SANKT-PETERBURG
Kaliningrad (Russia)
Stavanger
Kristiansand
Göteborg (Gothenburg)
Malmö
Gotland
Öland
Bornholm
Hiiumaa (Dagö)
Saaremaa (Ösel)
HAMBURG
Gdańsk
Gdynia
Szczecin
Poznań
Łódź
Kraków
Wrocław
Lviv
Brest
Hrodna
Homyel
Chernihiv
Smolensk
Bryansk
Novgorod
Pskov
Daugavpils
Kaunas
Klaipėda
Projection: Conical with two standard parallels
East from Greenwich
COPYRIGHT PHILIP'S
0 50 100 150 200 250 miles
0 100 200 300 400 km

Shetland Is.
(U.K.)
Unst
Fetlar
Yell
Mainland
Lerwick
Foula
Fair Isle
Orkney Is.
Westray
Sanday
Stronsay
Mainland
Kirkwall
Hoy
South Ronaldsay
Pentland Firth
C. Wrath
Thurso
Wick
Helmsdale
Lairg
Golspie
Tain
Moray Firth
Buckie
Banff
Fraserburgh
Peterhead
Ullapool
Invergordon
Dingwall
Nairn
Elgin
Huntly
Inverness
CAIRNGORMS
Inverurie
Aberdeen
L. Ness
Aviemore
Glen Mor
North West Highlands
North Minch
SCOTLAND
Grampian Mts.
Ballater
Stonehaven
Ben Nevis
1344
Fort William
Tobermory
Mull
Oban
L. Awe
L. Lomond
Forfar
Montrose
Arbroath
Dundee
Perth
St. Andrews
Glenrothes
Kirkcaldy
Stirling
Dunfermline
Dunbar
Edinburgh
Glasgow
Motherwell
Hamilton
Paisley
East Kilbride
Greenock
Dumbarton
Berwick-upon-Tweed
Jura
Islay
Colonsay
Tiree
Coll
Rhum
Eigg
Mallaig
Skye
Portree
Inner Hebrides
Sea of the Hebrides
Outer Hebrides
Lewis
Stornoway
789
Harris
North Uist
Benbecula
South Uist
Barra
St. Kilda
(U.K.)
1182
1214
973
1311
ATLANTIC OCEAN
NORTH SEA
1224
316
238
NORWAY
Askøyna
Bergen
Osøyro
Stord
Bømlo
Leirvik
Haugesund
Kopervik
Åkrahamn
Boknafjorden
Stavanger
Sandnes
Bryne
Nærbø
m
ft
2000
1000
500
200
100
50
0
6000
3000
1500
600
300
150

UNITED KINGDOM
IRELAND
ENGLAND
WALES
NETHERLANDS
BELGIUM
FRANCE
IRISH SEA
CELTIC SEA
English Channel
Bristol Channel
St. George's Channel
Str. of Dover
Cardigan Bay
The Wash
Galway B.
Channel Is. (U.K.)
Isles of Scilly
I. of Man
Anglesey
Isle of Wight
LONDON
Dublin
Belfast
BIRMINGHAM
MANCHESTER
Liverpool
Leeds
Sheffield
Bradford
Kingston upon Hull
Middlesbrough
Newcastle
Nottingham
Leicester
Coventry
Wolverhampton
Bristol
Cardiff
Swansea
Plymouth
Southampton
Portsmouth
Brighton
Norwich
Cork
Limerick
Galway
Waterford
BRUSSEL (Bruxelles)
ROTTERDAM
's-Gravenhage (Den Haag)
Antwerpen
Lille
Rouen
Le Havre
Projection: Conical with two standard parallels
West from Greenwich
East from Greenwich
COPYRIGHT PHILIP'S
km
miles

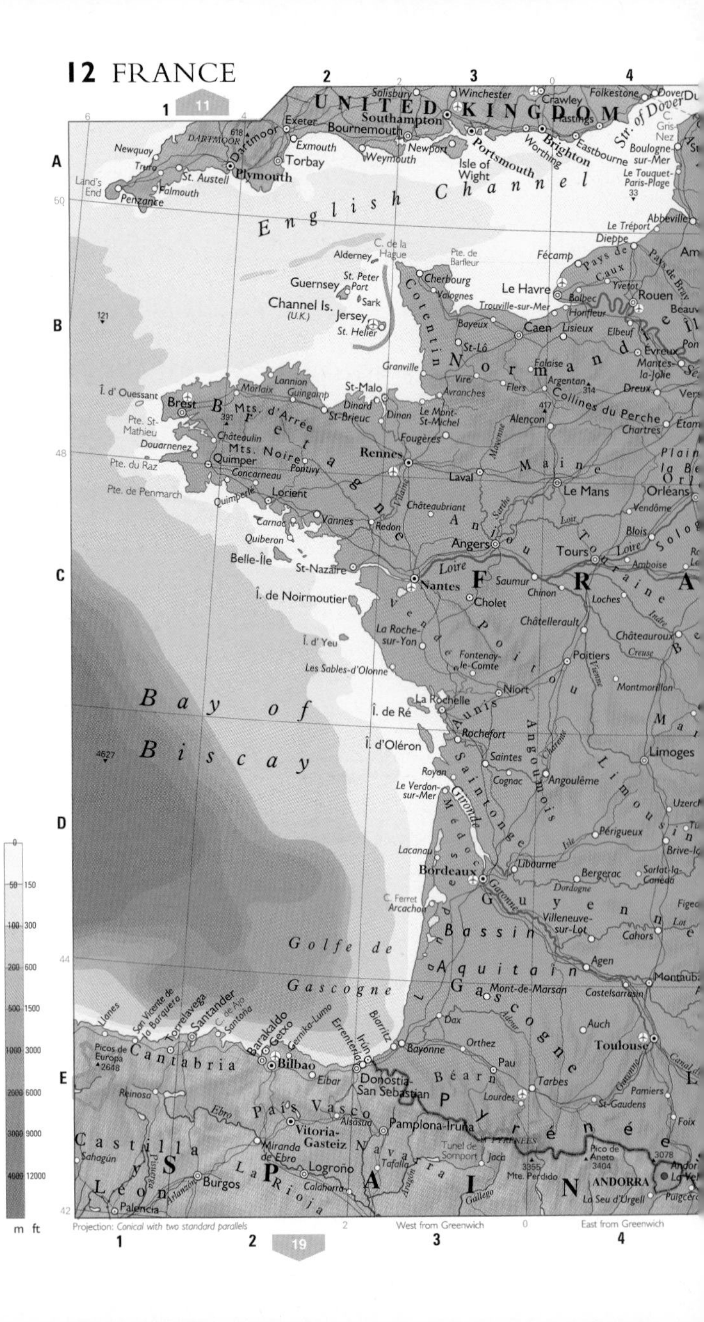
UNITED KINGDOM
Salisbury
Winchester
Crawley
Folkestone
Dover
Southampton
Exeter
Bournemouth
Hastings
Brighton
Portsmouth
Worthing
Eastbourne
Str. of Dover
Boulogne-sur-Mer
Le Touquet-Paris-Plage
Dartmoor
Exmouth
Torbay
Weymouth
Newport
Isle of Wight
Newquay
Truro
St. Austell
Plymouth
Land's End
Falmouth
Penzance
English Channel
Abbeville
Le Tréport
Dieppe
Fécamp
Pays de Caux
Yvetot
Rouen
Le Havre
Bolbec
Honfleur
Trouville-sur-Mer
Alderney
C. de la Hague
Pte. de Barfleur
Guernsey
St. Peter Port
Sark
Channel Is. (U.K.)
Jersey
St. Helier
Cherbourg
Valognes
Cotentin
Bayeux
Caen
Lisieux
Elbeuf
Évreux
St-Lô
Granville
Normandie
Falaise
Argentan
Mantes-la-Jolie
Vire
Flers
Dreux
Avranches
Collines du Perche
Chartres
Alençon
Le Mont-St-Michel
St-Malo
Dinard
Dinan
Lannion
Morlaix
Guingamp
St-Brieuc
Î. d' Ouessant
Brest
Mts. d'Arrée
Pte. St-Mathieu
Châteaulin
Douarnenez
Mts. Noires
Bretagne
Fougères
Rennes
Quimper
Pte. du Raz
Concarneau
Pontivy
Pte. de Penmarch
Quimperlé
Lorient
Laval
Maine
Le Mans
Orléans
Vendôme
Châteaubriant
Anjou
Carnac
Vannes
Redon
Quiberon
Belle-Île
St-Nazaire
Angers
Tours
Blois
Touraine
Amboise
Loire
Nantes
Saumur
Chinon
Loches
Î. de Noirmoutier
Cholet
Vendée
Châtellerault
Châteauroux
La Roche-sur-Yon
Î. d' Yeu
Fontenay-le-Comte
Poitiers
Poitou
Les Sables-d'Olonne
Montmorillon
Niort
Bay of Biscay
La Rochelle
Î. de Ré
Aunis
Rochefort
Î. d'Oléron
Saintes
Limoges
Limousin
Royan
Cognac
Angoulême
Angoumois
Le Verdon-sur-Mer
Saintonge
Gironde
Médoc
Périgueux
Lacanau
Libourne
Bordeaux
Bergerac
Sarlat-la-Canéda
Dordogne
C. Ferret
Arcachon
Garonne
Guyenne
Villeneuve-sur-Lot
Cahors
Bassin d'Aquitaine
Golfe de Gascogne
Agen
Montauban
Mont-de-Marsan
Castelsarrasin
Gascogne
Dax
Auch
Landes
Bayonne
Orthez
Toulouse
Biarritz
Irún
Pau
Béarn
Tarbes
Lourdes
Pamiers
St-Gaudens
Foix
Pyrénées
Pico de Aneto 3404
ANDORRA
La Seu d'Urgell
Puigcerdà
Mte. Perdido
Tunel de Somport
Jaca
Donostia-San Sebastián
Pamplona-Iruña
Navarra
Tafalla
Alsasua
País Vasco
Eibar
Errenteria
Gernika-Lumo
Getxo
Barakaldo
Bilbao
Santander
Santoña
Torrelavega
San Vicente de la Barquera
Llanes
Picos de Europa 2648
Cantabria
Reinosa
Ebro
Vitoria-Gasteiz
Miranda de Ebro
Logroño
La Rioja
Calahorra
Castilla y León
Sahagún
Burgos
Palencia
SPAIN
m ft
Projection: Conical with two standard parallels
West from Greenwich
East from Greenwich

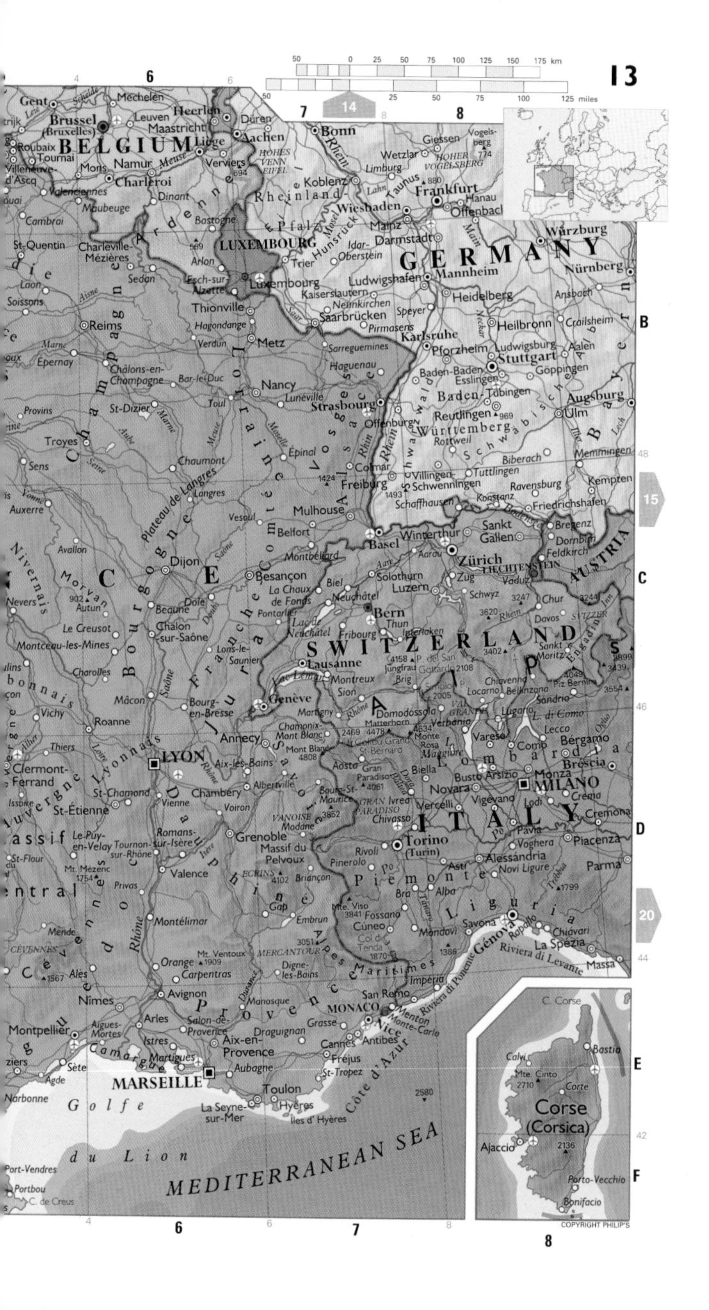
50 0 25 50 75 100 125 150 175 km
50 0 25 50 75 100 125 miles
14
15
20
BELGIUM
LUXEMBOURG
GERMANY
SWITZERLAND
AUSTRIA
LIECHTENSTEIN
ITALY
MONACO
MEDITERRANEAN SEA
Golfe du Lion
Corse (Corsica)
Gent
Mechelen
Brussel (Bruxelles)
Leuven
Heerlen
Maastricht
Düren
Aachen
Bonn
Roubaix
Tournai
Villeneuve-d'Ascq
Mons
Namur
Meuse
Liège
Verviers
HOHES VENN
EIFEL
Charleroi
Valenciennes
Maubeuge
Dinant
Cambrai
Ardenne
Bastogne
St-Quentin
Charleville-Mézières
Arlon
Sedan
Esch-sur-Alzette
Luxembourg
Thionville
Hagondange
Metz
Verdun
Reims
Laon
Soissons
Aisne
Marne
Épernay
Châlons-en-Champagne
Bar-le-Duc
Nancy
Lunéville
Toul
St-Dizier
Provins
Troyes
Sens
Chaumont
Épinal
Langres
Plateau de Langres
Vesoul
Auxerre
Yonne
Seine
Aube
Champagne
Lorraine
Vosges
Alsace
Koblenz
Rheinland-Pfalz
Hunsrück
Mosel
Idar-Oberstein
Trier
Wiesbaden
Mainz
Darmstadt
Frankfurt
Hanau
Offenbach
Giessen
Wetzlar
Limburg
Lahn
Taunus
HOHER VOGELSBERG
Vogelsberg
Würzburg
Main
Kaiserslautern
Neunkirchen
Saarbrücken
Pirmasens
Saar
Sarreguemines
Haguenau
Ludwigshafen
Mannheim
Heidelberg
Speyer
Karlsruhe
Pforzheim
Heilbronn
Neckar
Ludwigsburg
Stuttgart
Esslingen
Göppingen
Baden-Baden
Baden-Württemberg
Tübingen
Reutlingen
Rottweil
Schwäbische Alb
Ansbach
Nürnberg
Crailsheim
Aalen
Augsburg
Ulm
Iller
Lech
Bayern
Biberach
Memmingen
Kempten
Ravensburg
Friedrichshafen
Konstanz
Bodensee
Strasbourg
Offenburg
Rhein
Schwarzwald
Colmar
Freiburg
Villingen-Schwenningen
Tuttlingen
Schaffhausen
Mulhouse
Belfort
Basel
Montbéliard
Winterthur
Aarau
Zürich
Sankt Gallen
Bregenz
Dornbirn
Feldkirch
Vaduz
Solothurn
Biel
Aare
La Chaux de Fonds
Neuchâtel
Lac de Neuchâtel
Bern
Thun
Interlaken
Luzern
Zug
Schwyz
Chur
Davos
Fribourg
Pontarlier
Besançon
Dijon
Dole
Doubs
Saône
Beaune
Chalon-sur-Saône
Lons-le-Saunier
Lausanne
Lac Léman
Montreux
Sion
Genève
Martigny
Rhône
Jungfrau
P. del San Gottardo
Brig
Simplon P.
Chiavenna
Locarno
Bellinzona
Sondrio
Piz Bernina
Engadin
Inn
Sankt Moritz
Domodóssola
Matterhorn
Monte Rosa
Lugano
L. di Como
Lecco
Bergamo
Varese
Como
L. Maggiore
Verbania
Lombardia
Brescia
Monza
MILANO
Busto Arsizio
Novara
Vigevano
Lodi
Crema
Cremona
Biella
Vercelli
Ivrea
GRAN PARADISO
Gran Paradiso
Aosta
Col du Grand St-Bernard
Chamonix-Mont Blanc
Mont Blanc
Annecy
Aix-les-Bains
Chambéry
Albertville
Bourg-St-Maurice
VANOISE
Modane
Chivasso
Torino (Turin)
Rivoli
Pinerolo
Po
Asti
Alessándria
Novi Ligure
Voghera
Pavia
Piacenza
Parma
Trebbia
Piemonte
Bra
Alba
Tanaro
Mondovì
Cúneo
Fossano
Mte. Viso
Col di Tenda
Liguria
Savona
Génova
Rapallo
Chiávari
La Spézia
Massa
Riviera di Levante
Riviera di Ponente
Imperia
San Remo
Menton
Monte-Carlo
Nice
Antibes
Cannes
Grasse
Fréjus
St-Tropez
Côte d'Azur
Draguignan
Toulon
La Seyne-sur-Mer
Hyères
Îles d' Hyères
Aubagne
MARSEILLE
Aix-en-Provence
Martigues
Istres
Salon-de-Provence
Arles
Camargue
Aigues-Mortes
Montpellier
Sète
Agde
Narbonne
Port-Vendres
Portbou
C. de Creus
Nîmes
Avignon
Orange
Carpentras
Mt. Ventoux
Durance
Manosque
Digne-les-Bains
MERCANTOUR
Alpes Maritimes
Provence
Alès
Cévennes
CÉVENNES
Mende
Montélimar
Valence
Privas
Tournon-sur-Rhône
Romans-sur-Isère
Isère
Grenoble
Voiron
Vienne
Massif du Pelvoux
ECRINS
Briançon
Embrun
Gap
Dauphiné
LYON
St-Chamond
St-Étienne
Le Puy-en-Velay
Mt. Mézenc
St-Flour
Massif Central
Clermont-Ferrand
Issoire
Auvergne
Thiers
Allier
Loire
Lyonnais
Vichy
Roanne
Mâcon
Bourg-en-Bresse
Jura
Charolles
Montceau-les-Mines
Le Creusot
Autun
Morvan
Nevers
Nivernais
Bourbonnais
Avallon
Bourgogne
Franche-Comté
Savoie
Alpes
C. Corse
Bastia
Calvi
Mte. Cinto
Corte
Ajaccio
Porto-Vecchio
Bonifacio
B
C
D
E
F
COPYRIGHT PHILIP'S

NORTH SEA
UNITED KINGDOM
NETHERLANDS
AMSTERDAM
's-Gravenhage (Den Haag)
ROTTERDAM
BELGIUM
Brussel (Bruxelles)
LUXEMBOURG
FRANCE
PARIS
SWITZERLAND
Bern
LIECHTENSTEIN
Nordfriesische Inseln
Ostfriesische Inseln
Deutsche Bucht
Schleswig-Holstein
Niedersachsen
Nordrhein-Westfalen
Hessen
Rheinland-Pfalz
Baden-Württemberg
Bremen
Hamburg
Hannover
Frankfurt
Stuttgart
Köln (Cologne)
Bonn
Düsseldorf
Dortmund
Essen
Zürich
Basel
Genève
Lausanne
LYON
Strasbourg
Metz
Nancy
Dijon
Reims
Lille
Antwerpen
Gent
Brugge
Liège
Luxembourg
Ardenne
Lorraine
Alsace
Champagne
Bourgogne
Picardie
Île-de-France
Franche-Comté
Jura
Schwarzwald
Projection: Conical with two standard parallels

9
50 0 25 50 75 100 125 150 175 km
50 0 25 50 75 100 125 miles
7
8
9
10
BALTIC SEA
Zatoka Gdańska
Zalew Wiślany
Næstved
Møn
Nakskov
Falster
Lolland
Nykøbing
Rødbyhavn
Gedser
Fehmarn
Fehmarn Bælt
Mecklenburger Bucht
Rügen
Sassnitz
RÜGEN
Stralsund
Greifswald
Rostock
Wismar
Usedom
Wolin
Świnoujście
WOLIŃSKI
Güstrow
Mecklenburg
Stettiner Haff
Schwerin
Neubrandenburg
MÜRITZ
Parchim
Müritz
Neustrelitz
Elde
Brandenburg
Wittenberge
Neuruppin
Schwedt
Salzwedel
Stendal
Havel
Oranienburg
Eberswalde-Finow
Rathenow
BERLIN
Fürstenwalde
Brandenburg
Potsdam
Spree
Magdeburg
Luckenwalde
Sachsen-Anhalt
Dessau
Lutherstadt Wittenberg
Bernburg
Cottbus
Forst
Halle
Torgau
Lauchhammer
Leipzig
Riesa
Hoyerswerda
Naumburg
Bautzen
Zeitz
Meissen
Gera
Dresden
Görlitz
Sachsen
SÄCHSISCHE SCHWEIZ
Zwickau
Chemnitz
Děčín
Greiz
Reichenbach
Plauen
Erzgebirge
Teplice
Ústí nad Labem
Most
Chomutov
Ohře
Hof
1244
Karlovy Vary
Kladno
Cheb
Bayreuth
PRAHA (Prague)
Beroun
Plzeň
Weiden
Naab
Příbram
Amberg
Böhmerwald
1042
Klatovy
Písek
Grosser Arber
1456
ŠUMAVA
Regensburg
Straubing
Deggendorf
Plöckenstein
1378
Isar
Landshut
Passau
Inn
Freising
MÜNCHEN (Munich)
Braunau
Ried
Wels
Linz
Donau (Danube)
Salzburg
Chiemsee
Kufstein
BERCHTESGADEN
2351
Bad Ischl
2514
2995
Gmunden
Salzach
HOHE TAUERN
3797
Grossglockner
Badgastein
Lienz
2441
NOCKBERGE
3435
Kärnische Alpen
Villach
Klagenfurt
Kärnten
Wolfsberg
TRIGLAVSKI
Triglav
2863
2558
Karawanken
Kranj
Kobarid
Udine
Vittório Véneto
Pordenone
Gorizia
Conegliano
Ljubljana
Sava
SLOVENIA
Kalce
Tagliamento
Celje
Maribor
Drava
ZAGREB
1035
Słupsk
Lębork
SLOWIŃSKI
Wejherowo
Rumia
Gdynia
Sopot
Gdańsk
329
Tczew
Bytów
Darłowo
Kołobrzeg
Koszalin
Białogard
Starogard Gdański
Elbląg
Malbork
Kwidzyn
Iława
Pojezierze Pomorskie
Szczecinek
Chojnice
Wisła
Police
Goleniów
Szczecin
Stargard Szczeciński
Świecie
Grudziądz
Wałcz
Chełmno
Brodnica
Bydgoszcz
Piła
Choszczno
DRAWIEŃSKI
Noteć
Toruń
Rypin
Wisła (Vistula)
Gorzów Wielkopolski
Inowrocław
POLAND
Międzychód
Warta
Gniezno
Włocławek
Płock
Odra
Oder
Poznań
Września
Nowy Tomyśl
Frankfurt
Kutno
Świebodzin
WIELKOPOLSKI
Koło
Zielona Góra
Śrem
Konin
Łęczyca
Kościan
Turek
Prosna
Nowa Sól
Leszno
Kalisz
Łódź
Żagań
Zduńska Wola
Krotoszyn
Pabianice
Nysa
Żary
Bóbr
Głogów
Lubin
Ostrów Wielkopolski
Sieradz
Śląsk
Bolesławiec
Wieluń
Piotrków Trybunalski
Neisse
Oleśnica
Legnica
Radomsko
Zgorzelec
Wrocław
Kluczbork
Częstochowa
Jelenia Góra
Świdnica
Oława
Liberec
Wałbrzych
Opole
Myszków
1602
Śnieżka
KRKONOŠE
Dzierżoniów
Jablonec nad Nisou
Tarnowskie Góry
Zawiercie
Litoměřice
Mladá Boleslav
Trutnov
Kłodzko
Nysa
Zabrze
Bytom
Sudety
Gliwice
Katowice
Labe
Hradec Králové
Racibórz
Tychy
Oświęcim
Pardubice
1425
1492
Kolín
Opava
Karviná
Bielsko-Biała
Sázava
Šumperk
Ostrava
Havířov
Českomoravská Vrchovina
838
Olomouc
Frýdek-Místek
Cieszyn
Żywiec
CZECH REP.
Havlíčkův Brod
1324
Přerov
Vltava
Tábor
Prostějov
Jihlava
Vyškov
Zlín
Považská Bystrica
Žilina
Třebíč
Jindřichův Hradec
Jihlava
Brno
Bielé Karpaty
Martin
České Budějovice
2043
PODYJÍ
Znojmo
Trenčín
Gmünd
Hodonín
Prievidza
Banská Bystrica
Horn
768
Malé Karpaty
SLOVAK REP.
Zwettl
Morava
Váh
Freistadt
Krems
Stockerau
Trnava
Nitra
Topoľčany
Zvolen
Nitra
Hron
Levice
Melk
Sankt Pölten
WIEN (Vienna)
Bratislava
Traun
Amstetten
Baden
Bruck an der Leitha
Steyr
Enns
Neusiedler See
Dunaj (Danube)
Nové Zámky
Wiener Neustadt
Moson-magyaróvár
Komárno
Vác
SÖLKTALER
Semmering P.
Győr
Esztergom
Dunakeszi
AUSTRIA
985
Mürzzuschlag
Sopron
Eisenerz
Kapfenberg
Rába
Tatabánya
BUDAPEST
Tauern
2449
Bruck an der Mur
Leoben
PÖLLAUER TAL
Pápa
709
Szombathely
Steiermark
Ajka
Bakony
Székesfehérvár
Graz
Veszprém
Mur
BALATON FELVIDÉKI
Dunaújváros
Balaton
Siófok
KISKUNSÁGI
Zalaegerszeg
HUNGARY
Kalocsa
Nagykanizsa
Szekszárd
Duna (Danube)
Varaždin
Kaposvár
681
DUNA-DRAVA
Koprivnica
Baja
Pécs
Bjelovar
Virovitica
Mohács
Drava
ITALY
Dolomiti
0
50
100
150
300
m
ft
East from Greenwich
12
14
16
18
54
52
50
48
46
A
B
C
D
E
F
16
20
COPYRIGHT PHILIP'S

GERMANY
POLAND
CZECH REP.
SLOVAKIA
AUSTRIA
HUNGARY
SLOVENIA
CROATIA
SERBIA
BERLIN
WARSZAWA (Warsaw)
PRAHA (Prague)
WIEN (Vienna)
Bratislava
BUDAPEST
Ljubljana
ZAGREB
Zatoka Gdańska
Zalew Wiślany
Stettiner Haff
Pojezierze Pomorskie
Pojezierze Mazurskie
Gdańsk
Gdynia
Sopot
Słupsk
Koszalin
Kołobrzeg
Szczecin
Świnoujście
Bydgoszcz
Toruń
Grudziądz
Elbląg
Olsztyn
Kaliningrad
Poznań
Gorzów Wielkopolski
Zielona Góra
Wrocław
Łódź
Częstochowa
Kraków
Katowice
Opole
Kielce
Płock
Włocławek
Legnica
Wałbrzych
Jelenia Góra
Bielsko-Biała
Ostrava
Olomouc
Brno
Plzeň
České Budějovice
Jihlava
Hradec Králové
Pardubice
Liberec
Ústí nad Labem
Karlovy Vary
Cheb
Chemnitz
Dresden
Cottbus
Frankfurt
Linz
Salzburg
Graz
Klagenfurt
Sankt Pölten
Wiener Neustadt
Maribor
Győr
Székesfehérvár
Kecskemét
Szeged
Pécs
Miskolc
Zvolen
Nitra
Trenčín
Žilina
Poprad
Prešov
Banská Bystrica
Osijek
Novi Sad
Subotica
Rijeka
Trieste
Erzgebirge
Böhmerwald
Sudety
Karpaty
Tatry
Nízke Tatry
Západné Beskydy
Steiermark
Kärnten
Karawanken
Bakony
Balaton
Wisła
Odra
Warta
Dunaj (Danube)
Donau (Danube)
Drava
Sava
Tisza
Vojvodina
Projection: Conical with two standard parallels

50 0 25 50 75 100 125 150 175 km
50 0 25 50 75 100 125 miles
7
8
9
10
B
C
D
E
F
6
7
8
24
25
22
East from Greenwich
COPYRIGHT PHILIP'S
BELARUS
UKRAINE
MOLDOVA
ROMANIA
MINSK
Dzyarzhynsk
Hrodzyanka
Asipovichy
Babruysk
Bykhaw
Slawharad
Ragachow
Zhlobin
Homyel
Lida
Nyoman
Navahrudak
Hrodna
Masty
Dzyatlava
Stowbtsy
Nyasvizh
Slutsk
Baranavichy
Vawkavysk
Slonim
Klyetsk
Glusk
Aktsyabrski
Svyetlahorsk
Rechytsa
Byarezina
Białystok
Svislach
Lyakhavichy
Hantsavichy
Salihorsk
Hajnówka
Ivatsevichy
Byaroza
Tsyelyakhany
Vasilevichi
Pyetrikaw
Kalinkavichy
Pruzhany
Yaselda
Luninyets
Pripyats
Kobryn
Dragichyn
Loyew
Khoyniki
Mazyr
Zhabinka
Ivanava
Pinsk
Davyd Haradok
PRIPYATSKY
Yelsk
Biała Podlaska
Brest
Stolin
Malaryta
Międzyrzec Podlaski
Pripet Marshes
Kamin-Kashyrskyy
Dubrovytsya
Ovruch
Chornobyl
Prypyat
Oster
Włodawa
Olevsk
Belokorovichi
Uzh
Kyyivske Vdskh.
Lyuboml
Kovel
Staryy Chortoriysk
Sluch
Korosten
Dymer
Irpin
Chełm
Rozhyshche
Kivertsi
Kostopil
Novohrad-Volynskyy
Malyn
Teterev
KYYIV (Kiev)
Novovolynsk
Volodymyr-Volynskyy
Lutsk
Oleksandriya
Rivne
Zdolbuniv
Korets
Radomyshl
Korostyshev
Vasylkiv
Zamość
Horokhiv
Dubno
Ostroh
Slavuta
Zhytomyr
Pershotravensk
Fastiv
Sokal
Chervonohrad
Radekhiv
Berestechko
Kremenets
Shepetivka
Izyaslav
Polonne
Berdychiv
Bila Tserkva
Rava-Ruska
Kamyanka-Buzka
Brody
Skvyra
Tarashcha
Nesterov
Yavoriv
Starokonstyantyniv
Khmelnik
Kozyatyn
Tetiyev
Mostyska
Lviv (Lvov)
Zolochiv
Zbarazh
Horodok
Ternopil
Skalat
Podilska Vysochyna
Khmelnytskyy
Vinnytsya
Lipovets
Zhashkiv
Sambir
Khodoriv
Berezhany
Hrymayliv
Drohobych
Rogatyn
Terebovlya
Horodok
Bar
Zhmerynka
Haysyn
Boryslav
Kopychyntsi
Truskavets
Stryy
Dnister
Buchach
Chortkiv
Tulchyn
Uman
Skole
Kalush
Skala-Podilska
Kamyanets-Podilskyy
Vapnyarka
Hayvoron
Bolekhiv
Zalishchyky
Ivano-Frankivsk
Horodenka
Mohyliv-Podilskyy
Bershad
Uzhhorod
Volovets
Nadvirna
Kolomyya
Khotyn
Pechenizhyn
Snyatyn
Ocnița
Yarempil
Balta
Yaremcha
Novoselytsya
Lipcani
Mukacheve
Chernivtsi
Drochia
Soroca
Ananyiv
Berehove
Yasinya
Hlyboka
Edineț
Florești
Khust
Storozhynets
Kotovsk
Rakhiv
Dorohoi
Râbnița
Bălți
Vynohradiv
Tyachiv
Siret
Dubăsari Vdkhr.
Transnistria
Sighetu-Marmatiei
Rădăuți
Fălești
Satu Mare
Botoșani
Suceava
Dubăsari
Borșa
Cornești
Baia Mare
Pietrosul
Fălticeni
Orhei
Carei
Someș
Pașcani
Ungheni
Chișinău
Tiraspol
Vatra-Dornei
Iași
Bistrița
Pietrosul
Roman
Tighina
Zalău
Dej
Bistrița
Piatra Neamț
Huși
Leova
Cimișlia
Dnister
Nistru
Vaslui
Mureș
Reghin
Prut
Cluj-Napoca
Bacău
Basarabeasca
Bilhorod-Dnistrovskyy
Târgu Mureș
Comrat
Turda
Miercurea-Ciuc
Bârlad
Artsyz
Munții Bihor
Odorheiu Secuiesc
Onești
Ciadâr-Lunga
Abrud
Cahul
Tatarbunary
Tecuci
Brad
Târnăveni
Sighișoara
Sfântu Gheorghe
Alba-Iulia
Aiud
Mediaș
Bolhrad
Ozero Sasyk
Vulcanești
Kiliya
Vylkove
Focșani
Deva
Sibiu
Olt
Făgăraș
Brașov
Izmayil
Reni
Simeria
Galați
Sulina
Săcele
Râmnicu Sărat
Brăila
Hunedoara
Carpații Meridionali
P. Turnu Roșu
Vf. Moldoveanu
Petroșani
Câmpulung
Vf. Omul
Câmpina
Buzău
Dunărea (Danube)
Vf. Peleaga
Vulcan
RETEZAT
Parângul Mare
Curtea de Argeș
Alytus
Druskininkai
Sokółka
Wola
Zhashkiv

# 18 SPAIN AND PORTUGAL

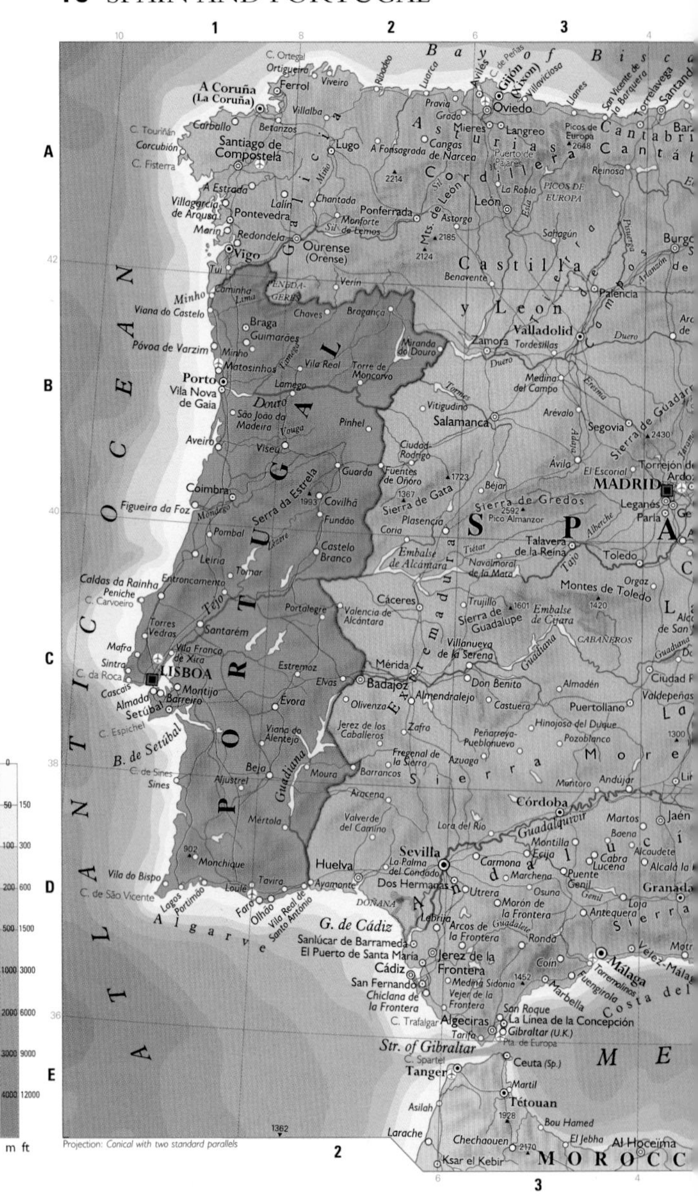

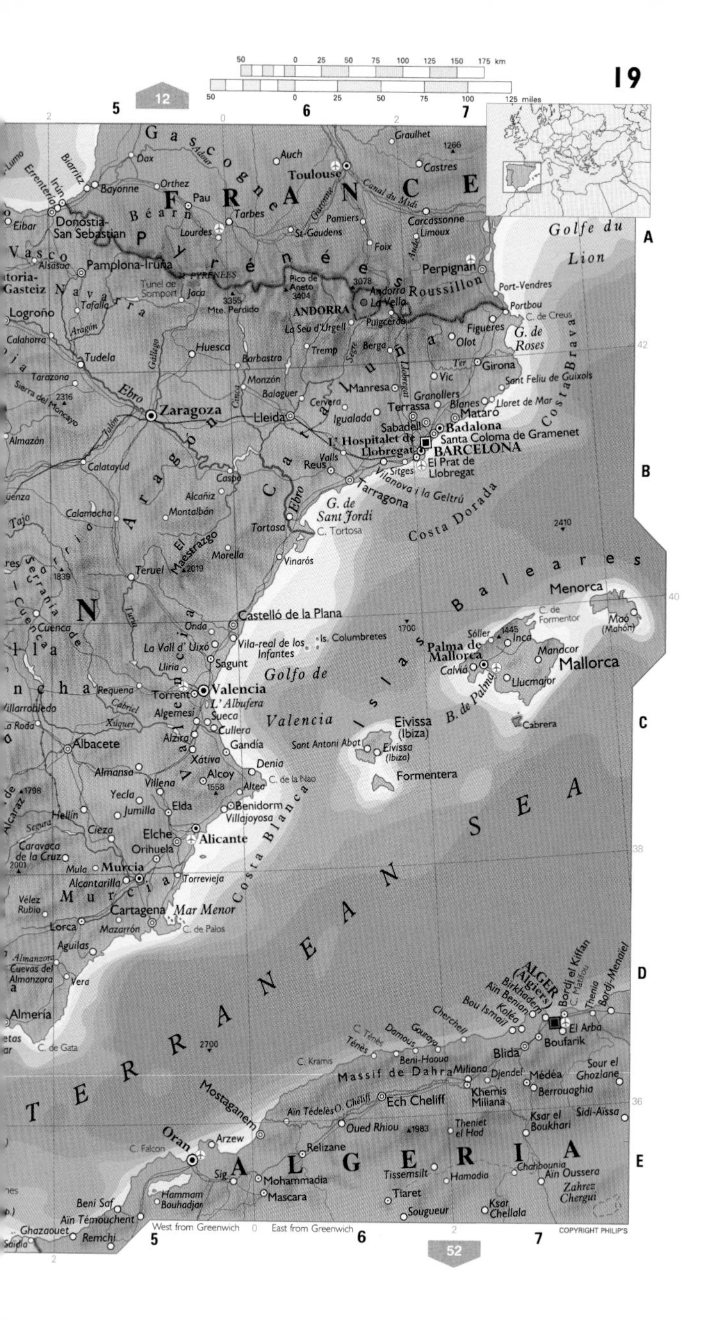

FRANCE
Gascogne
Béarn
Pyrénées
Toulouse
Bayonne
Biarritz
Dax
Auch
Orthez
Pau
Tarbes
Lourdes
St-Gaudens
Pamiers
Foix
Carcassonne
Limoux
Castres
Graulhet
Canal du Midi
Perpignan
Roussillon
Golfe du Lion
Port-Vendres
Portbou
C. de Creus
Donostia-San Sebastian
Irún
Errenteria
Eibar
Pamplona-Iruña
Vasco
Alsasua
Navarra
Vitoria-Gasteiz
Logroño
Tafalla
Túnel de Somport
Jaca
Mte. Perdido
3355
Pico de Aneto
3404
3078
ANDORRA
Andorra La Vella
Puigcerdà
La Seu d'Urgell
Tremp
Berga
Olot
Figueres
G. de Roses
Girona
Vic
Manresa
Catalunya
Costa Brava
Sant Feliu de Guíxols
Lloret de Mar
Blanes
Granollers
Terrassa
Mataró
Sabadell
Badalona
Santa Coloma de Gramenet
L'Hospitalet de Llobregat
BARCELONA
El Prat de Llobregat
Sitges
Vilanova i la Geltrú
Tarragona
Reus
Valls
Costa Dorada
Calahorra
Tudela
Huesca
Barbastro
Monzón
Balaguer
Cervera
Igualada
Lleida
Zaragoza
Aragón
Ebro
Tarazona
Sierra del Moncayo
2316
Almazán
Calatayud
Caspe
Alcañiz
Montalbán
Calamocha
Teruel
El Maestrazgo
2019
Morella
Tortosa
G. de Sant Jordi
C. Tortosa
Vinarós
2410
Islas Baleares
Menorca
Maó (Mahón)
C. de Formentor
Sóller
1445
Inca
Manacor
Palma de Mallorca
Calvià
Llucmajor
Mallorca
B. de Palma
Cabrera
Eivissa (Ibiza)
Sant Antoni Abat
Formentera
1700
Is. Columbretes
Castelló de la Plana
Onda
La Vall d'Uixó
Vila-real de los Infantes
Sagunt
Llíria
Golfo de Valencia
Valencia
Torrent
L'Albufera
Requena
Algemesí
Sueca
Cullera
Alzira
Gandía
Xàtiva
Denia
C. de la Nao
Alcoy
1558
Altea
Benidorm
Villajoyosa
Valenciana
Albacete
Almansa
Villena
Yecla
Jumilla
Elda
Hellín
Cieza
Elche
Alicante
Orihuela
Costa Blanca
Caravaca de la Cruz
2001
Mula
Murcia
Alcantarilla
Torrevieja
Cartagena
Mar Menor
C. de Palos
Mazarrón
Lorca
Vélez Rubio
Águilas
Cuevas del Almanzora
Vera
Almería
C. de Gata
Cuenca
Serranía de Cuenca
1839
Tajo
Mancha
Villarrobledo
Cabriel
Xúquer
1798
MEDITERRANEAN SEA
2700
ALGER (Algiers)
Bordj el Kiffan
C. Matifou
Thenia
Bordj-Menaiel
Birkhadem
Aïn Benian
Koléa
Bou Ismaïl
Cherchell
Gouraya
Damous
C. Ténès
Ténès
Beni-Haoua
C. Kramis
El Arba
Boufarik
Blida
Massif de Dahra
Miliana
Djendel
Médéa
Sour el Ghozlane
Khemis Miliana
Berrouaghia
Ech Cheliff
Aïn Tédelès
O. Chéliff
Mostaganem
Oued Rhiou
1983
Theniet el Had
Ksar el Boukhari
Sidi-Aïssa
Oran
C. Falcon
Arzew
Relizane
ALGERIA
Sig
Mohammadia
Mascara
Tissemsilt
Hamadia
Tiaret
Chahbounia
Aïn Oussera
Zahrez Chergui
Sougueur
Ksar Chellala
Hammam Bouhadjar
Beni Saf
Aïn Témouchent
Ghazaouet
Remchi
Saïda
West from Greenwich
East from Greenwich
km
miles
A
B
C
D
E
5
6
7
12
52

SWITZERLAND
AUSTRIA
SLOVENIA
CROATIA
HUNGARY
BOSNIA-
HERZEGOVINA
FRANCE
MONACO
SAN MARINO
VATICAN CITY
ITALIA
ADRIATIC SEA
LIGURIAN SEA
Golfo di Génova
Golfo di Venézia
Alpes Maritimes
Dolomiti
Kärnische Alpen
Karawanken
Steiermark
Kärnten
Lombárdia
Piemonte
Liguria
Toscana
Lazio
Dalmacija
Istra
Kvarner
Kvarnerić
Velika Kapela
Velebit Planina
Dinara Planina
Riviera di Ponente
Riviera di Levante
Côte d'Azur
Bouches de Bonifacio
Corse (Corsica)
ROMA
MILANO
ZAGREB
Ljubljana
Sarajevo
Torino (Turin)
Génova
Venézia (Venice)
Firenze (Florence)
Trieste
Rijeka
Split
Zadar
Dubrovnik
Mostar
Banja Luka
Graz
Klagenfurt
Villach
Maribor
Pécs
Bologna
Verona
Pádova
Ancona
Pescara
Nice
Grenoble
Chambéry
Annecy
Ajaccio
Bastia
Elba
Livorno
Pisa
Parma
Ferrara
Ravenna
Rímini
Perugia
Viterbo
Latina
Foggia
16
14
22
1 2 3 4 5 6 7
A B C

# ITALY AND THE ADRIATIC

m
4000
3000
2000
1000
500
200
100
50
ft
12000
9000
6000
3000
1500
600
300
150
0
17
20
BLACK SEA
ADRIATIC
UKRAINE
ROMANIA
HUNGARY
CROATIA
BOSNIA-HERZEGOVINA
SERBIA
MONTENEGRO
KOSOVO
MACEDONIA
BULGARIA
Vojvodina
Transilvania
Carpatii Meridionali
Stara Planina
Rhodopi Planina
Dobrogea
Valahia
Yildiz Dağlari
BUCUREŞTI (Bucharest)
BEOGRAD (Belgrade)
SOFIYA
ISTANBUL
Sarajevo
Skopje
Podgorica
Priština
Constanţa
Varna
Burgas
Galaţi
Brăila
Ploieşti
Braşov
Craiova
Timişoara
Novi Sad
Szeged
Subotica
Pécs
Osijek
Niš
Plovdiv
Ruse
Pleven
Mostar
Tuzla
Zenica
Kragujevac
Edirne
Dunărea (Danube)
Sava
Drava
Tisa
Morava
İstanbul Boğazi (Bosporus)

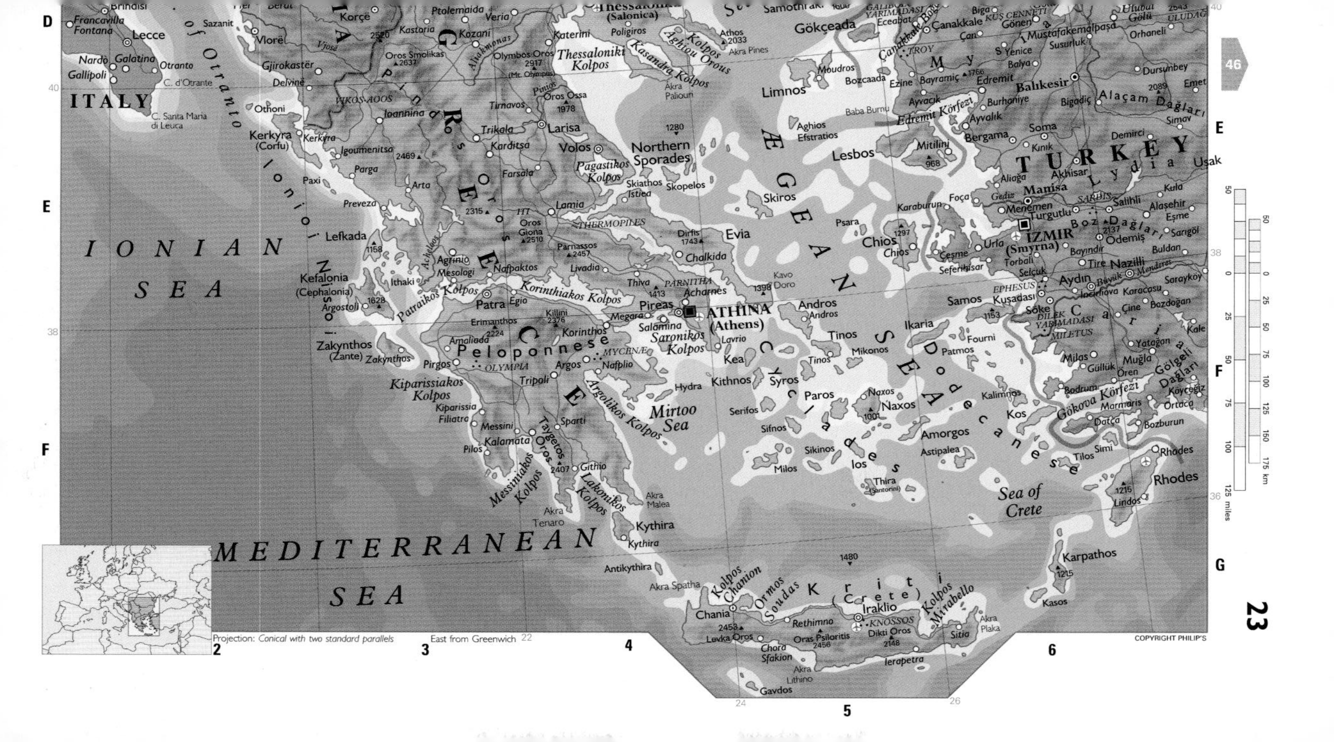
ITALY
GREECE
TURKEY
IONIAN SEA
AEGEAN SEA
MEDITERRANEAN SEA
Sea of Crete
Mirtoo Sea
Ionioi Nisoi
Peloponnese
Cyclades
Dodecanese
Northern Sporades
Kriti (Crete)
Lydia
Caria
Mysia
Pindos Oros
ATHINA (Athens)
IZMIR (Smyrna)
Thessaloniki (Salonica)
Brindisi
Francavilla Fontana
Lecce
Nardò
Galatina
Gallipoli
Otranto
C. d'Otrante
C. Santa Maria di Leuca
Vlorë
Gjirokastër
Delvinë
Korçë
Sazanit
Othoni
Kerkyra (Corfu)
Paxi
Lefkada
Kefalonia (Cephalonia)
Argostoli
Ithaki
Zakynthos (Zante)
Ioannina
Igoumenitsa
Parga
Preveza
Arta
Agrinio
Mesologi
Nafpaktos
Patra
Egio
Pirgos
Amaliada
Tripoli
Argos
Nafplio
Korinthos
Sparti
Kalamata
Messini
Pilos
Kiparissia
Filiatra
Githio
Kythira
Antikythira
Akra Tenaro
Akra Malea
Kastoria
Ptolemaida
Kozani
Veria
Katerini
Larisa
Volos
Trikala
Karditsa
Farsala
Tirnavos
Lamia
Livadia
Thiva
Chalkida
Evia
Skiros
Skiathos
Skopelos
Istiea
Megara
Salamina
Pireas
Acharnes
Lavrio
Kea
Kithnos
Serifos
Sifnos
Milos
Sikinos
Ios
Thira (Santorini)
Syros
Paros
Naxos
Tinos
Mikonos
Andros
Amorgos
Astipalea
Kalimnos
Kos
Patmos
Fourni
Ikaria
Samos
Chios
Psara
Lesbos
Mitilini
Limnos
Moudros
Aghios Efstratios
Gökçeada
Bozcaada
Hydra
Chania
Rethimno
Iraklio
Sitia
Ierapetra
Gavdos
Karpathos
Kasos
Rhodes
Lindos
Tilos
Simi
Çanakkale
Ezine
Ayvacık
Ayvalık
Edremit
Balıkesir
Bergama
Soma
Manisa
Menemen
Aliağa
Foça
Karaburun
Çeşme
Urla
Torbalı
Selçuk
Kuşadası
Söke
Aydın
Nazilli
Ödemiş
Turgutlu
Salihli
Alaşehir
Muğla
Milas
Bodrum
Marmaris
Datça
Bozburun
Uşak
Akhisar
Demirci
Dursunbey
Mustafakemalpaşa
Susurluk
Gönen
Biga
Çan
Yenice
Balya
Burhaniye
Bayramiç
Bigadiç
Alaçam Dağları
Boz Dağlar
Edremit Körfezi
Gökova Körfezi
Thessaloniki Kolpos
Kasandra Kolpos
Aghiou Orous Kolpos
Pagastikos Kolpos
Patraikos Kolpos
Korinthiakos Kolpos
Saronikos Kolpos
Argolikos Kolpos
Lakonikos Kolpos
Messiniakos Kolpos
Kiparissiakos Kolpos
Kolpos Chanion
Ormos Soudas
Kolpos Mirabello
Oros Smolikas
Olymbos Oros (Mt. Olympus)
Oros Ossa
Oros Giona
Parnassos
Taygetos Oros
Lefka Oros
Oras Psiloritis
Dikti Oros
Athos
Akra Pines
Akra Spatha
Akra Plaka
Akra Lithino
Kavo Doro
TROY
THERMOPYLAE
MYCENAE
OLYMPIA
EPHESUS
MILETUS
SARDIS
KNOSSOS
Projection: Conical with two standard parallels
East from Greenwich
0 25 50 75 100 125 150 175 km
0 25 50 75 100 125 miles
COPYRIGHT PHILIP'S
46

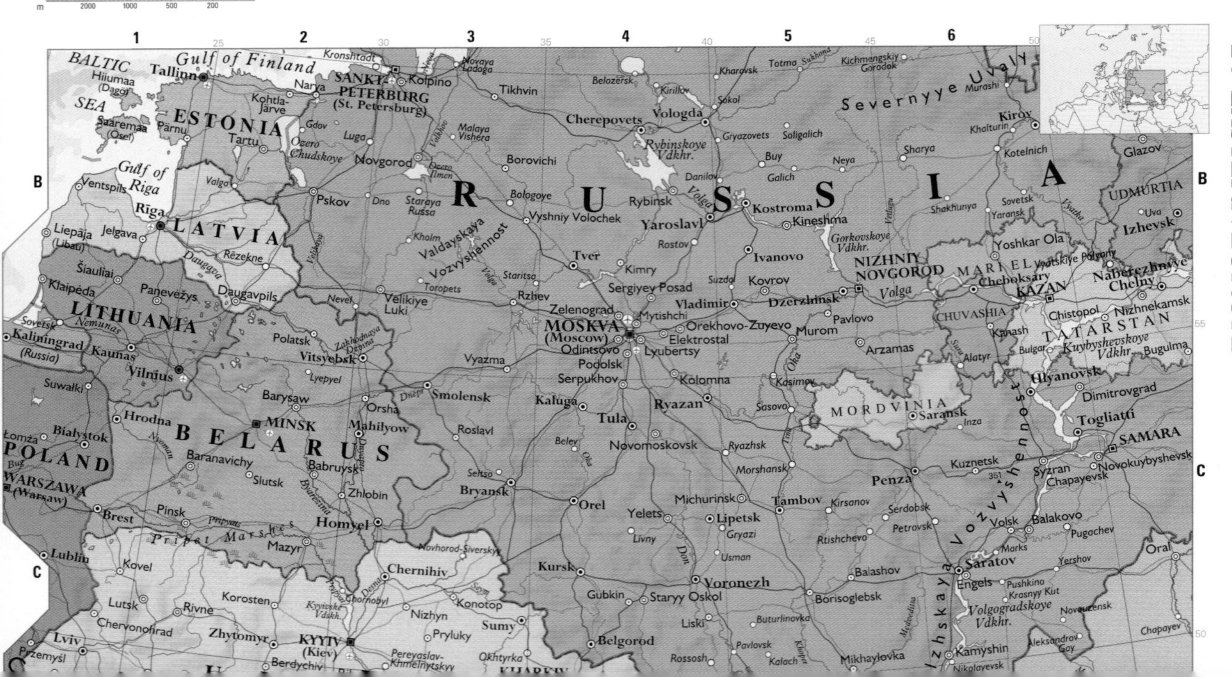

ft 6000 3000 1500 600 0
m 2000 1000 500 200
RUSSIA
ESTONIA
LATVIA
LITHUANIA
BELARUS
POLAND
UDMURTIA
TATARSTAN
CHUVASHIA
MARI EL
MORDVINIA
BALTIC SEA
Gulf of Finland
Gulf of Riga
Severnyye Uvaly
Valdayskaya Vozvyshennost
Privolzhskaya Vozvyshennost
Rybinskoye Vdkhr.
Gorkovskoye Vdkhr.
Kuybyshevskoye Vdkhr.
Volgogradskoye Vdkhr.
Pripet Marshes
MOSKVA (Moscow)
SANKT-PETERBURG (St. Petersburg)
NIZHNIY NOVGOROD
KAZAN
SAMARA
MINSK
KYYIV (Kiev)
WARSZAWA (Warsaw)
Tallinn
Riga
Vilnius
Kaliningrad (Russia)
Izhevsk
Kirov
Glazov
Yoshkar Ola
Cheboksary
Naberezhnyye Chelny
Nizhnekamsk
Chistopol
Dimitrovgrad
Ulyanovsk
Togliatti
Syzran
Novokuybyshevsk
Chapayevsk
Balakovo
Saratov
Engels
Volsk
Kuznetsk
Penza
Saransk
Arzamas
Dzerzhinsk
Murom
Pavlovo
Ivanovo
Kovrov
Kostroma
Kineshma
Yaroslavl
Rybinsk
Vologda
Cherepovets
Tver
Vladimir
Orekhovo-Zuyevo
Elektrostal
Lyubertsy
Podolsk
Serpukhov
Kolomna
Ryazan
Tula
Novomoskovsk
Kaluga
Orel
Bryansk
Smolensk
Kursk
Belgorod
Voronezh
Lipetsk
Tambov
Michurinsk
Yelets
Staryy Oskol
Balashov
Borisoglebsk
Kamyshin
Pskov
Novgorod
Velikiye Luki
Vitsyebsk
Orsha
Mahilyow
Babruysk
Homyel
Hrodna
Brest
Pinsk
Baranavichy
Barysaw
Chernihiv
Zhytomyr
Rivne
Lutsk
Lviv
Sumy
Konotop
Kaunas
Klaipėda
Šiauliai
Panevėžys
Daugavpils
Liepāja (Libau)
Jelgava
Tartu
Pärnu
Narva
Lublin
Białystok
Volga
Oka
Don
Dnyapro
Pripyat
Nyoman

ROMANIA
MOLDOVA
BULGARIA
TURKEY
GEORGIA
ARMENIA
AZERBAIJAN
IRAN
KALMYKIA
CRIMEA
DAGESTAN
CHECHENIA
ABKHAZIA
AJARIA
BLACK SEA
Sea of Azov
CASPIAN SEA
Caspian Depression
Caucasus Mountains
Kuzey Anadolu Dağları
Anadolu
Bessarabia
Botoșani
Bălți
Iași
Chișinău
Tiraspol
Tighina
Bacău
Brașov
Focșani
Galați
Brăila
Izmayil
Buzău
Pitești
Ploiești
BUCUREȘTI (Bucharest)
Constanța
Ruse
Silistra
Dobrich
Veliko Tŭrnovo
Varna
Sliven
Burgas
Khaskovo
Edirne
İSTANBUL
Tekirdağ
Marmara Denizi
Bandırma
Çanakkale
BURSA
Balıkeşir
İZMİR (Smyrna)
Manisa
Aydın
Kütahya
Eskişehir
ANKARA
Zonguldak
Sakarya
Kocaeli (İzmit)
Samsun
Sinop
Trabzon
Rize
Erzurum
Sivas
Kayseri
Malatya
Elazığ
Van Gölü
Van
ODESA
Mykolayiv
Kherson
Kryvyy Rih
Zaporizhzhya
Nikopol
Melitopol
DONETSK
Horlivka
Mariupol
Berdyansk
Taganrog
ROSTOV
Novocherkassk
Shakhty
Volgodonsk
Yevpatoriya
Simferopol
Sevastopol
Yalta
Kerch
Feodosiya
Novorossiysk
Krasnodar
Maykop
Armavir
Stavropol
Elista
Astrakhan
Tuapse
Sochi
Sokhumi
Kutaisi
Poti
Batumi
TBILISI
Rustavi
Nalchik
Vladikavkaz
Groznyy
Makhachkala
Derbent
Gyumri
YEREVAN
Gäncä
Sumqayıt
BAKI (Baku)
TABRĪZ
Ardabīl
Projection: Conical with two standard parallels
East from Greenwich
COPYRIGHT PHILIP'S

100 0 200 400 600 800 1000 1200 1400 km

100 0 200 400 600 800 1000 miles

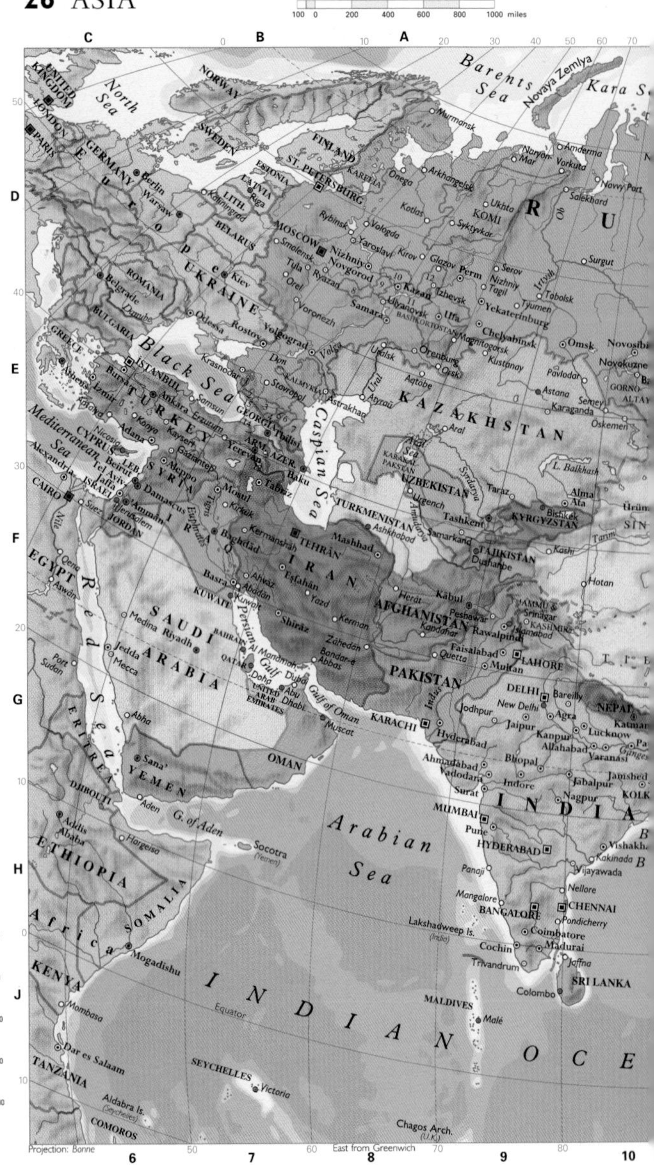


0
200 600
1000 3000
2000 6000
4000 12000
6000 18000
8000 24000

m ft

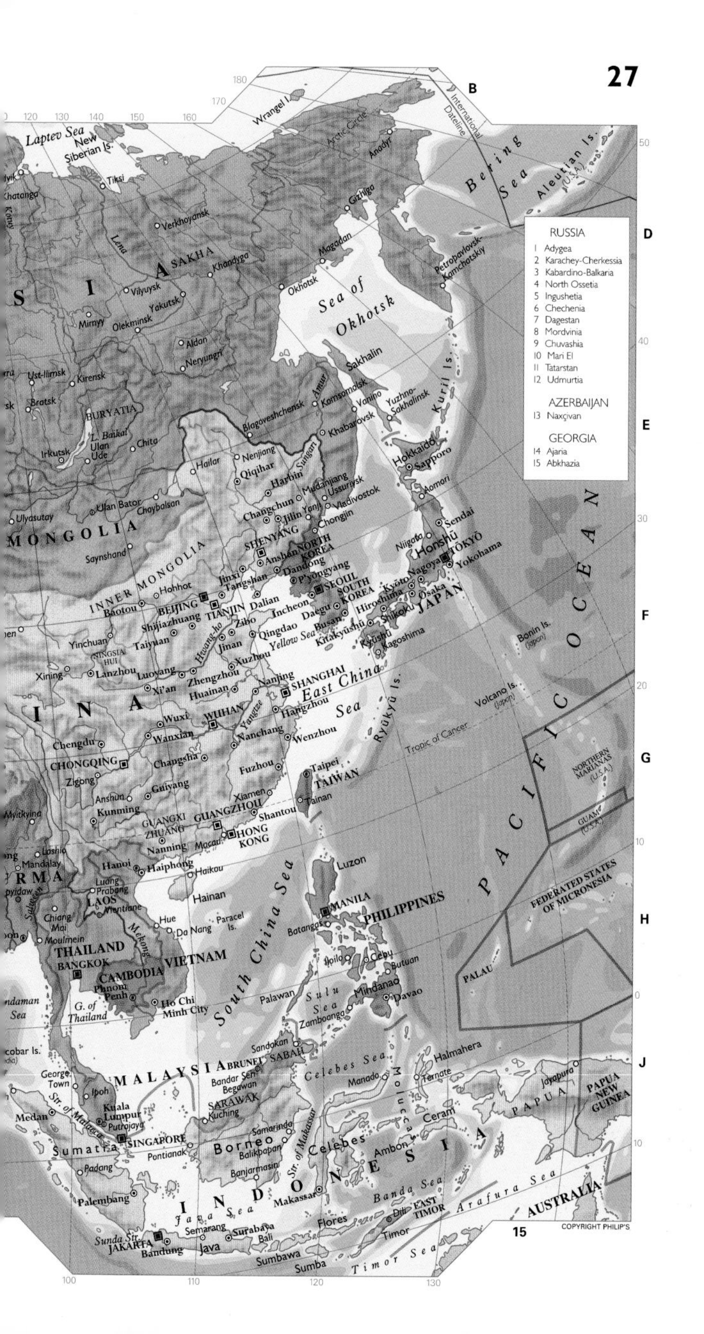
RUSSIA
1 Adygea
2 Karachey-Cherkessia
3 Kabardino-Balkaria
4 North Ossetia
5 Ingushetia
6 Chechenia
7 Dagestan
8 Mordvinia
9 Chuvashia
10 Mari El
11 Tatarstan
12 Udmurtia
AZERBAIJAN
13 Naxçivan
GEORGIA
14 Ajaria
15 Abkhazia
Laptev Sea
New Siberian Is.
Wrangel I.
Arctic Circle
International Dateline
Bering Sea
Aleutian Is. (U.S.A.)
Anadyr
Tiksi
Khatanga
Verkhoyansk
Lena
SAKHA
Khandyga
Magadan
Gizhiga
Petropavlovsk-Kamchatskiy
Okhotsk
Sea of Okhotsk
Vilyuysk
Yakutsk
Mirnyy
Olekminsk
Aldan
Neryungri
Sakhalin
Kuril Is.
Ust-Ilimsk
Kirensk
Bratsk
BURYATIA
L. Baikal
Irkutsk
Ulan Ude
Chita
Amur
Komsomolsk
Vanino
Yuzhno-Sakhalinsk
Blagoveshchensk
Khabarovsk
Hailar
Nenjiang
Qiqihar
Harbin
Sungari
Hokkaido
Sapporo
Mudanjiang
Ussuriysk
Vladivostok
Aomori
Ulan Bator
Choybalsan
Uliastay
MONGOLIA
Changchun
Jilin
Yanji
Chongjin
SHENYANG
NORTH KOREA
Sendai
Niigata
Honshu
TOKYO
Yokohama
Saynshand
INNER MONGOLIA
Anshan
Dandong
P'yongyang
SEOUL
SOUTH KOREA
Kyoto
Nagoya
Osaka
JAPAN
Hohhot
Jinxi
Tangshan
BEIJING
TIANJIN
Dalian
Incheon
Daegu
Hiroshima
Baotou
Shijiazhuang
Zibo
Qingdao
Yellow Sea
Busan
Kitakyushu
Shikoku
Kyushu
Kagoshima
Bonin Is. (Japan)
Yinchuan
NINGSIA HUI
Taiyuan
Hwang-ho
Jinan
Xuzhou
Xining
Lanzhou
Luoyang
Zhengzhou
Nanjing
SHANGHAI
East China Sea
Xi'an
Huainan
Ryukyu Is.
Volcano Is. (Japan)
Wuxi
WUHAN
Yangtze
Hangzhou
Wanxian
Nanchang
Wenzhou
Tropic of Cancer
Chengdu
CHONGQING
Changsha
Fuzhou
Taipei
TAIWAN
Tainan
Zigong
Guiyang
Xiamen
Anshun
Kunming
GUANGZHOU
Shantou
NORTHERN MARIANAS (U.S.A.)
GUAM (U.S.A.)
PACIFIC OCEAN
Myitkyina
GUANGXI ZHUANG
Macau
HONG KONG
Nanning
Lashio
Mandalay
Hanoi
Haiphong
Haikou
Luzon
Luang Prabang
LAOS
Vientiane
Hainan
South China Sea
MANILA
PHILIPPINES
FEDERATED STATES OF MICRONESIA
Chiang Mai
Hue
Da Nang
Paracel Is.
Batangas
Moulmein
Mekong
THAILAND
VIETNAM
Iloilo
Cebu
Butuan
BANGKOK
CAMBODIA
PALAU
Phnom Penh
Palawan
Sulu Sea
Mindanao
Davao
Andaman Sea
G. of Thailand
Ho Chi Minh City
Zamboanga
Nicobar Is.
Sandakan
SABAH
Halmahera
BRUNEI
Bandar Seri Begawan
Celebes Sea
Manado
Ternate
Jayapura
George Town
MALAYSIA
Ipoh
SARAWAK
Moluccas
PAPUA
PAPUA NEW GUINEA
Kuala Lumpur
Putrajaya
Medan
Str. of Malacca
Kuching
Samarinda
Ceram
SINGAPORE
Sumatra
Pontianak
Borneo
Balikpapan
Str. of Makassar
Celebes
Ambon
Padang
Banjarmasin
INDONESIA
Banda Sea
Arafura Sea
Palembang
Makassar
Dili
EAST TIMOR
AUSTRALIA
Java Sea
Flores
Timor
Sunda Str.
JAKARTA
Semarang
Surabaya
Bali
Bandung
Java
Sumbawa
Sumba
Timor Sea
B
D
E
F
G
H
J
15
COPYRIGHT PHILIP'S

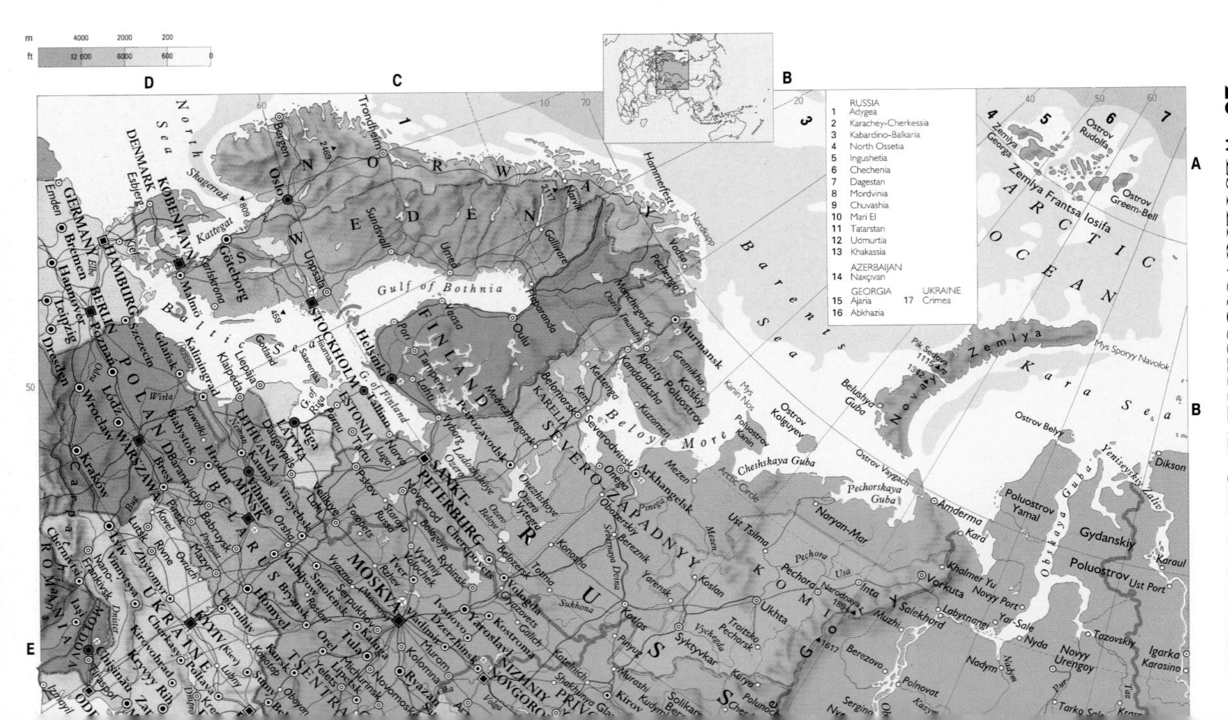
m 4000 2000 200
ft 12 000 6000 600 0
RUSSIA
1 Adygea
2 Karachey-Cherkessia
3 Kabardino-Balkaria
4 North Ossetia
5 Ingushetia
6 Chechenia
7 Dagestan
8 Mordvinia
9 Chuvashia
10 Mari El
11 Tatarstan
12 Udmurtia
13 Khakassia
AZERBAIJAN
14 Naxçıvan
GEORGIA
15 Ajaria
16 Abkhazia
UKRAINE
17 Crimea
A R C T I C O C E A N
Zemlya Frantsa Iosifa
Zemlya Georga
Ostrov Rudolfa
Ostrov Greem-Bell
Kara Sea
Barents Sea
Novaya Zemlya
Mys Sporyy Navolok
Pik Sedova
Belushya Guba
Ostrov Belyy
Poluostrov Yamal
Obskaya Guba
Gydanskiy Poluostrov
Yeniseyskiy Zaliv
Dikson
Ostrov Vaygach
Pechorskaya Guba
Naryan-Mar
Ostrov Kolguyev
Cheshskaya Guba
Poluostrov Kanin
Mys Kanin Nos
Arctic Circle
Beloye More
Kolskiy Poluostrov
Murmansk
Nordkapp
Hammerfest
Vadsø
Pechenga
Arkhangelsk
Severodvinsk
Onega
Kandalaksha
Apatity
Monchegorsk
Kem
Belomorsk
KARELIA
Narvik
Gällivare
Haparanda
Oulu
Gulf of Bothnia
Umeå
Vaasa
FINLAND
Tampere
Pori
Lahti
Helsinki
G. of Finland
Tallinn
ESTONIA
Tartu
Pärnu
Hiiumaa
Saaremaa
G. of Riga
Rīga
LATVIA
Daugavpils
LITHUANIA
Kaunas
Vilnius
Klaipėda
Liepāja
Gotland
Baltic Sea
STOCKHOLM
Uppsala
Sundsvall
Trondheim
Bergen
Oslo
NORWAY
SWEDEN
Göteborg
Karlskrona
Malmö
Skagerrak
Kattegat
North Sea
KØBENHAVN
DENMARK
Esbjerg
Kiel
HAMBURG
Emden
Bremen
Hannover
GERMANY
Elbe
BERLIN
Leipzig
Dresden
Szczecin
Gdańsk
Kaliningrad (Russia)
POLAND
Poznań
Łódź
WARSZAWA
Wrocław
Kraków
Białystok
Suwałki
Hrodna
MINSK
BELARUS
Brest
Pinsk
Baranavichy
Babruysk
Mahilyow
Vitsyebsk
Orsha
Homyel
Mazyr
UKRAINE
Kovel
Lutsk
Rivne
Lviv
Ivano-Frankivsk
Chernivtsi
Zhytomyr
KYYIV (Kiev)
Chernihiv
Cherkasy
Poltava
Kirovohrad
Kryvyy Rih
Vinnytsya
Dnister
MOLDOVA
Chişinău
Tiraspol
Iaşi
ROMANIA
SANKT-PETERBURG
Vyborg
Petrozavodsk
Medvezhyegorsk
Ladozhskoye Ozero
Onezhskoye Ozero
Novgorod
Pskov
Luga
Narva
Staraya Russa
Velikiye Luki
Toropets
Smolensk
Roslavl
Bryansk
MOSKVA
Tver
Rzhev
Vyazma
Kaluga
Tula
Serpukhov
Orel
Kursk
Vladimir
Ivanovo
Yaroslavl
Rybinsk
Kostroma
Vologda
Cherepovets
Belozersk
Kotlas
Syktyvkar
Ukhta
Pechora
Vorkuta
Inta
Salekhard
Labytnangi
Nadym
Novyy Urengoy
Igarka
Karasino
SEVERO-ZAPADNYY
KOMI
Severnaya Dvina
Mezen
Kirov
Ryazan
Kolomna
Murom
NIZHNIY NOVGOROD
Volga
Dnipro
Izmayil

KAZAKHSTAN
UZBEKISTAN
TURKMENISTAN
KYRGYZSTAN
TAJIKISTAN
AFGHANISTAN
IRAN
IRAQ
TURKEY
GEORGIA
ARMENIA
AZERBAIJAN
CHINA
SIBIRSKIY
NOVOSIBIRSK
OMSK
YEKATERINBURG
CHELYABINSK
SAMARA
UFA
VOLGOGRAD
ROSTOV
TOSHKENT (Tashkent)
ALMATY
BAKI (Baku)
TBILISI
YEREVAN
TEHRĀN
TABRĪZ
MASHHAD
EŞFAHĀN
SHĪRĀZ
BAGHDĀD
AL MAWSIL (Mosul)
ÜRÜMQI
Astana
Qaraghandy
Bishkek
Dushanbe
Ashgabat
Aral Sea
Caspian Sea
Black Sea
Ustyurt Plateau
Kyzyl Kum
Garagum
Junggar Pendi
Pamir
Kūhhā-ye Zāgros
Dasht-e Kavīr
D
E
F
G
6
7
8
9
40
60
70
80
90
30
100 0 100 200 300 400 500 600 700 800 km
100 0 100 200 300 400 500 miles
Projection: Conical Orthomorphic with two standard parallels
East from Greenwich
COPYRIGHT PHILIP'S

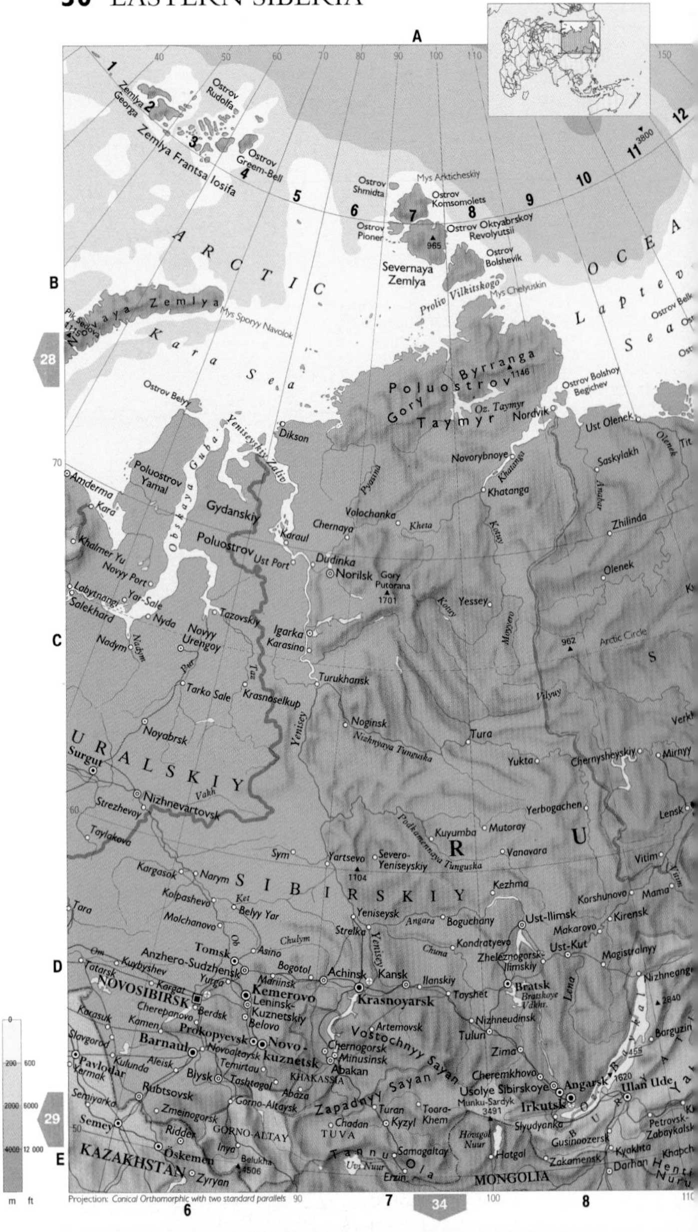

A
B
C
D
E
1
2
3
4
5
6
7
8
9
10
11
12
40
50
60
70
80
90
100
110
150
Ostrov Rudolfa
Zemlya Georga
Zemlya Frantsa Iosifa
Ostrov Greem-Bell
Ostrov Shmidta
Mys Arkticheskiy
Ostrov Komsomolets
Ostrov Pioner
965
Ostrov Oktyabrskoy Revolyutsii
Ostrov Bolshevik
Severnaya Zemlya
Proliv Vilkitskogo
Mys Chelyuskin
3800
A R C T I C
O C E A
L a p t e v S e a
Ostrov Belk
Novaya Zemlya
Pik Sedova 1150
Mys Sporyy Navolok
Kara Sea
Ostrov Belyy
Poluostrov Taymyr
Gory Byrranga
1146
Oz. Taymyr
Nordvik
Ostrov Bolshoy Begichev
Ust Olenek
Olenek
Dikson
Yeniseyskiy Zaliv
70
Amderma
Poluostrov Yamal
Obskaya Guba
Gydanskiy Poluostrov
Pyasina
Novorybnoye
Khatanga
Saskylakh
Anabar
Kara
Volochanka
Kheta
Kotuy
Zhilinda
Chernaya
Karaul
Khalmer Yu
Ust Port
Dudinka
Norilsk
Gory Putorana 1701
Olenek
Novyy Port
Labytnangi
Yar-Sale
Salekhard
Nyda
Tazovskiy
Yessey
Kotuy
Moyyero
Nadym
Nadym
Novyy Urengoy
Igarka
Karasino
962
Arctic Circle
S
Pur
Taz
Tarko Sale
Krasnoselkup
Turukhansk
Vilyuy
Yenisey
Noginsk
Nizhnyaya Tunguska
Tura
Noyabrsk
U R A L S K I Y
Surgut
Yukta
Chernyshevskiy
Mirnyy
Verkh
Vakh
Nizhnevartovsk
60
Strezhevoy
Yerbogachen
Lensk
Taylakova
Podkamennaya Tunguska
Kuyumba
Mutoray
R
U
Sym
Yartsevo
Severo-Yeniseyskiy
Vanavara
Vitim
1104
Kargasok
Narym
S I B I R S K I Y
Kezhma
Vitim
Kolpashevo
Ket
Korshunovo
Mama
Tara
Belyy Yar
Yeniseysk
Angara
Boguchany
Ust-Ilimsk
Kirensk
Molchanovo
Makarovo
Strelka
Ob
Chulym
Yenisey
Kondratyevo
Ust-Kut
Chuna
Tomsk
Asino
Zheleznogorsk-Ilimskiy
Magistralnyy
Om
Anzhero-Sudzhensk
Bogotol
Achinsk
Kansk
Tatarsk
Kuybyshev
Yurga
Mariinsk
Ilanskiy
Bratsk
Bratskoye Vdkhr.
Lena
Nizhneangarsk
NOVOSIBIRSK
Kargat
Kemerovo
Krasnoyarsk
Tayshet
2840
Berdsk
Leninsk-Kuznetskiy
Karasuk
Cherepanovo
Belovo
Artemovsk
Nizhneudinsk
Kamen
Prokopyevsk
Novokuznetsk
Vostochnyy Sayan
Tulun
Barguzin
Slavgorod
Barnaul
Novoaltaysk
Chernogorsk
Zima
Baykal
455
Pavlodar
Kulunda
Aleisk
Temirtau
Minusinsk
Yermak
Abakan
Cheremkhovo
Biysk
Tashtagol
KHAKASSIA
1620
Angarsk
Ulan Ude
Usolye Sibirskoye
Semiyarka
Rubtsovsk
Abaza
Zapadnyy Sayan
Munku-Sardyk 3491
Irkutsk
Zmeinogorsk
Gorno-Altaysk
Turan
Toora-Khem
Petrovsk-Zabaykalsk
Semey
Ridder
GORNO-ALTAY
Chadan
Kyzyl
Hövsgöl Nuur
Slyudyanka
BURYATIYA
TUVA
Gusinoozersk
Öskemen
Inya
Tannu Ola
Samagaltay
Hatgal
Zakamensk
Kyakhta
Khapcheranga
KAZAKHSTAN
Belukha 4506
Uvs Nuur
Erzin
MONGOLIA
Darhan
Hentiyn Nuruu
Zyryan

0
200 600
2000 6000
4000 12 000
m ft

Projection: Conical Orthomorphic with two standard parallels

90
6
7
100
8
110

28
29
34

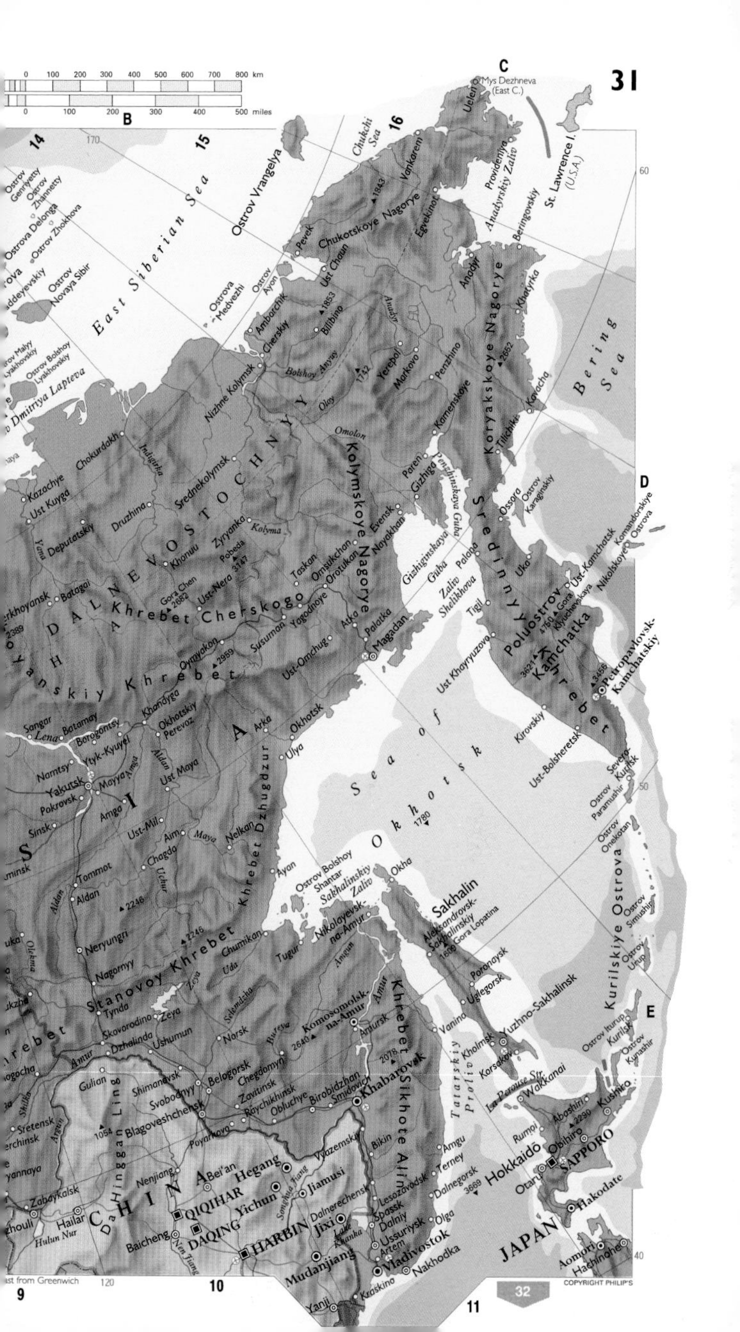
0 100 200 300 400 500 600 700 800 km
0 100 200 300 400 500 miles
B
C
D
E
14
15
16
170
60
50
40
120
Mys Dezhneva
(East C.)
Uelen
St. Lawrence I.
(U.S.A.)
Provideniya
Anadyrskiy Zaliv
Chukchi Sea
Vankarem
Beringovskiy
Egvekinot
1843
Chukotskoye Nagorye
Pevek
Ostrov Vrangelya
East Siberian Sea
Ostrov Genrietty
Ostrov Zhannetty
Ostrova Delonga
Ostrov Zhokhova
Ostrov Novaya Sibir
Ostrova Medvezhi
Ostrov Ayon
Ust Chaun
1853
Bilibino
Anadyr
Anadyr
Ambarchik
Cherskiy
Koryakskoye Nagorye
Khatyrka
Bering Sea
2562
Ostrov Malyy Lyakhovskiy
Ostrov Bolshoy Lyakhovskiy
Proliv Dmitriya Lapteva
Nizhne Kolymsk
Bolshoy Anyuy
1712
Yeropol
Markovo
Penzhino
Oloy
Kamenskoye
Kaiacha
Omolon
Tilichiki
Chokurdakh
Indigirka
Srednekolymsk
DALNEVOSTOCHNYY
Kolymskoye Nagorye
Paren
Gizhiga
Penzhinskaya Guba
Ossora
Ostrov Karaginskiy
Kazachye
Ust Kuyga
Druzhina
Zyryanka
Kolyma
Evensk
Sredinnyy
Deputatskiy
Yana
Khonuu
Pobeda 3147
Omsukchan
Noyakhan
Gizhiginskaya Guba
Palana
Ust-Kamchatsk
Komandorskiye Ostrova
Nikolskoye
Taskan
Orotukan
Zaliv Shelikhova
Ukal
Verkhoyansk
Batagai
Gora Chen 2682
Ust-Nera
Yagodnoye
Atka
Palatka
Tigil
Poluostrov Kamchatka
Gora Klyuchevskaya 4750
2389
Khrebet Cherskogo
Susuman
Magadan
Ust-Omchug
Oymyakon
2959
Ust Khayryuzova
3621
3456
Petropavlovsk-Kamchatskiy
Khrebet
Verkhoyanskiy Khrebet
Khandyga
Okhotskiy Perevoz
Arka
Okhotsk
Sea of Okhotsk
Kirovskiy
Sangar
Lena
Batamay
Borogontsy
Ytyk-Kyuyel
Aldan
Amga
Ulya
Ust-Bolsheretsk
Severo-Kurilsk
Namtsy
Yakutsk
Maya
Ust Maya
Pokrovsk
Amga
SIBIRIA
Ostrov Paramushir
Sinsk
Ust-Mil
Aim
Maya
Nelkan
Khrebet Dzhugdzur
1780
Ostrov Onekotan
Chagda
Uchur
Tommot
Aldan
Aldan
2246
Ayan
Ostrov Bolshoy Shantar
Sakhalinskiy Zaliv
Okha
Sakhalin
Ostrov Simushir
Aleksandrovsk-Sakhalinskiy
Gora Lopatina 1609
Nikolayevsk-na-Amur
Amgun
Olekma
Neryungri
2246
Chumikan
Tugur
Kurilskiye Ostrova
Ostrov Urup
Nagornyy
Stanovoy Khrebet
Uda
Poronaysk
Uglegorsk
Zeya
Tynda
Selemdzha
Komsomolsk-na-Amur
Amur
Amursk
Khrebet Sikhote Alin
Yuzhno-Sakhalinsk
Vanino
Skovorodino
Zeya
Ushumun
Norsk
Bureya
2640
Kholmsk
Korsakov
Ostrov Iturup
Kurilsk
Ostrov Kunashir
Dzhalinda
Amur
2078
Chegdomyn
Zavitinsk
Tatarskiy Proliv
La Perouse Str.
Wakkanai
Gulian
Shimanovsk
Belogorsk
Svobodnyy
Raychikhinsk
Birobidzhan
Obluchye
Smidovich
Khabarovsk
Abashiri
Kushiro
2290
Sretensk
Blagoveshchensk
Shilka
Argun
Nerchinsk
1054
Poyarkovo
Bikin
Rumoi
Obihiro
SAPPORO
Amgu
Vyazemskiy
Terney
Hokkaido
Hegang
Bei'an
Nenjiang
Da Hinggan Ling
CHINA
QIQIHAR
Jiamusi
Songhua Jiang
Lesozavodsk
Dalnegorsk
3669
Otaru
Zabaykalsk
Hailar
Yichun
DAQING
Dalnerechensk
Spassk Dalniy
Hulun Nur
Baicheng
Nen Jiang
HARBIN
Jixi
Lake Khanka
Ussuriysk
Olga
Hakodate
Artem
Vladivostok
Nakhodka
JAPAN
Aomori
Hachinohe
Mudanjiang
Kraskino
Yanji
East from Greenwich
9
10
11
32
COPYRIGHT PHILIP'S

CHINA
RUSSIA
NORTH KOREA
SEA OF JAPAN (EAST SEA)
Hokkaidō
Khrebet Sikhote Alin
Jixi
Linkou
Novokachalinsk
Kamen-Rybolov
Pogranichnyy
Suifenhe
Hunchun
1498
Khasan
Najin
Ch'ŏngjin
L. Khanka
Lesozavodsk
Kirovskiy
Spassk Dalniy
Sibirtsevo
Ussuriysk
Artem
Vladivostok
Trudovoye
Slavyanka
Zaliv Petra Velikogo
Nakhodka
Arsenev
Yakovlevka
Gornyy
Rakitnoye
Ariadnoye
1855
Lazo
Preobrazheniye
Margaritovo
Kavalerovo
Dalnegorsk
Plastun
Terney
Wakkanai
Rebun-Tō
Rishiri-Tō
Teshio
Embetsu
Teshio-Gawa
Haboro
Rumoi
Nayoro
Shibetsu
Otoineppu
Esashi
Kitami-Sammyaku
Ōmu
Mombetsu
Yūbetsu
Abashiri-Wan
Abashiri
Rausu Dake
1661
Nemuro Kaikyō
Ostrov Kunashir
Shari
Kussharo-Ko
Nemuro
Nakashibetsu
Shibecha
Akkeshi
Kushiro
Honbetsu
Kitami
Engaru
Asahikawa
Ishikari-Gawa
Daisetsu-Zan
2290
Ishikari-Sammyaku
2077
Takikawa
Akabira
Bibai
Iwamizawa
Ishikari-Wan
Atsuta
Kamui-Misaki
Otaru
SAPPORO
Ebetsu
Chitose
Obihiro
Poroshiri-Dake
2052
Hidaka-Sammyaku
Hiroo
Iwanai
Sikotu-Ko
Toya-Ko
Suttsu
Tomakomai
Setana
Uchiura-Wan
Muroran
Urakawa
Samani
Erimo-misaki
Yakumo
Okushiri-Tō
Esashi
Hakodate
Esan-Misaki
Tsugaru Kaikyō
Shiriya-Zaki
Matsumae
Shiragami-Misaki
Ohata
Mutsu
Mutsu-Wan
Kanagi
Aomori
Goshogawara
Towada-Ko
Towada
Hachinohe
Henashi-Misaki
Hirosaki
Odate
Kitakami-Sammyaku
Kuji
Noshiro
Kazuno
Iwaizumi
Oga
Oga-Hantō
Iwate-San
2041
Morioka
Miyako
Hayachine-San
Akita
Omagari
1914
Kamaishi
Honjō
Hanamaki
Chōkai-San
2230
Mizusawa
Kesennuma
Sakata
Mogami-Gawa
Ichinoseki
Tsuruoka
Furukawa
Ishinomaki
Gas-San
1980
A
B
C
D
2
3
4
5
6
7
8
9
132
134
136
138
140
142
144
38
40
42
44
m
ft
8000
6000
4000
2000
200
24 000
18 000
12 000
6000
600
0
31

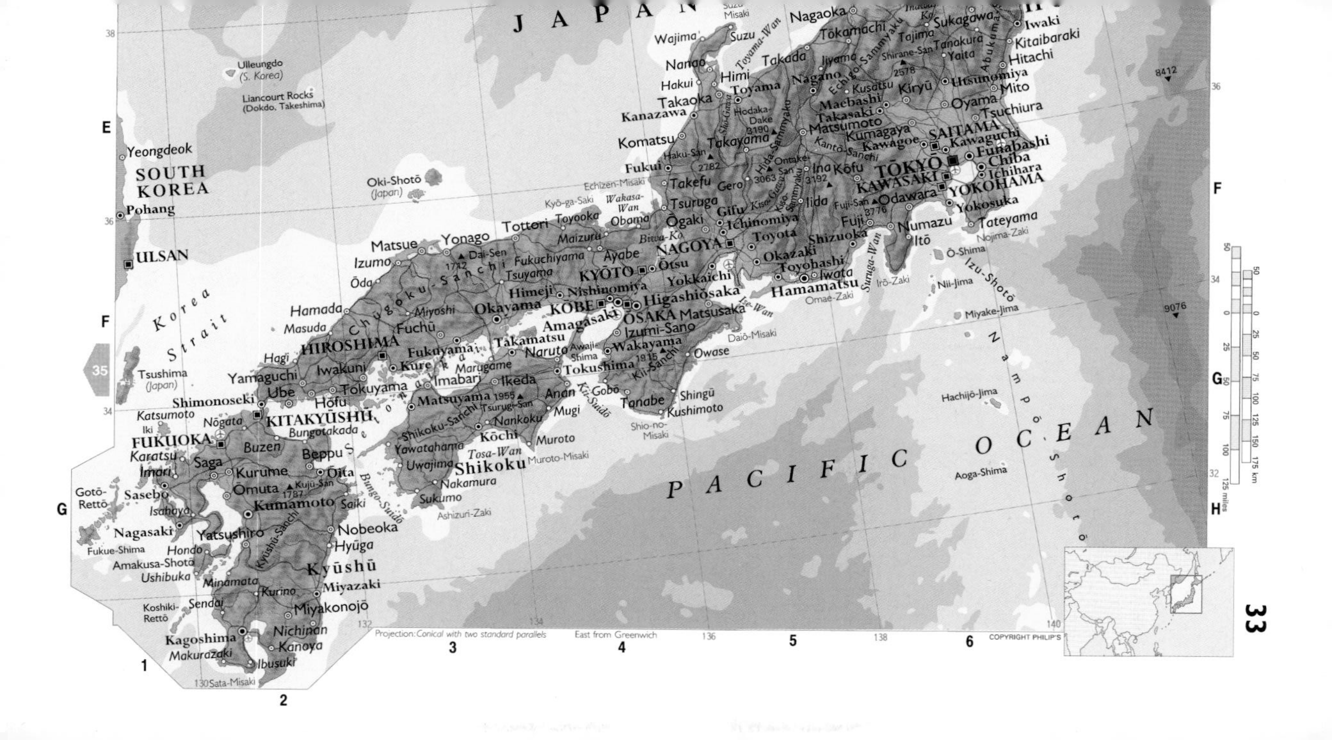
JAPAN
SOUTH KOREA
Yeongdeok
Pohang
ULSAN
Ulleungdo (S. Korea)
Liancourt Rocks (Dokdo, Takeshima)
Oki-Shotō (Japan)
Korea Strait
Tsushima (Japan)
Iki
Gotō-Rettō
Fukue-Shima
Koshiki-Rettō
Amakusa-Shotō
Katsumoto
FUKUOKA
Karatsu
Imari
Sasebo
Isahaya
Nagasaki
Hondo
Ushibuka
Minamata
Sendai
Kagoshima
Makurazaki
Ibusuki
Sata-Misaki
Nōgata
Saga
Kurume
Ōmuta
Kumamoto
Yatsushiro
Kyūshū-Sanchi
Kurino
Miyakonojō
Nichinan
Kanoya
Kyūshū
Miyazaki
Hyūga
Nobeoka
Saiki
Ōita
Beppu
Kujū-San 1787
Buzen
Bungotakada
KITAKYŪSHŪ
Shimonoseki
Ube
Yamaguchi
Hagi
Hōfu
Tokuyama
Iwakuni
HIROSHIMA
Masuda
Hamada
Ōda
Izumo
Matsue
Yonago
Dai-Sen 1712
Chūgoku-Sanchi
Miyoshi
Fuchū
Fukuyama
Kure
Tottori
Tsuyama
Okayama
Himeji
Takamatsu
Marugame
Imabari
Matsuyama
Shikoku-Sanchi
Yawatahama
Uwajima
Shikoku
Nakamura
Sukumo
Ashizuri-Zaki
Bungo-Suidō
Tosa-Wan
Kōchi
Nankoku
Tsurugi-San 1955
Ikeda
Naruto
Tokushima
Anan
Mugi
Muroto
Muroto-Misaki
Awaji-Shima
Kii-Suidō
Gobō
Tanabe
Shio-no-Misaki
Kushimoto
Shingū
Owase
Kii-Sanchi
Wakayama
Izumi-Sano
ŌSAKA
Amagasaki
KŌBE
Nishinomiya
Higashiōsaka
Fukuchiyama
Toyooka
Kyō-ga-Saki
Maizuru
Ayabe
KYŌTO
Ōtsu
Biwa-Ko
Obama
Wakasa-Wan
Echizen-Misaki
Tsuruga
Takefu
Fukui
Komatsu
Kanazawa
Takaoka
Hakui
Nanao
Wajima
Suzu
Himi
Toyama
Toyama-Wan
Haku-San 2782
Takayama
Hodaka-Dake 3190
Hida-Sammyaku
Ontake-San 3063
Gero
Gifu
Ōgaki
Ichinomiya
NAGOYA
Yokkaichi
Matsusaka
Ise-Wan
Daiō-Misaki
Toyota
Okazaki
Toyohashi
Hamamatsu
Iwata
Omae-Zaki
Shizuoka
Suruga-Wan
Irō-Zaki
Ina
Iida
Kiso-Sammyaku
Kōfu
Fuji
Fuji-San 3776
Numazu
Itō
Odawara
Kantō-Sanchi
Matsumoto
Nagano
Takada
Nagaoka
Tōkamachi
Iiyama
Echigo-Sammyaku
Shirane-San 2578
Kusatsu
Maebashi
Takasaki
Kumagaya
Kawagoe
Kiryū
Tajima
Sukagawa
Tanakura
Yaita
Utsunomiya
Oyama
Mito
Hitachi
Kitaibaraki
Iwaki
Tsuchiura
SAITAMA
Kawaguchi
TŌKYŌ
KAWASAKI
YOKOHAMA
Yokosuka
Funabashi
Chiba
Ichihara
Tateyama
Nojima-Zaki
Ō-Shima
Izu-Shotō
Nii-Jima
Miyake-Jima
Hachijō-Jima
Aoga-Shima
Nampō-Shotō
PACIFIC OCEAN
8412
9076
Projection: Conical with two standard parallels
East from Greenwich
COPYRIGHT PHILIP'S
0 25 50 75 100 125 150 175 km
0 25 50 75 100 125 miles
35

KAZAKHSTAN
Astana
Qaraghandy
Semey
Öskemen
Rubtsovsk
Biysk
Gorno-Altaysk
Kyzyl
Ulaangom
Ölgiy
Balqash Köl
Taldyqorghan
Almaty
Bishkek
Ysyk-Köl
KYRGYZSTAN
Tian Shan
Pik Pobedy 7439
Junggar Pendi
Gurbantünggüt Shamo
Ürümqi
Karamay
Tacheng
Altay
Yining
Shihezi
Changji
Turpan
Turpan Pendi
Hami
XINJIANG UYGUR ZIZHIQU (SINKIANG)
Tarim Pendi
Taklamakan Shamo
Kashi
Shache
Hotan
Aksu
Korla
Lop Nur
Dunhuang
Yumen
Altun Shan
Kunlun Shan
Qilian Shan
Qaidam Pendi
Golmud
QINGHAI
Qinghai Hu
Xining
K2 8611
Karakoram
Aksai Chin
XIZANG ZIZHIQU (TIBET)
Tanggula (Dangla) Shan
Nyainqentanglha Shan
Lhasa
Xigazê
Mt. Everest 8850
Kanchenjunga
Himalaya
NEPAL
KATMANDU
BHUTAN
Thimphu
Assam
Guwahati
Brahmaputra
INDIA
LUCKNOW
KANPUR
VARANASI
ALLAHABAD
PATNA
Ganga
BANGLADESH
DHAKA
KOLKATA (Calcutta)
CHITTAGONG
JAMSHEDPUR
Cuttack
BAY OF BENGAL
VISHAKHAPATNAM
BURMA (MYANMAR)
Mandalay
Kachin
Myitkyina
YUNNAN
Dali
SICHUAN
THAILAND (SIAM)
Projection: Bonne
East from Greenwich
m ft
0
200 600
2000 6000
4000 12 000
6000 18 000

29
38

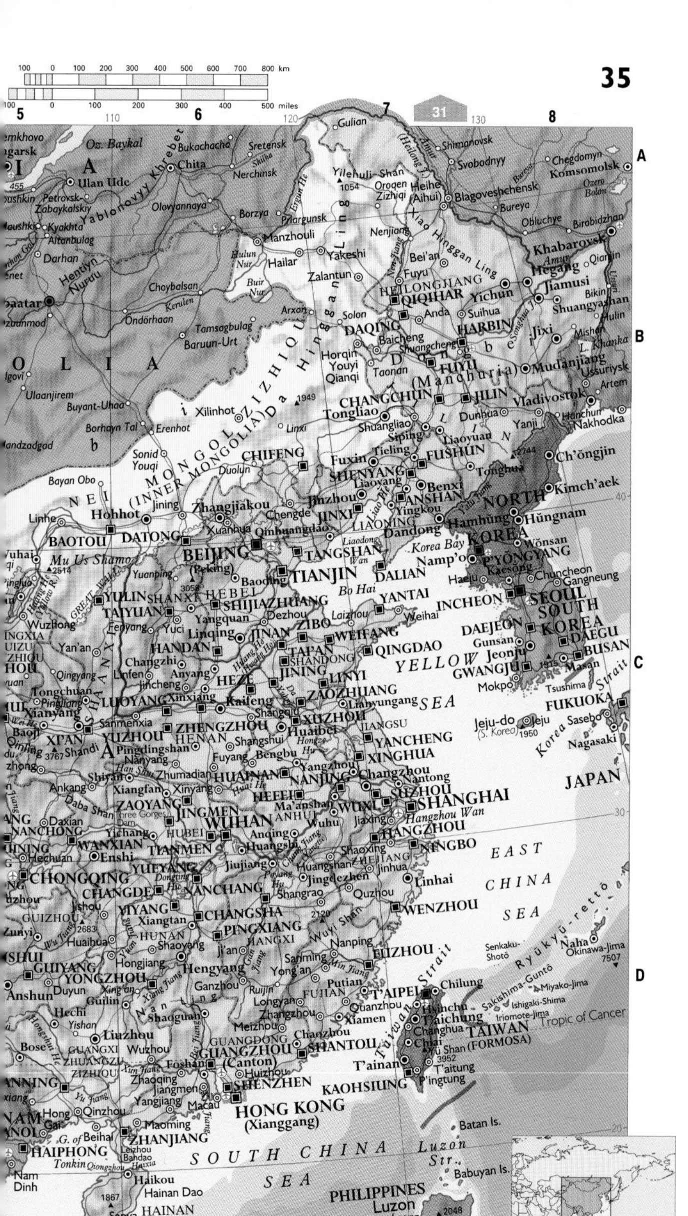
100 0 100 200 300 400 500 600 700 800 km
100 0 100 200 300 400 500 miles
5
6
7
8
31
A
B
C
D
Oz. Baykal
Bukachacha
Sretensk
Shilka
Chita
Nerchinsk
Ulan Ude
Petrovsk-Zabaykalskiy
Yablonovyy Khrebet
Olovyannaya
Borzya
Kyakhta
Altanbulag
Darhan
Hentiyn Nuruu
Choybalsan
Kerulen
Öndörhaan
Tamsagbulag
Baruun-Urt
Ulaanjirem
Buyant-Uhaa
Borhoyn Tal
Erenhot
Dandzadgad
Sonid Youqi
Bayan Obo
Gulian
Yilehuli Shan
1054
Oroqen Zizhiqi
Heihe (Aihui)
Blagoveshchensk
Shimanovsk
Svobodnyy
Amur
(Heilong J.)
Chegdomyn
Komsomolsk
Bureya
Ozero Bolon
Obluchye
Birobidzhan
Khabarovsk
Argun
Priargunsk
Manzhouli
Hulun Nur
Hailar
Yakeshi
Buir Nur
Zalantun
Nenjiang
Bei'an
Xiao Hinggan Ling
Fuyu
HEILONGJIANG
QIQIHAR
Yichun
Hegang
Jiamusi
Qianjin
Bikin
Shuangyashan
Hulin
Arxan
Solon
Anda
Suihua
DAQING
HARBIN
Jixi
Mishan
L. Khanka
Baicheng
Shuangcheng
Horqin Youyi Qianqi
Taonan
FUYU
Manchuria
Mudanjiang
Ussuriysk
Artem
Vladivostok
Nakhodka
CHANGCHUN
JILIN
Da Hinggan Ling
1949
Xilinhot
NEI MONGOL ZIZHIQU (INNER MONGOLIA)
Tongliao
Shuangliao
Siping
Liaoyuan
Dunhua
Yanji
Hunchun
Linxi
CHIFENG
Tieling
FUSHUN
2744
Ch'ŏngjin
Fuxin
SHENYANG
Liaoyang
Benxi
Tonghua
Kimch'aek
Duolun
Jinzhou
ANSHAN
Yingkou
Yalu Jiang
NORTH KOREA
Hamhŭng
Hŭngnam
Jining
Zhangjiakou
Chengde
JINXI
LIAONING
Dandong
Wŏnsan
Linhe
Hohhot
DATONG
Xuanhua
Qinhuangdao
Korea Bay
BAOTOU
BEIJING (Peking)
TANGSHAN
Liaodong Wan
Namp'o
P'YŎNGYANG
Wuhai
Mu Us Shamo
2514
Yuanping
Baoding
TIANJIN
DALIAN
Haeju
Kaesŏng
Chuncheon
Gangneung
SEOUL
3058
HEBEI
Bo Hai
YANTAI
INCHEON
SOUTH KOREA
YULIN
SHANXI
SHIJIAZHUANG
Dezhou
Laizhou
Weihai
TAIYUAN
Yangquan
Yuci
Fenyang
Linqing
JINAN
ZIBO
WEIFANG
DAEJEON
Gunsan
DAEGU
Wuzhong
Yan'an
HANDAN
TAI'AN
SHANDONG
QINGDAO
Jeonju
BUSAN
Changzhi
Anyang
JINING
YELLOW SEA
GWANGJU
1915
Masan
Qingyang
Linfen
Jincheng
HEZE
LINYI
Mokpo
Tsushima
Tongchuan
Pingliang
LUOYANG
Xinxiang
Kaifeng
ZAOZHUANG
Lianyungang
FUKUOKA
Xianyang
Sanmenxia
Shangqiu
XUZHOU
JIANGSU
Jeju-do (S. Korea)
Jeju
1950
Sasebo
Baoji
XI'AN
YUZHOU
ZHENGZHOU
HENAN
Shangshui
Huaibei
YANCHENG
Korea Strait
Nagasaki
Qinling Shandi
3767
Pingdingshan
Nanyang
Fuyang
Bengbu
Hongze Hu
XINGHUA
Zhumadian
HUAINAN
Yangzhou
Shiyan
Han Shui
Xiangfan
Xinyang
NANJING
Changzhou
Nantong
JAPAN
Ankang
Huai He
HEFEI
SUZHOU
Daba Shan
ZAOYANG
JINGMEN
Ma'anshan
WUXI
SHANGHAI
Three Gorges Dam
ANHUI
Wuhu
Jiaxing
Hangzhou Wan
Daxian
NANCHONG
Yichang
HUBEI
WUHAN
Anqing
HANGZHOU
WANXIAN
TIANMEN
Huangshi
Shaoxing
NINGBO
EAST CHINA SEA
Hechuan
Enshi
ZHEJIANG
Jinhua
YUEYANG
Jiujiang
Huangshan
CHONGQING
Dongting Hu
Poyang Hu
Jingdezhen
Linhai
CHANGDE
NANCHANG
Shangrao
Quzhou
Jishou
YIYANG
CHANGSHA
WENZHOU
GUIZHOU
2683
Xiangtan
2120
Zunyi
Wu Jiang
HUNAN
PINGXIANG
JIANGXI
Wuyi Shan
Ryūkyū-rettō
Huaihua
Shaoyang
Ji'an
Nanping
Senkaku-Shotō
Naha
Okinawa-Jima
7507
Hongjiang
Sanming
FUZHOU
GUIYANG
Hengyang
Yong'an
Min Jiang
Strait
YONGZHOU
Ganzhou
Putian
Sakishima-Guntō
Miyako-Jima
Anshun
Duyun
Guilin
Ruijin
FUJIAN
T'AIPEI
Chilung
Ishigaki-Shima
Nan Ling
Longyan
Quanzhou
Hsinchu
Iriomote-Jima
Hechi
Shaoguan
Zhangzhou
Xiamen
T'aichung
Tropic of Cancer
Yishan
Meizhou
Changhua
TAIWAN
Liuzhou
GUANGDONG
Chaozhou
Chiai
Bose
GUANGXI ZHUANGZU ZIZHIQU
Wuzhou
GUANGZHOU (Canton)
SHANTOU
Yü Shan (FORMOSA)
3952
Foshan
Huizhou
T'ainan
T'aitung
Zhaoqing
Jiangmen
SHENZHEN
KAOHSIUNG
P'ingtung
NANNING
Yu Jiang
Yangjiang
Macau
Hong Gai
Qinzhou
HONG KONG (Xianggang)
Maoming
Batan Is.
HANOI
G. of Beihai
ZHANJIANG
HAIPHONG
Leizhou Bandao
SOUTH CHINA SEA
Luzon Str.
Tonkin
Haixia
Babuyan Is.
Nam Dinh
Haikou
Hainan Dao
PHILIPPINES
1867
Luzon
Sanya
HAINAN
Laoag
2048
110
120
130
40
30
20
COPYRIGHT PHILIP'S

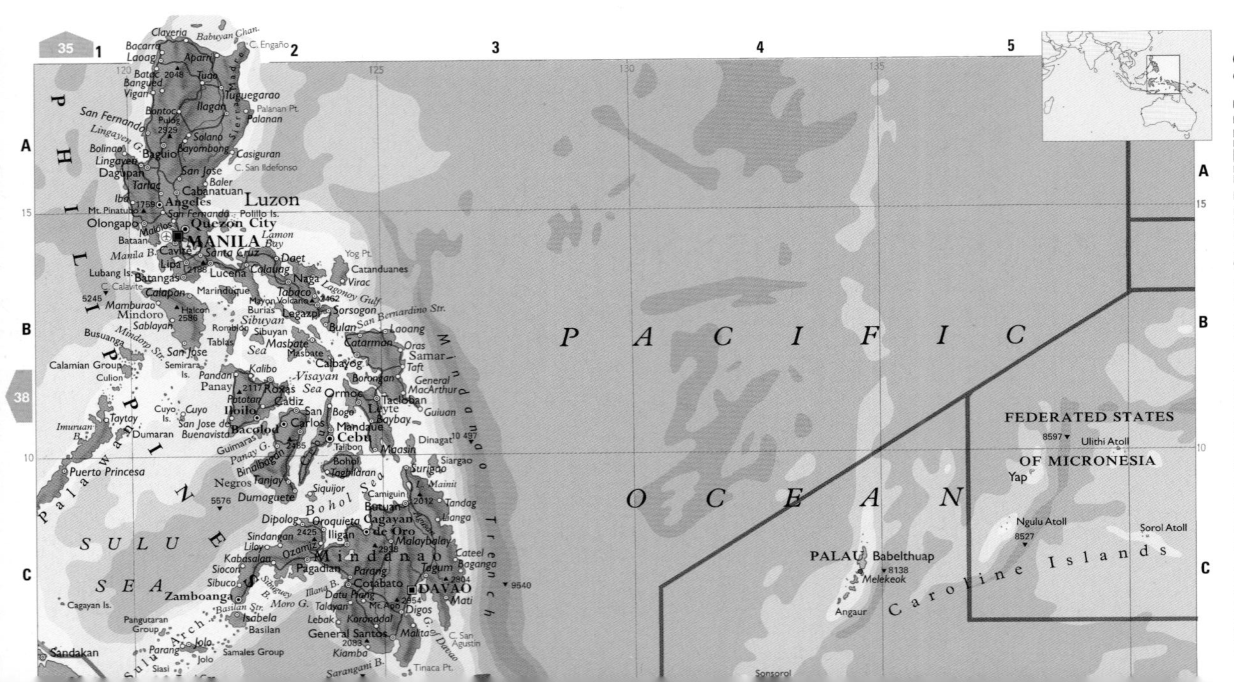
PACIFIC OCEAN
PHILIPPINES
FEDERATED STATES OF MICRONESIA
Caroline Islands
PALAU
Babelthuap
Melekeok
Angaur
Sonsorol
Yap
Ulithi Atoll
Ngulu Atoll
Sorol Atoll
Luzon
MANILA
Quezon City
Mindoro
Panay
Negros
Cebu
Bohol
Leyte
Samar
Mindanao
DAVAO
Zamboanga
SULU SEA
Bohol Sea
Sibuyan Sea
Visayan Sea
Palawan
Puerto Princesa
Mindanao Trench
Babuyan Chan.
C. Engaño
Sierra Madre
Lingayen G.
Manila B.
Lamon Bay
Lagonoy Gulf
San Bernardino Str.
Mindoro Str.
Moro G.
G. of Davao
Sarangani B.
Sulu Archipelago
Jolo
Basilan
Sandakan
Cagayan Is.
Calamian Group
Busuanga
Culion
Iloilo
Bacolod
Dumaguete
Tacloban
Ormoc
Cagayan de Oro
Iligan
General Santos
Cotabato
Surigao
Legazpi
Naga
Sorsogon
Catanduanes
Virac
Masbate
Lucena
Batangas
Calapan
Olongapo
Baguio
Laoag
Vigan
Aparri
Tuguegarao
Ilagan
Dagupan
Angeles
Cabanatuan
Baler
Casiguran
Palanan
Siargao
Dinagat
Camiguin
Siquijor
Tagbilaran
Dipolog
Ozamiz
Pagadian
Mati
Digos
Tagum
Roxas
Kalibo
Romblon
Tablas
Sibuyan
Burias
Marinduque
Lubang Is.
Mayon Volcano
Mt. Pinatubo
Mt. Apo
Halcon
5245
9540
10 497
8597
8527
8138

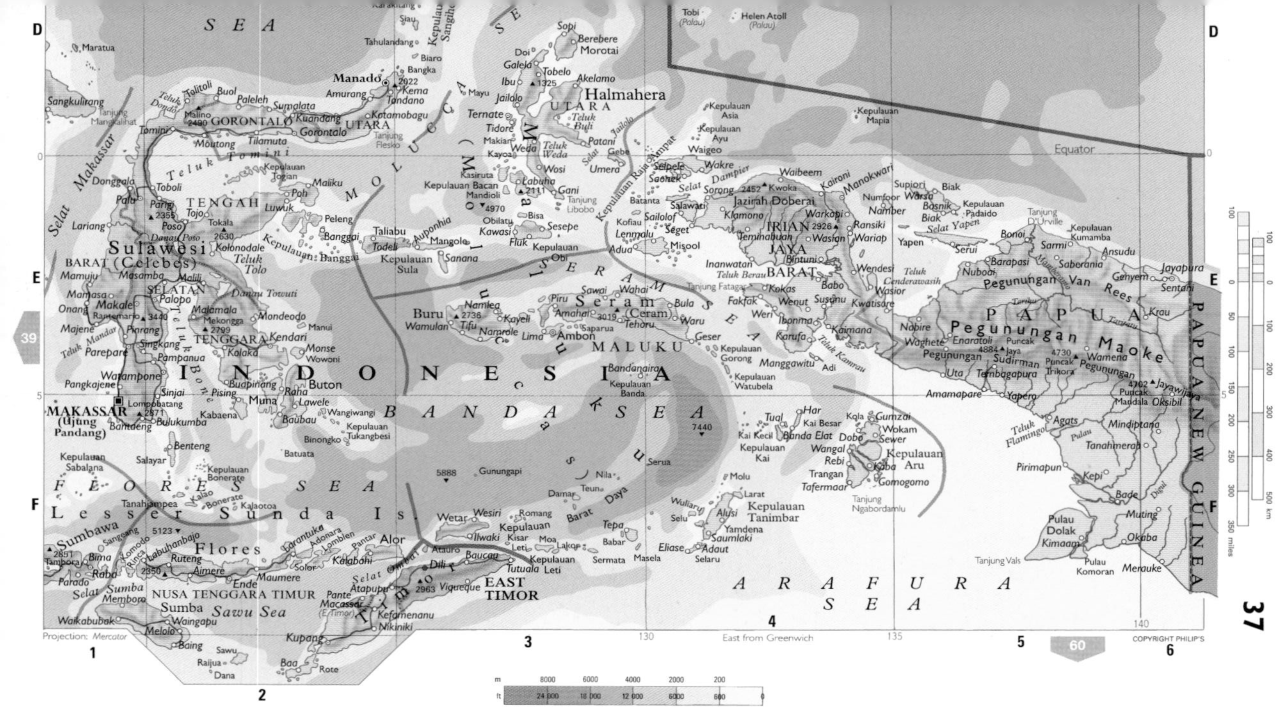

SEA
Maratua
Sangkulirang
Tanjung Mangkalihat
Selat Makassar
Tolitoli
Buol
Teluk Dondo
Paleleh
Sumalata
Malino 2490
GORONTALO
Kuandang
Gorontalo
Tomini
Moutong
Tilamuta
Teluk Tomini
Kepulauan Togian
Donggala
Palu
Toboli
Parigi
2355
Tojo
Poso
Danau Poso
Tokala 2630
Kolonodale
Teluk Tolo
TENGAH
Luwuk
Poh
Maliku
Peleng
Banggai
Kepulauan Banggai
Lariang
Sulawesi (Celebes)
BARAT
Mamuju
Masamba
Malili
SELATAN
Palopo
Danau Towuti
Mamasa
Makale
Onang
Rantemario 3440
Majene
Pinrang
Teluk Mandar
Parepare
Singkang
Pampanua
Teluk Bone
Malamala
Mekongga 2799
TENGGARA
Mondeodo
Kendari
Kolaka
Manui
Monse
Wowoni
Watampone
Pangkajene
Sinjai
MAKASSAR (Ujung Pandang)
Lompobatang 2871
Bantaeng
Bulukumba
Pising
Budpinang
Muna
Raha
Buton
Lawele
Baubau
Kabaena
Wangiwangi
Kepulauan Tukangbesi
Binongko
Benteng
Salayar
Kepulauan Sabalana
Kepulauan Bonerate
Kalao
Bonerate
Kalaotoa
Batuata
Tahanjampea
FLORES SEA
Lesser Sunda Is.
Sumbawa
2851 Tambora
Sangeang
5123
Bima
Raba
Komodo
Rinca
Labuhanbajo
Ruteng
2350
Flores
Aimere
Ende
Maumere
Larantuka
Adonara
Lomblen
Pantar
Alor
Kalabahi
Solor
Parado
Selat Sumba
Sumba
Memboro
Waikabubak
Waingapu
Melolo
Baing
NUSA TENGGARA TIMUR
Sawu Sea
Sawu
Raijua
Dana
Selat Ombai
Atapupu
Pante Macassar (E. Timor)
Timor
Kefamenanu
Nikiniki
Kupang
Baa
Rote
Atauro
Dili
Baucau
2963
Viqueque
EAST TIMOR
Wetar
Wesiri
Ilwaki
Romang
Kepulauan Kisar
Leti
Moa
Lakor
Kepulauan Leti
Tutuala
Siau
Tahulandang
Kepulauan Sangihe
Karakitang
Biaro
Bangka
Manado
2022
Kema
Amurang
Tondano
Kotamobagu
UTARA
Tanjung Flesko
MOLUCCA SEA
Mayu
Taliabu
Mangole
Todeli
Kepulauan Sula
Sanana
Auponhia
Kepulauan Bacan
Mandioli
4970
Kasiruta
Obilatu
Bisa
Kawasi
Sesepe
Fluk
Kepulauan Obi
Maluku
Sopi
Berebere
Morotai
Doi
Galela
Tobelo
Ibu
1325
Akelamo
Jailolo
Halmahera
UTARA
Ternate
Tidore
Makian
Kayoa
Weda
Teluk Buli
Teluk Weda
Patani
Labuha
2111
Wosi
Gani
Tanjung Libobo
Selat Jailolo
Gebe
Umera
Buru
Wamulan
Namlea
2736
Kayeli
Tifu
Namrole
Seram Sea
Piru
Sawai
Wahai
Seram (Ceram)
Bula
Amahai
3019
Saparua
Tehoru
Waru
Lima
Ambon
Geser
MALUKU
INDONESIA
Bandanaira
Kepulauan Banda
BANDA SEA
Banda Sea
5888
Gunungapi
Damar
Teun
Nila
Serua
7440
Barat Daya
Tepa
Babar
Sermata
Masela
Tobi (Palau)
Helen Atoll (Palau)
Kepulauan Asia
Kepulauan Ayu
Waigeo
Kepulauan Raja Ampat
Selpele
Saonek
Wakre
Selat Dampier
Batanta
Salawati
Sorong
Sailolof
Seget
Kofiau
Lenmalu
Misool
Adua
Kepulauan Mapia
Equator
Waibeem
2452 Kwoka
Kaironi
Manokwari
Jazirah Doberai
Klamono
Warkopi
IRIAN JAYA BARAT
2926
Wasian
Ransiki
Teminabuan
Wariap
Inanwatan
Teluk Berau
Bintuni
Tanjung Fatagar
Kokas
Babo
Fakfak
Wenut
Susunu
Weri
Ibonma
Kaimana
Karufa
Teluk Kamrau
Manggawitu
Adi
Kepulauan Gorong
Kepulauan Watubela
Supiori
Biak
Warsa
Bosnik
Numfoor
Namber
Biak
Kepulauan Padaido
Selat Yapen
Yapen
Serui
Teluk Cenderawasih
Wendesi
Wasior
Kwatisore
Tanjung D'Urville
Kepulauan Kumamba
Bonoi
Sarmi
Barapasi
Saborania
Mamberamo
Ansudu
Nubooi
Pegunungan Van Rees
Genyem
Jayapura
Sentani
PAPUA
Tariku
Taritatu
Krau
Nabire
Waghete
Enarotali
Pegunungan Maoke
Puncak Jaya 4884
Pegunungan Sudirman
Puncak Trikora 4730
Wamena
Pegunungan
Uta
Tembagapura
Amamapare
Yapero
4702
Puncak Mandala
Jayawijaya
Oksibil
Teluk Flamingo
Agats
Mindiptana
Pulau
Tanahmerah
Pirimapun
Kepi
Bade
Digul
Muting
Pulau Dolak
Kimaam
Okaba
Pulau Komoran
Merauke
Tanjung Vals
PAPUA NEW GUINEA
Tual
Har
Kai Besar
Kai Kecil
Banda Elat
Kepulauan Kai
Kola
Gumzai
Wokam
Dobo
Sewer
Wangal
Rebi
Kepulauan Aru
Koba
Trangan
Tafermaar
Gomogomo
Tanjung Ngabordamlu
Molu
Larat
Kepulauan Tanimbar
Wuliaru
Alusi
Selu
Yamdena
Saumlaki
Eliase
Adaut
Selaru
ARAFURA SEA
D
E
F
1
2
3
4
5
6
0
5
130
135
140
East from Greenwich
Projection: Mercator
COPYRIGHT PHILIP'S

39
60

| m | 8000 | 6000 | 4000 | 2000 | 200 | 0 |
|---|---|---|---|---|---|---|
| ft | 24 000 | 18 000 | 12 000 | 6000 | 600 | 0 |

100 0 100 200 300 400 500 km
100 0 50 100 150 200 250 300 350 miles

BURMA
RANGOON (Yangon)
(MYANMAR)
G. of Martaban
THAILAND
BANGKOK
LAOS
Vientiane (Viangchan)
VIETNAM
CAMBODIA
PHNOM PENH
THANH PHO HO CHI MINH (Saigon)
PHILIPPINES
Palawan
SABAH
SOUTH CHINA SEA
MALAYSIA
ANDAMAN SEA
Gulf of Thailand
Malay Pen.
Straits of
Paracel Is.
Spratly Is.
Mergui Arch.
Kho Khot Kra (Isthmus of Kra)
Tonle Sap
Phnom Dangrek
Da Nang
Hue
Nha Trang
Cam Ranh
Qui Nhon
Da Lat
Buon Ma Thuot
Can Tho
Kampong Cham
Batdambang
Siemreab
Nakhon Ratchasima
Khon Kaen
Udon Thani
Ubon Ratchathani
Phitsanulok
Nakhon Sawan
Hat Yai
Songkhla
Nakhon Si Thammarat
Surat Thani
Phuket
Kota Bharu
Kota Kinabalu
Sandakan
Alor Setar
George Town
Moulmein
Tavoy
Mergui
Ranong
Chumphon
Hua Hin
Pattaya
Rayong
Kampot
Rach Gia
Ca Mau
Vung Tau
Bien Hoa
Pakxe
Savannakhet
Sakon Nakhon
Nong Khai

INDONESIA
Greater Sunda Islands
INDIAN OCEAN
JAVA SEA
Java Trench
Selat Karimata
Selat Makassar
Selat Sunda
Selat Berhala
Selat Bangka
Sumatera
Kalimantan (Borneo)
Jawa (Java)
SARAWAK
KUALA LUMPUR
SINGAPORE
JAKARTA
BANDUNG
SURABAYA
PALEMBANG
Pekanbaru
Padang
Jambi
Bengkulu
Bandar Lampung
Pontianak
Banjarmasin
Balikpapan
Samarinda
Palangkaraya
Semarang
Yogyakarta
Surakarta
Malang
Denpasar
Mataram
Kuching
Johor Bahru
Tanjungpinang
Pangkalpinang
Bogor
Cirebon
Tegal
Kediri
Madiun
Jember
Banyuwangi
Probolinggo
Madura
Bangka
Belitung
BALI
Lombok
Sumbawa Besar
Kepulauan Riau
Kepulauan Lingga
Kepulauan Anambas
Kepulauan Natuna Selatan
Kepulauan Karimata
Kepulauan Karimunjawa
Kepulauan Mentawai
Kepulauan Batu
Kepulauan Banyak
Siberut
Nias
Simeulue
Enggano
RIAU
JAMBI
BENGKULU
LAMPUNG
BANTEN
UTARA
BARAT
SELATAN
TENGAH
TIMUR
NUSA TENGGARA BARAT
Equator
East from Greenwich
Projection: Mercator
100 0 100 200 300 400 500 km
100 0 50 100 150 200 250 300 350 miles
m 8000 6000 4000 2000 200 0
ft 24 000 18 000 12 000 6000 600 0
COPYRIGHT PHILIP'S

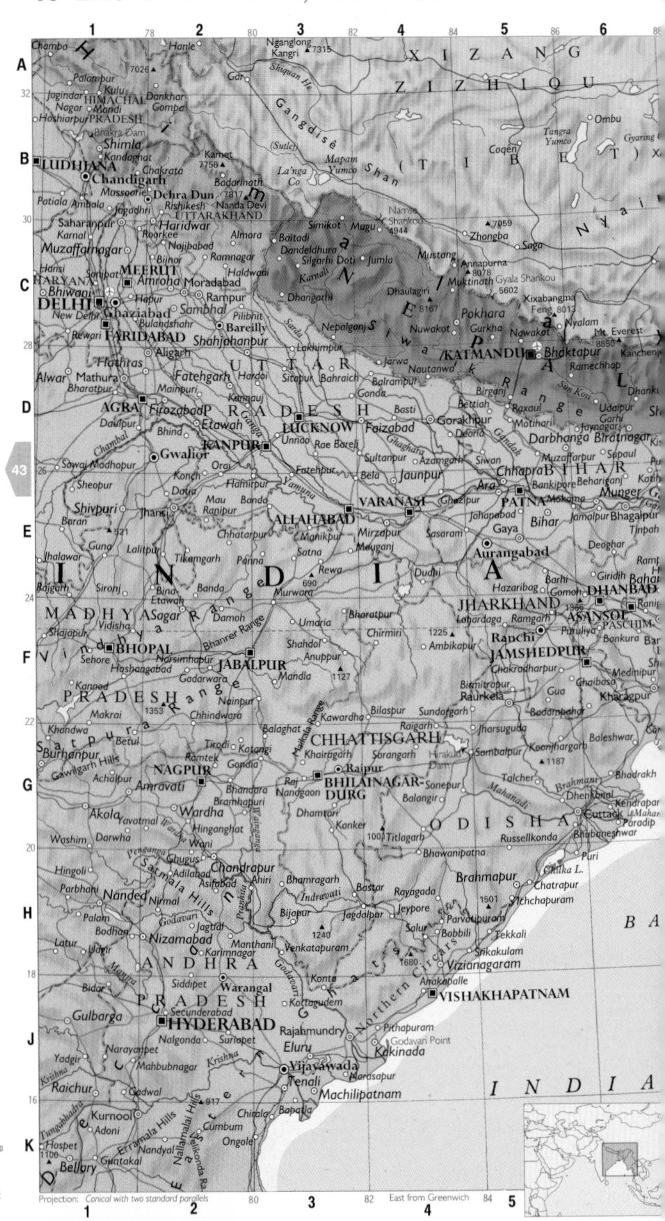
Projection: Conical with two standard parallels
East from Greenwich
INDIA
XIZANG ZIZHIQU
NEPAL
UTTAR PRADESH
MADHYA PRADESH
CHHATTISGARH
JHARKHAND
BIHAR
ODISHA
ANDHRA PRADESH
HIMACHAL PRADESH
UTTARAKHAND
HARYANA
DELHI
LUCKNOW
KANPUR
AGRA
VARANASI
ALLAHABAD
PATNA
BHOPAL
JABALPUR
NAGPUR
HYDERABAD
VISHAKHAPATNAM
KATMANDU
JAMSHEDPUR
DHANBAD
ASANSOL
BHILAINAGAR-DURG
MEERUT
FARIDABAD
LUDHIANA
Chandigarh
Dehra Dun
Gwalior
Raipur
Ranchi
Cuttack
Bhubaneshwar
Vijayawada
Warangal
Himalaya
Gangdisê Shan
Siwalik Range
Vindhya Range
Satpura Range
Eastern Ghats
Northern Circars
INDIAN OCEAN
Ganga
Yamuna
Godavari
Krishna
Mahanadi
Mt. Everest 8850
Annapurna 8078
Dhaulagiri 8167
Nanda Devi 7817
Kamet 7756
43

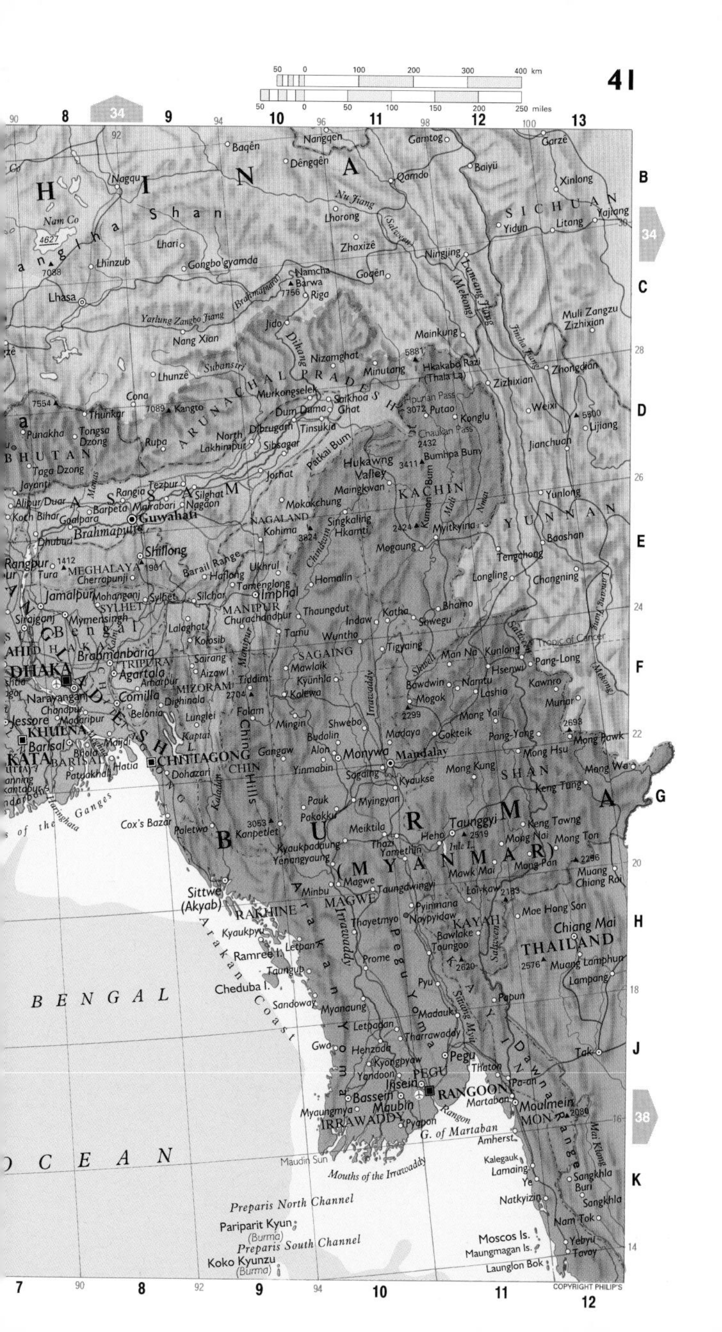
CHINA
Lhasa
Nagqu
Nam Co
Yarlung Zangbo Jiang
Brahmaputra
Namcha Barwa
Qamdo
Nu Jiang
(Salween)
Lancang Jiang
(Mekong)
Jinsha Jiang
SICHUAN
YUNNAN
BHUTAN
ARUNACHAL PRADESH
ASSAM
Guwahati
Shillong
MEGHALAYA
NAGALAND
Kohima
MANIPUR
Imphal
MIZORAM
Aizawl
TRIPURA
Agartala
BANGLADESH
DHAKA
CHITTAGONG
Cox's Bazar
KACHIN
Myitkyina
Bhamo
SAGAING
Irrawaddy
Chindwin
Mandalay
Monywa
SHAN
Taunggyi
BURMA (MYANMAR)
CHIN
Chin Hills
RAKHINE
Sittwe (Akyab)
MAGWE
Arakan Coast
Arakan Yoma
Pegu Yoma
Naypyidaw
KAYAH
THAILAND
Chiang Mai
Mae Hong Son
Tropic of Cancer
PEGU
RANGOON
IRRAWADDY
Bassein
Moulmein
MON
G. of Martaban
Mouths of the Irrawaddy
Preparis North Channel
Preparis South Channel
BAY OF BENGAL
OCEAN
Tavoy
Moscos Is.
COPYRIGHT PHILIP'S

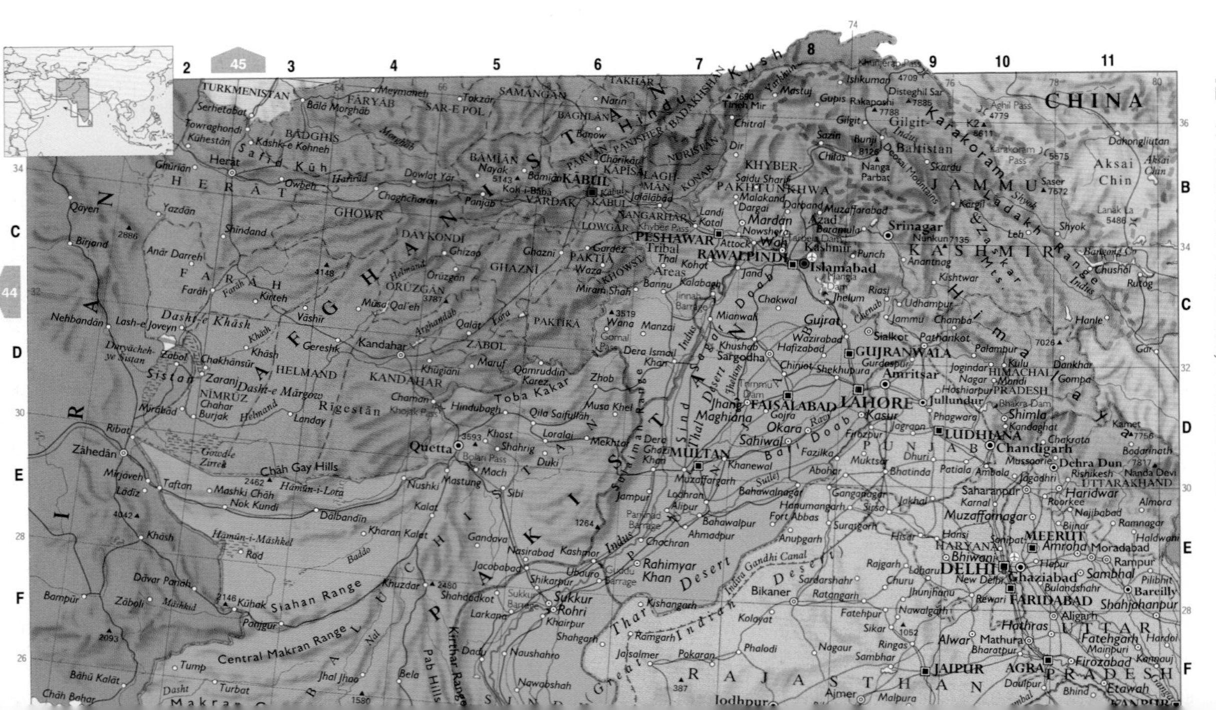

CHINA
Aksai Chin
Karakoram
JAMMU
KASHMIR
Srinagar
Islamabad
RAWALPINDI
PESHAWAR
GUJRANWALA
LAHORE
FAISALABAD
MULTAN
Amritsar
LUDHIANA
Chandigarh
Dehra Dun
DELHI
New Delhi
FARIDABAD
Ghaziabad
MEERUT
Moradabad
Bareilly
AGRA
JAIPUR
Ajmer
Bikaner
Jaisalmer
Sukkur
Quetta
Kandahar
KABUL
Jalalabad
Herat
Zahedan
Kirthar Range
Pab Hills
Central Makran Range
Siahan Range
Chah Gay Hills
Rigestan
Thar Desert
TURKMENISTAN

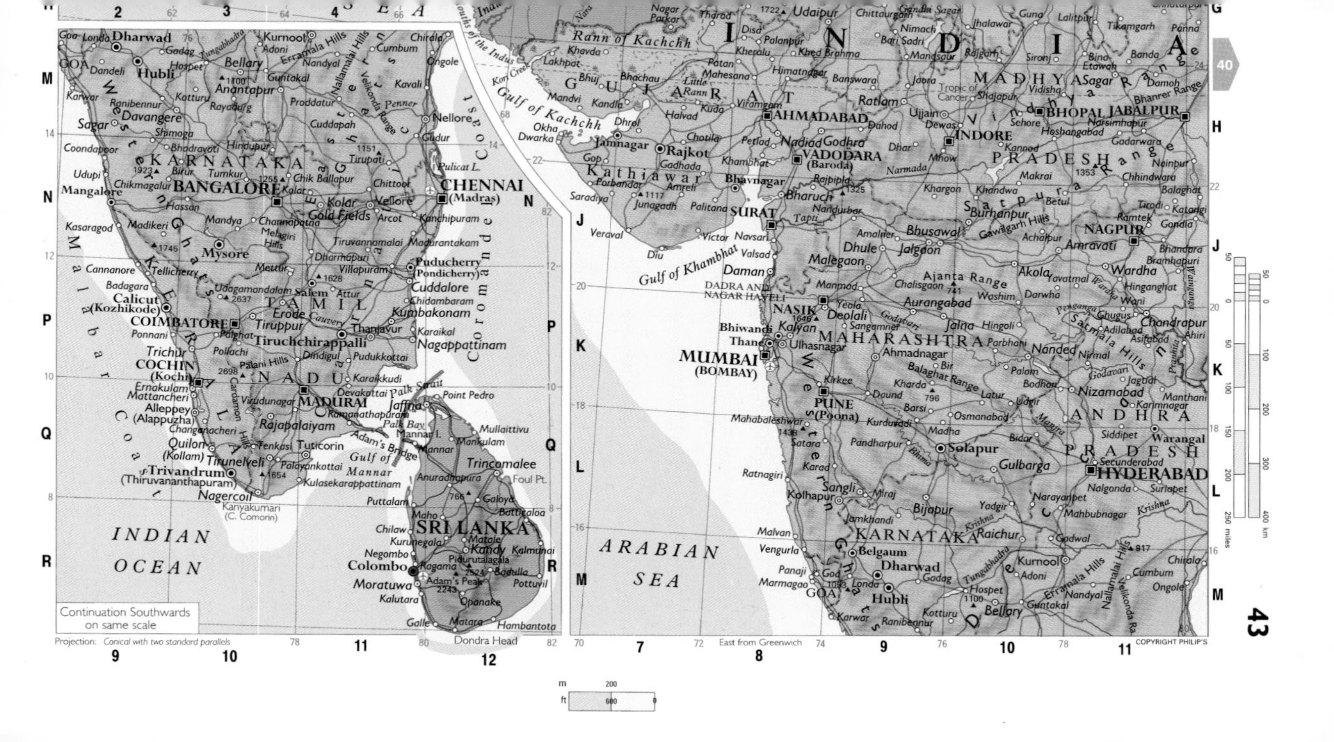
INDIA
GUJARAT
MADHYA PRADESH
MAHARASHTRA
ANDHRA PRADESH
KARNATAKA
TAMIL NADU
KERALA
SRI LANKA
ARABIAN SEA
INDIAN OCEAN
Rann of Kachchh
Gulf of Kachchh
Gulf of Khambhat
Kathiawar
Gulf of Mannar
Palk Strait
Palk Bay
Adam's Bridge
Coromandel Coast
Malabar Coast
Western Ghats
Eastern Ghats
Vindhya Range
Satpura Range
Ajanta Range
Balaghat Range
Satmala Hills
Nallamalai Hills
Erramala Hills
Velikonda Range
Palani Hills
Cardamon Hills
Tropic of Cancer
DADRA AND NAGAR HAVELI
MUMBAI (BOMBAY)
CHENNAI (Madras)
BANGALORE
HYDERABAD
AHMADABAD
NAGPUR
PUNE (Poona)
SURAT
VADODARA (Baroda)
INDORE
BHOPAL
JABALPUR
NASIK
COIMBATORE
MADURAI
COCHIN (Kochi)
Tiruchchirappalli
Colombo
Kandy
Trincomalee
Jaffna
Trivandrum (Thiruvananthapuram)
Mysore
Solapur
Rajkot
Jamnagar
Hubli
Dharwad
Belgaum
Kanyakumari (C. Comorin)
Dondra Head
Point Pedro
Foul Pt.
Continuation Southwards on same scale
Projection: Conical with two standard parallels
East from Greenwich
COPYRIGHT PHILIP'S
m 200
ft 600
0 50 100 200 300 400 km
0 50 100 150 200 250 miles
40
43

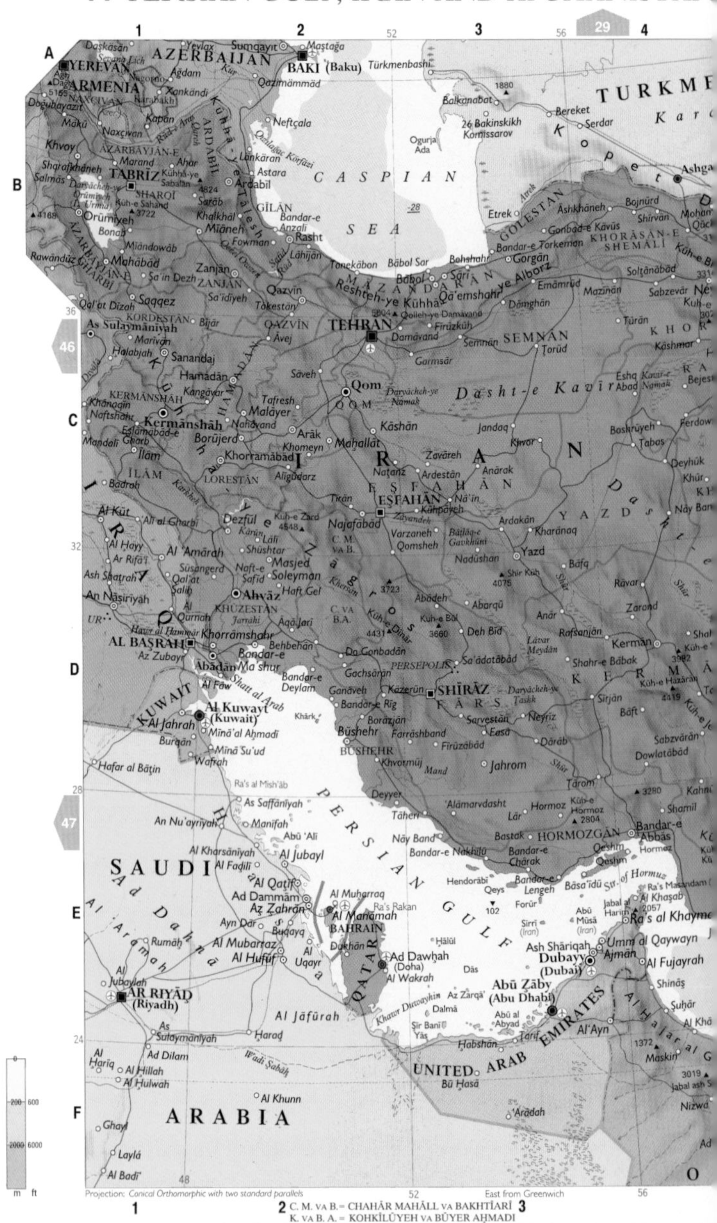


Projection: *Conical Orthomorphic with two standard parallels* 48 52 East from Greenwich 56

1 2 C. M. va B. = CHAHĀR MAHĀLL va BAKHTĪARĪ 3
K. va B. A. = KOHKĪLŪYEH va BŪYER AḨMADI

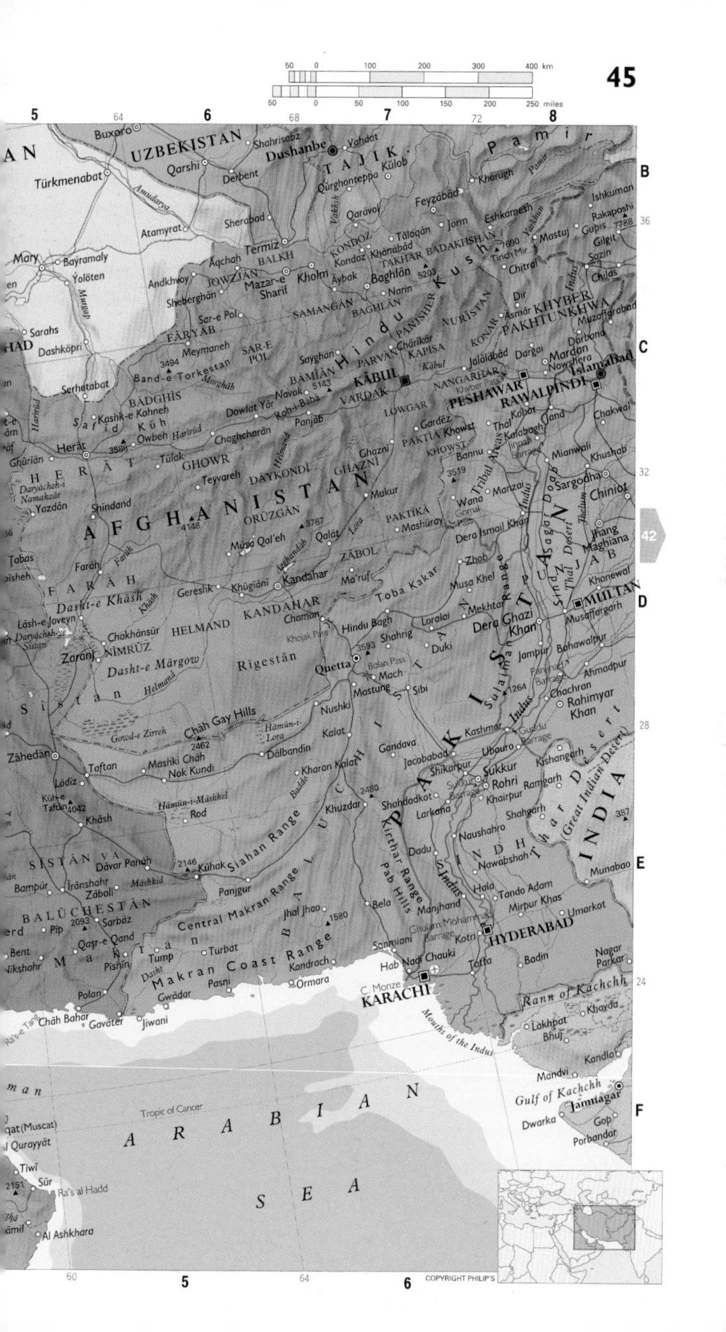

45
50 0 100 200 300 400 km
50 0 50 100 150 200 250 miles
5
6
7
8
64
68
72
B
C
D
E
F
36
32
28
24
42
UZBEKISTAN
TAJIK.
Pamir
Buxoro
Shahrisabz
Dushanbe
Vahdat
Türkmenabat
Qarshi
Derbent
Qŭrghonteppa
Kŭlob
Khorugh
Amudarya
Sherabad
Qarāvol
Feyzābād
Ishkuman
Atamyrat
Termiz
Tāloqān
Jorm
Eshkamesh
Rakaposhi
7788
Gupis
Mastuj
Mary
Bayramaly
Ýolöten
Murgap
Āqchah
BALKH
KONDOZ
Kondoz
Khānābād
TAKHAR
BADAKHSHAN
7690
Tirich Mir
Gilgit
Sazin
Chitral
Chilas
Andkhvoy
JOWZJĀN
Mazar-e Sharif
Kholm
Āybak
Baghlān
5203
Narin
Kush
Hindu
Sheberghān
SAMANGĀN
BAGHLĀN
PANJSHER
NŪRISTĀN
Dir
Sar-e Pol
Asmār
KHYBER PAKHTUNKHWA
Muzaffgrabad
Sarahs
FĀRYĀB
SAR-E POL
Meymaneh
Sayghān
Chārikār
KAPISA
PARVĀN
KONAR
Jalālābād
Dargai
Mardan
Nowshera
Darband
Islamabad
Dashköpri
3494
Band-e Torkestan
Morghāb
BĀMIĀN
Navak
5143
KĀBUL
Kābul
NANGARHĀR
Khyber Pass
PESHAWAR
RAWALPINDI
Serhetabat
BĀDGHĪS
Kashk-e Kohneh
Safīd Kūh
Dowlat Yār
Koh-i-Bābā
VARDAK
LOWGAR
Kohat
Jand
Chakwal
Harīrūd
Panjāb
Gardēz
PAKTIA
Khowst
Thal
Kalabagh
Jinnah Barrage
Herāt
3588
Owbeh
Chaghcharān
Ghaznī
KHOWST
Bannu
Mianwali
Khushab
Ghūriān
HERĀT
Tūlak
GHOWR
Helmand
GHAZNI
Tribal Areas
Sargodha
Daryācheh-i Namakzār
Teyvareh
DAYKONDI
3519
Chiniot
Yazdān
Shīndand
AFGHANISTAN
Mukur
Wana
Manzai
Gomal Pass
Jhelum
4148
ORŪZGĀN
3787
PAKTĪKA
Mashūray
Dera Ismail Khan
Jhang Maghiana
Tabas
Farāh
Mūsá Qal'eh
Qalāt
Lora
Zhob
Sind Sagar Doab
Thal Desert
PUNJAB
FARĀH
Arghandāb
ZĀBOL
Musa Khel
Khanewal
Dasht-e Khāsh
Khāsh
Gereshk
Khūgīāni
Kandahar
Ma'ruf
Toba Kakar
Mekhtar
MULTAN
Lāsh-e Joveyn
HELMAND
KANDAHAR
Chaman
Hindu Bagh
Loralai
Dera Ghazi Khan
Musaffargarh
Daryācheh-ye Sīstān
Chakhānsūr
Khojak Pass
Shahrig
Sulaiman Range
Zaranj
NĪMRŪZ
Dasht-e Mārgow
Rīgestān
3593
Quetta
Duki
Jampur
Bahawalpur
Bolan Pass
Mach
Panjnad Barrage
Ahmadpur
Sīstān
Mastung
Sibi
1264
Chachran
Rahimyar Khan
Nushki
Chāh Gay Hills
Hāmūn-i-Lora
Kalat
Indus
Gowd-e Zirreh
2462
Kashmor
Guddu Barrage
Zāhedān
Taftān
Mashki Chāh
Dālbandin
Gandava
Jacobabad
Ubauro
Kishangarh
Nok Kundi
Kharan Kalat
Shikarpur
Sukkur
Rohri
Ramgarh
Lādīz
Kūh-e Taftān
4042
Hāmūn-i-Māshkel
Baddo
2480
Sukkur Barrage
Khairpur
Rod
Khuzdar
Shahdadkot
Larkana
Shahgarh
387
Khāsh
BALUCHISTAN
PAKISTAN
Thar Desert
(Great Indian Desert)
INDIA
Kirthar Range
Naushahro
Dadu
SINDH
SĪSTĀN VA BALŪCHESTĀN
Dāvar Panāh
2146
Kūhak
Siahan Range
Pab Hills
Nawabshah
Munabao
Bampūr
Īrānshahr
Mashkid
Zāboli
Panjgur
Hala
Tando Adam
Central Makran Range
Jhal Jhao
Bela
Manjhand
Mirpur Khas
Umarkot
2093
Sarbāz
1580
Pīp
Qasr-e Qand
Turbat
Sonmiani
Ghulam Mohammad Barrage
Kotri
HYDERABAD
Bent
Nīkshahr
Makran
Pīshīn
Tump
Makran Coast Range
Kandrach
Hab Nadi Chauki
Tatta
Badin
Nagar Parkar
Dasht
Pasni
Ormara
C. Monze
KARACHI
Polan
Gwādar
Rann of Kachchh
Ra's-e Tang
Chāh Bahār
Gavāter
Jiwani
Mouths of the Indus
Khavda
Lakhpat
Bhuj
Kandla
Mandvi
Gulf of Kachchh
Jamnagar
ARABIAN SEA
Tropic of Cancer
Masqat (Muscat)
Al Qurayyāt
Dwarka
Gop
Porbandar
Tīwī
2151
Sūr
Ra's al Hadd
Al Ashkhara
60
64
5
6

BLACK SEA
CASPIAN SEA
MEDITERRANEAN SEA
RUSSIA
GEORGIA
ARMENIA
AZERBAIJAN
TURKEY
SYRIA
IRAN
CYPRUS
LEBANON
ISRAEL
GREECE
BULGARIA
ANKARA
İSTANBUL
İZMIR
BURSA
ADANA
TBILISI
YEREVAN
BAKI (Baku)
TABRĪZ
HALAB (Aleppo)
DIMASHQ (Damascus)
BAYRŪT (Beirut)
AL MAWṢIL (Mosul)
Konya
Kayseri
Gaziantep
Diyarbakır
Erzurum
Trabzon
Samsun
Sinop
Sivas
Malatya
Antalya
Eskişehir
Nicosia
Limassol
Sochi
Derbent
Rhodes
Dodecanese
Kuzey Anadolu Dağları (Pontine Mts.)
Toros Dağları (Taurus Mts.)
Caucasus Mountains
Al Jazīrah
Nahr Dijlah (Tigris)
Van Gölü
Tuz Gölü

PERSIAN
GULF
RED
SEA
SAUDI
ARABIA
EGYPT
SUDAN
KUWAIT
HALAIB TRIANGLE
An Nafūd
Ad Dahnā'
Al Ḥijāz
Jabal Shammar
Al Qaṣīm
Ṣafājah
Ḥarrat Khaybar
Ḥarrat al 'Uwairidh
Ḥarrat al Kishb
Ḥarrat Nawāṣīf
'Urūq Subay
Al 'Aramah
Al Jāfūrah
Ṣaḥrā' al Ḥijārah
Aṭ Ṭubayq
Wādī Ṣabāḥ
Wadi ar Rimah
Es Sahrâ
Esh Sharqîya
Es Sahrâ en Nûbîya
Es Sînâ'
Khalig el Suweis
Gulf of Aqaba
Tropic of Cancer
Buheirat en Naser (Lake Nasser)
Sadd el Aali (Aswan High Dam)
AR RIYĀḌ (Riyadh)
Makkah (Mecca)
JIDDAH (Jedda)
Al Madīnah (Medina)
Aṭ Ṭā'if
Al Kuwayt (Kuwait)
AL BAṢRAH
EL QÂHIRA (Cairo)
El Suweis (Suez)
Ad Dammām
Aẓ Ẓahrān
Al Qaṭīf
Al Jubayl
Al Hufūf
Al Mubarraz
Buraydah
'Unayzah
Ḥā'il
Tabūk
Taymā
Al 'Ulā
Madā'in Ṣāliḥ
Al Jawf
Sakākah
'Ar'ar
Ḥafar al Bāṭin
Al Wajh
Umm Lajj
Yanbu 'al Baḥr
Rābigh
Al Qaḍīmah
Ḥaql
Al Muwayliḥ
Ḍubā
Aswân
Qena
El Uqsur
Asyûṭ
El Minyâ
Beni Suef
El Faiyûm
Helwân
Hurghada
Bûr Safâga
Wadi Halfa
An Nāṣirīyah
Al 'Amārah
Ahvāz
Khorramshahr
Ābādān
Bandar-e Ma'shur
Ma'ān
Al 'Aqabah
Elat
PETRA
UR
THEBES
Projection: Conical Orthomorphic with two standard parallels
East from Greenwich
50 0 100 200 300 400 km
50 0 50 100 150 200 250 miles

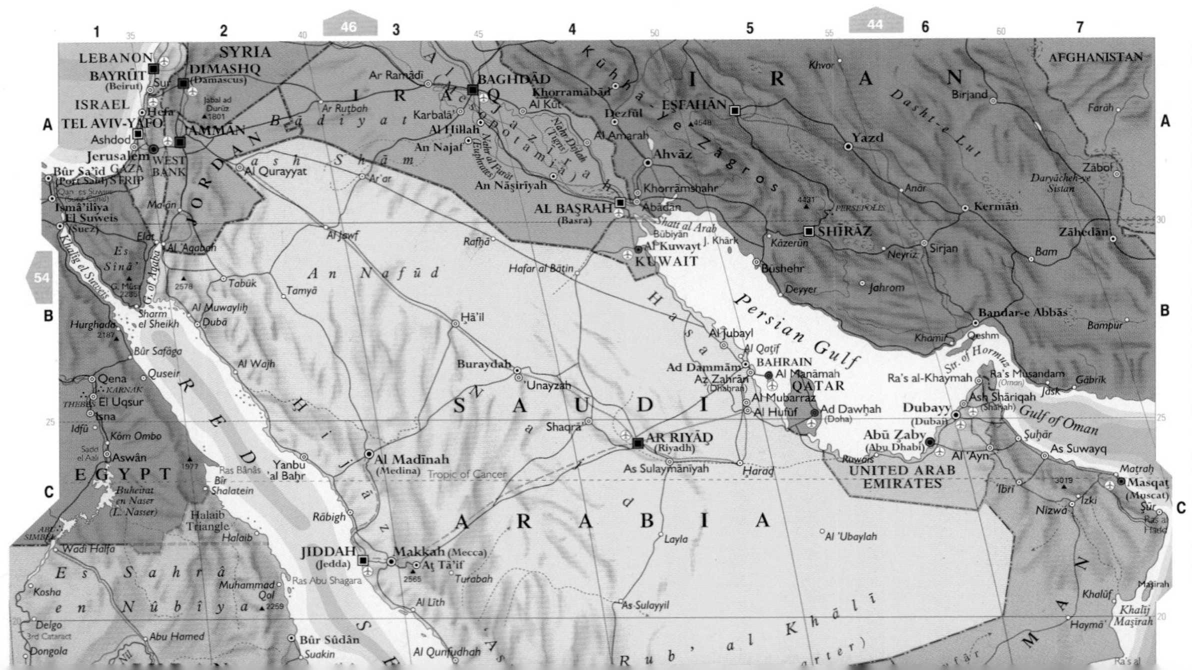
AFGHANISTAN
IRAN
Dasht-e Lut
Kūhhā-ye Zāgros
Zāhedān
Kermān
Yazd
ESFAHĀN
SHĪRĀZ
Bandar-e Abbās
Ahvāz
Ābādān
Khorramshahr
Dezfūl
Būshehr
Persian Gulf
Gulf of Oman
Str. of Hormuz
IRAQ
BAGHDĀD
AL BAŞRAH (Basra)
An Nāşirīyah
Karbalā'
An Najaf
Al Kūt
Nahr al Furāt (Euphrates)
Nahr Dijlah (Tigris)
Ar Ramādī
Ar Rutbah
KUWAIT
Al Kuwayt
BAHRAIN
Al Manāmah
QATAR
Ad Dawhah (Doha)
UNITED ARAB EMIRATES
Abū Zaby (Abu Dhabi)
Dubayy (Dubai)
Ra's al-Khaymah
OMAN
Masqat (Muscat)
Şūr
Nizwá
SAUDI ARABIA
AR RIYĀD (Riyadh)
Ad Dammām
Az Zahrān (Dhahran)
Al Jubayl
Al Hufūf
Hā'il
Buraydah
'Unayzah
Al Madīnah (Medina)
Makkah (Mecca)
Aţ Tā'if
JIDDAH (Jedda)
Tabūk
Yanbu 'al Bahr
An Nafūd
Rub' al Khālī
Tropic of Cancer
RED SEA
SYRIA
DIMASHQ (Damascus)
LEBANON
BAYRŪT (Beirut)
ISRAEL
TEL AVIV-YAFO
Jerusalem
JORDAN
AMMAN
EGYPT
Aswân
El Uqsur
Qena
Hurghada
Es Sînâ'
Khalîg el Suweis
G. of Aqaba
Bûr Sûdân
Halaib Triangle
Wadi Halfa
Dongola
Es Sahrâ en Nûbîya

INDIAN OCEAN
Gulf of Aden
ETHIOPIA
Ethiopian Highlands
ERITREA
DJIBOUTI
Djibouti
YEMEN
Hadramawt
SOMALIA
Somaliland
Puntland
Galmudug
Ogaden
SOUTH SUDAN
Sudd
KENYA
UGANDA
Jibalan Nubah
El Gezira
Danakil Desert
Elemi Triangle
Omdurmân
EL KHARTÛM
(Khartoum)
Kassalâ
Khashm el Girba
Wâd Medanî
Gedaref
Ed Dueim
Kôstî
Singa
Umm Ruwaba
Ed Damazin
Roseires Res.
Nil el Abyad
Nil el Azraq
Malakâl
Sobat
Bahr el Jebel (Nile)
Pibor Post
Bôr
Tali Post
Mongalla
Juba
Kapoeta
Torit
Kajo Kaji
Yei
Akordat
Asmera
Mitsiwa
Zula
Dahlak Kebir
Adigrat
Aksum
Adwa
Mekele
Ras Dashen 4620
Gonder
Lalibela
L. Tana
Debre Tabor
Bahir Dar
Bure
Debre Markos
Dese
Abay (Blue Nile)
Nekemte
ADDIS ABEBA
Debre Zeyit
Nazret
Asela
L. Ziway
Dembidolo
Metu
Gore
Jima
Awasa
Shashemene
Yirga Alem
Dila
L. Abaya
Arba Minch
L. Shamo
Omo
Mt. Batu 4307
Goba
Ginir
Kibre Mengist
Negele
Dire Dawa
Awash
Harer
Jijiga
Tendaho
L. Assal
L. Abbé
Dikhil
Tadjoura
Saylac
Aseb
Bab el Mandeb
Imi
Scebeli
Genale
Kebri Dehar
Dolo
Mega
Moyale
Chew Bahir
Lokitaung
L. Turkana
Lodwar
South Horr
Marsabit
Wajir
El Wak
Kitale
Mt. Elgon
Gulu
Lira
Moroto
Soroti
Mbale
L. Kyoga
Arua
Pakwach
Murchison Falls
L. Albert
Masindi
Albert Nile
Turkwel
Hajjah
Khamir
Al Luhayyah
Kamaran
SANA'
Al Hudaydah
Hanish
Dhamar
Djebel Marar
Ibb
Ta'izz
Al Mukha
Madinat ash Sha'b
'Adan
Shuqra
Ahwar
Nisab
Shibam
Al Mukalla
Sayhut
Ras Fartak
'Abd al Kuri (Yemen)
Socotra (Yemen)
Hadiboh
Berbera
Karin
Hargeisa
Burco
Boosaaso
Ceerigaabo
Bereeda
Ras Asir
Xaafuun
Ras Xaafuun
Qardho
Bender Beyla
Garoowe
Las Anod (Laascaanood)
Eyl
Gaalkacyo
Hobyo
Beledweyne
Luuq
Baydhabo
Buurhakaba
Jawhar
Wanleweyne
MUQDISHO
(Mogadishu)
Marka
Shabeelle
Baardheere
Giuba (Juba)
Jilib
Dif
Equator
Kismaayo
(Chisimaio)
Projection: Sanson-Flamsteed's Sinusoidal
East from Greenwich
COPYRIGHT PHILIP S
km
miles
m
ft

55
57

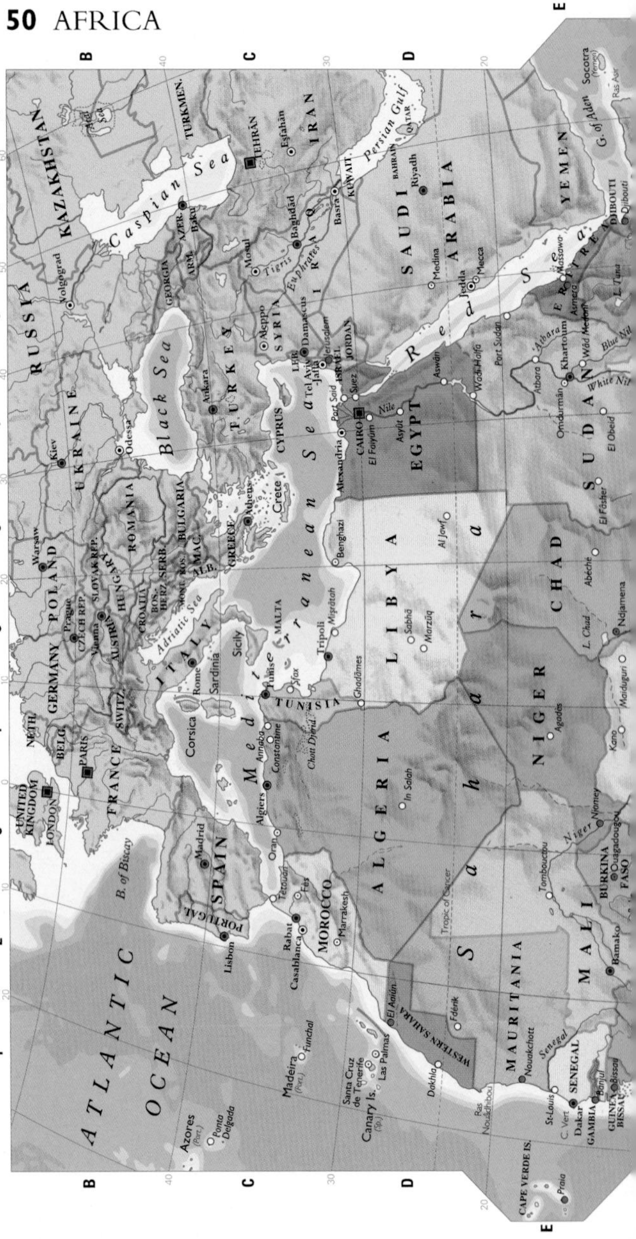

ATLANTIC OCEAN
Azores (Port.)
Ponta Delgada
Madeira (Port.)
Funchal
Canary Is. (Sp.)
Santa Cruz de Tenerife
Las Palmas
CAPE VERDE IS.
Praia
B. of Biscay
UNITED KINGDOM
LONDON
FRANCE
PARIS
BELG.
NETH.
GERMANY
SWITZ.
PORTUGAL
Lisbon
SPAIN
Madrid
MOROCCO
Rabat
Casablanca
Fès
Tétouan
Marrakesh
WESTERN SAHARA
El Aaiún
Dakhla
Ras Nouâdhibou
MAURITANIA
Nouakchott
Fdérik
SENEGAL
Dakar
St-Louis
C. Vert
Senegal
GAMBIA
Banjul
GUINEA-BISSAU
Bissau
MALI
Bamako
Tombouctou
Tropic of Cancer
BURKINA FASO
Ouagadougou
Niger
Niamey
NIGER
Agadès
Kano
Maiduguri
ALGERIA
Algiers
Oran
Annaba
Constantine
Chott Djerid
In Salah
Ghadāmes
TUNISIA
Tunis
Sfax
Sahara
LIBYA
Tripoli
Misrātah
Benghazi
Sabhā
Marzūq
Al Jawf
CHAD
L. Chad
Ndjamena
Abéché
Mediterranean Sea
Corsica
Sardinia
Sicily
MALTA
ITALY
Rome
Adriatic Sea
AUSTRIA
Vienna
CZECH REP.
Prague
SLOVAK REP.
POLAND
Warsaw
HUNGARY
CROATIA
BOS.-HERZ.
SERB.
MONT.
KOS.
ALB.
MAC.
GREECE
Athens
Crete
ROMANIA
BULGARIA
UKRAINE
Kiev
Odessa
Black Sea
RUSSIA
Volgograd
KAZAKHSTAN
Aral Sea
TURKMEN.
Caspian Sea
GEORGIA
ARM.
AZER.
Baku
TURKEY
Ankara
CYPRUS
SYRIA
Aleppo
LEB.
Damascus
ISRAEL
Tel Aviv-Jaffa
Jerusalem
JORDAN
IRAQ
Mosul
Baghdād
Basra
Tigris
Euphrates
IRAN
TEHRĀN
Eşfahān
KUWAIT
BAHRAIN
QATAR
Persian Gulf
SAUDI ARABIA
Riyadh
Medina
Jedda
Mecca
EGYPT
CAIRO
Alexandria
Port Said
Suez
El Faiyûm
Asyût
Aswân
Nile
Wadi Halfa
Red Sea
SUDAN
Port Sudan
Atbara
Khartoum
Omdurmân
Wad Medani
El Obeid
El Fâsher
White Nile
Blue Nile
ERITREA
Asmera
Massawa
L. Tana
YEMEN
G. of Aden
DJIBOUTI
Djibouti
Socotra (Yemen)
Ras Asir

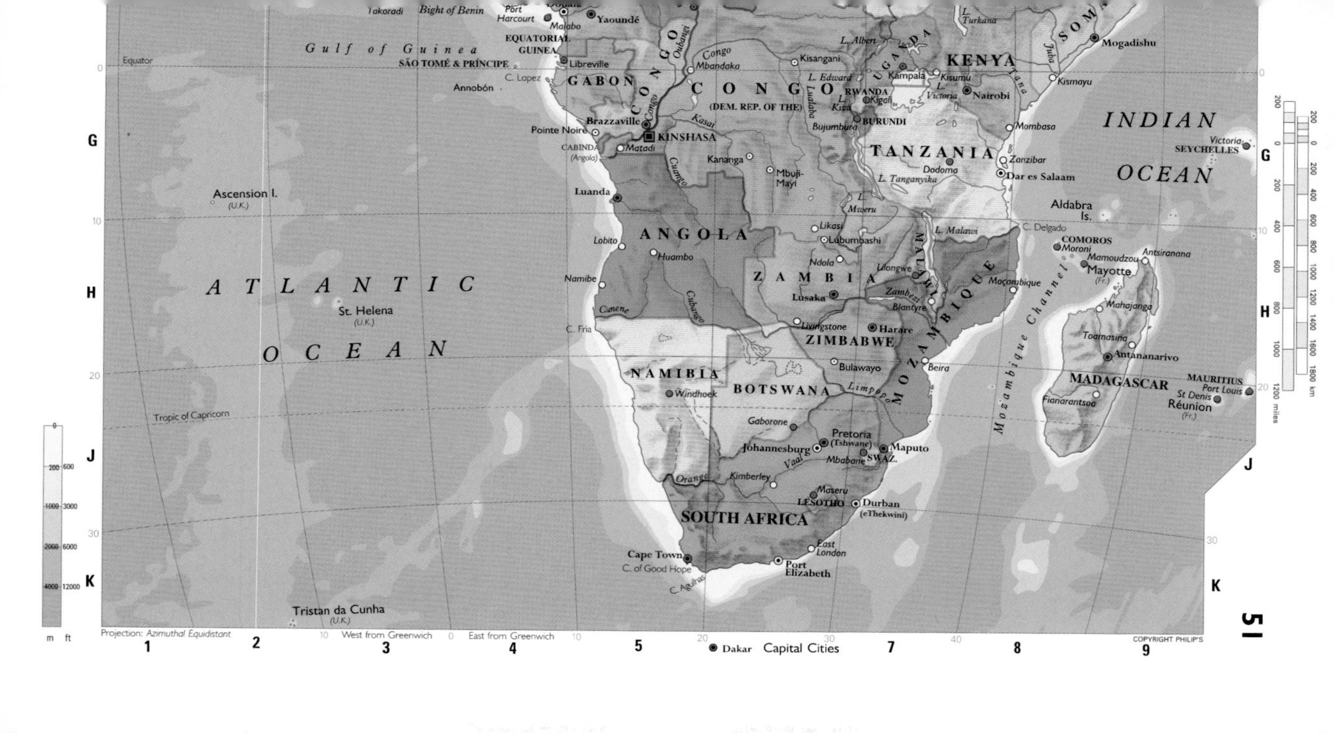

ATLANTIC OCEAN
INDIAN OCEAN
Gulf of Guinea
Bight of Benin
Takoradi
Port Harcourt
Malabo
Yaoundé
EQUATORIAL GUINEA
SÃO TOMÉ & PRÍNCIPE
Libreville
Annobón
C. Lopez
GABON
CONGO
Oubangi
Congo
Mbandaka
Kisangani
CONGO (DEM. REP. OF THE)
Brazzaville
Pointe Noire
KINSHASA
Kasai
CABINDA (Angola)
Matadi
Cuango
Kananga
Mbuji-Mayi
Lualaba
L. Edward
L. Albert
L. Kivu
RWANDA
Kigali
Bujumbura
BURUNDI
UGANDA
Kampala
L. Victoria
Kisumu
KENYA
Nairobi
L. Turkana
Tana
Juba
Kismayu
SOMALIA
Mogadishu
Mombasa
TANZANIA
Dodoma
Zanzibar
Dar es Salaam
L. Tanganyika
L. Mweru
L. Malawi
C. Delgado
Aldabra Is.
SEYCHELLES
Victoria
Ascension I. (U.K.)
Luanda
ANGOLA
Lobito
Huambo
Namibe
Cunene
Cubango
C. Fria
Likasi
Lubumbashi
Ndola
ZAMBIA
Lusaka
Lilongwe
MALAWI
Zambezi
Blantyre
Livingstone
Harare
ZIMBABWE
Bulawayo
MOZAMBIQUE
Moçambique
Beira
COMOROS
Moroni
Mamoudzou
Mayotte (Fr.)
Antsiranana
Mozambique Channel
Mahajanga
Toamasina
Antananarivo
MADAGASCAR
Fianarantsoa
MAURITIUS
Port Louis
St Denis
Réunion (Fr.)
St. Helena (U.K.)
NAMIBIA
Windhoek
BOTSWANA
Limpopo
Gaborone
Pretoria (Tshwane)
Johannesburg
Maputo
Mbabane
SWAZ.
Vaal
Orange
Kimberley
Maseru
LESOTHO
Durban (eThekwini)
SOUTH AFRICA
Cape Town
C. of Good Hope
C. Agulhas
Port Elizabeth
East London
Tropic of Capricorn
Equator
Tristan da Cunha (U.K.)
Projection: Azimuthal Equidistant
West from Greenwich
East from Greenwich
Dakar Capital Cities
COPYRIGHT PHILIP'S
m ft
200 600
1000 3000
2000 6000
4000 12000
km 200 0 200 400 600 800 1000 1200 1400 1600 1800
miles 200 0 200 400 600 800 1000 1200

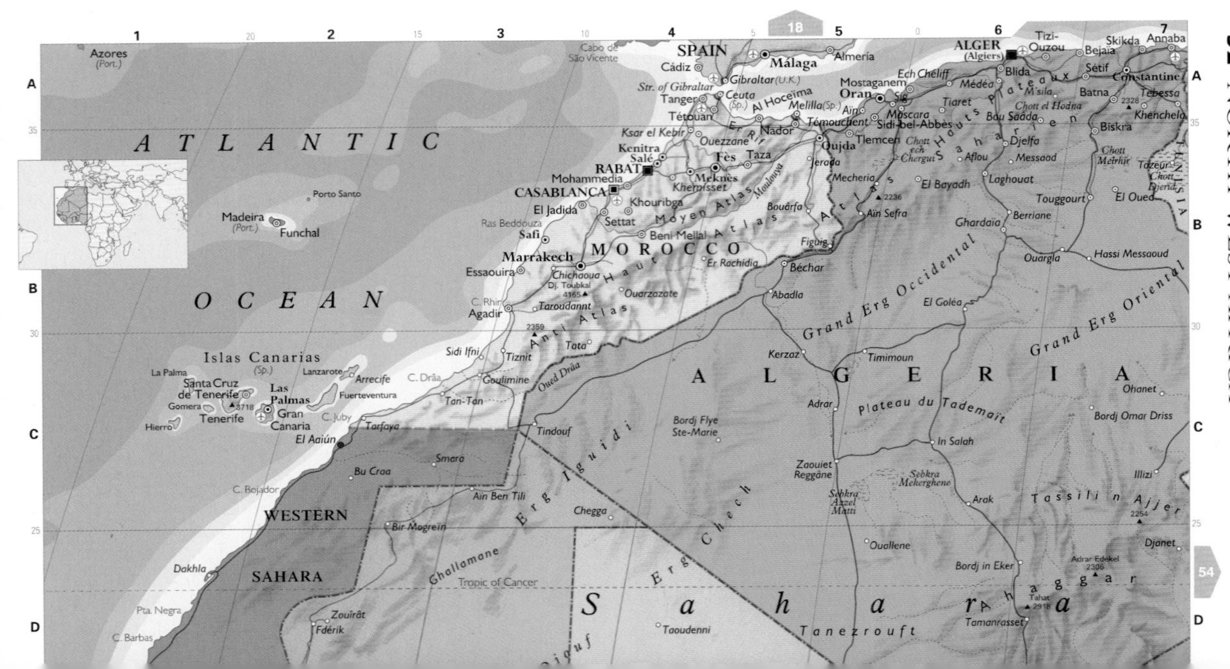
ATLANTIC
OCEAN
MOROCCO
ALGERIA
WESTERN
SAHARA
SPAIN
Sahara
ALGER (Algiers)
RABAT
CASABLANCA
Marrakech
Fès
Meknès
Tanger
Tétouan
Oran
Constantine
Annaba
Skikda
Bejaïa
Sétif
Batna
Biskra
Blida
Médéa
Tiaret
Mostaganem
Tlemcen
Oujda
Nador
Melilla (Sp.)
Ceuta (Sp.)
Gibraltar (U.K.)
Málaga
Almería
Cádiz
Str. of Gibraltar
Cabo de São Vicente
Kenitra
Salé
Mohammedia
El Jadida
Safi
Essaouira
Agadir
Settat
Khouribga
Beni Mellal
Ouarzazate
Taza
Al Hoceima
Béchar
Ghardaia
Ouargla
Touggourt
Laghouat
Djelfa
El Oued
Hassi Messaoud
El Goléa
In Salah
Adrar
Timimoun
Tindouf
Tamanrasset
Djanet
Illizi
Ohanet
Bordj Omar Driss
Grand Erg Occidental
Grand Erg Oriental
Plateau du Tademaït
Tassili n Ajjer
Ahaggar
Haut Atlas
Moyen Atlas
Anti Atlas
Hauts Plateaux
Erg Iguidi
Erg Chech
Tanezrouft
Islas Canarias (Sp.)
Las Palmas
Gran Canaria
Santa Cruz de Tenerife
Tenerife
Fuerteventura
Lanzarote
Arrecife
La Palma
Gomera
Hierro
Madeira (Port.)
Funchal
Porto Santo
Azores (Port.)
El Aaiún
Dakhla
Smara
Bu Craa
Tarfaya
Tan-Tan
Sidi Ifni
Tiznit
Goulimine
Tata
Taroudannt
Dj. Toubkal 4165
Tropic of Cancer
Taoudenni
Zouîrât
Fdérik
Chegga
Aïn Ben Tili
Bir Mogreïn
Kerzaz
Abadla
Zaouiet Reggâne
Arak
Bordj in Eker
Ouallene
18
54

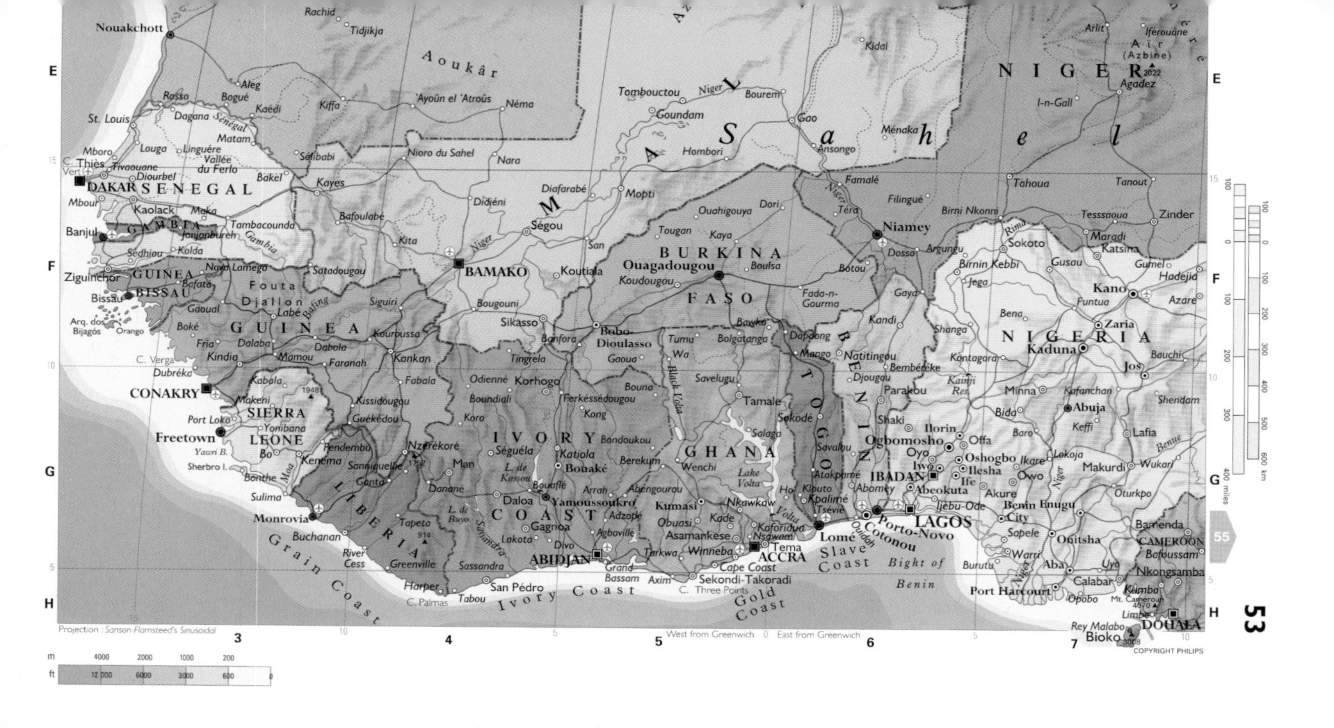
100 0 100 200 300 400 500 600 km
100 0 100 200 300 400 miles
55
E
F
G
H
15
10
5
3
4
5
6
7
NIGER
Aïr (Azbine)
Agadez
2022
Arlit
Iférouane
I-n-Gall
Tahoua
Tanout
Zinder
Maradi
Tessaoua
Katsina
Birni Nkonni
Niamey
Dosso
Filingué
Ménaka
Kidal
Gao
Ansongo
Bourem
Tombouctou
Goundam
Hombori
Niger
Téra
Famalé
Sahel
MALI
Mopti
Diafarabé
Ségou
San
Koutiala
BAMAKO
Sikasso
Bougouni
Kita
Kayes
Bafoulabé
Nioro du Sahel
Didiéni
Nara
Néma
'Ayoûn el 'Atroûs
Aoukâr
Kiffa
Tidjikja
Rachid
Sélibabi
Kaédi
Aleg
Bogué
Rosso
Nouakchott
Matam
Bakel
Dagana
Sénégal
Linguère
Vallée du Ferlo
Louga
St. Louis
Mboro
Thiès
Tivaouane
Diourbel
DAKAR
C. Vert
Mbour
Kaolack
Maka
SENEGAL
Tambacounda
Gambia
GAMBIA
Banjul
Janjanbureh
Kolda
Sédhiou
Ziguinchor
Nova Lamego
Bafatá
GUINEA-BISSAU
Bissau
Arq. dos Bijagós
Orango
Gaoual
Boké
Fria
Kindia
Dubréka
C. Verga
CONAKRY
Fouta Djallon
Bafing
Labé
Dalaba
Mamou
Dabola
Faranah
Kouroussa
Kankan
Siguiri
Satadougou
Fabala
GUINEA
Kissidougou
Guékédou
Nzérékoré
1752
SIERRA LEONE
Freetown
Port Loko
Makeni
Kabala
1948
Yonibana
Bo
Kenema
Pendembu
Sherbro I.
Yawri B.
Bonthe
Sulima
Moa
Monrovia
Buchanan
River Cess
Greenville
Harper
C. Palmas
LIBERIA
Sanniquellie
Ganta
Tapeta
914
Grain Coast
IVORY COAST
Odienné
Boundiali
Korhogo
Tingréla
Ferkéssédougou
Kong
Koro
Séguéla
Katiola
Bouaké
Man
Danané
Daloa
Yamoussoukro
Bouaflé
Arrah
Gagnoa
Divo
Lakota
Sassandra
San Pédro
Tabou
ABIDJAN
Grand Bassam
Agboville
Adzopé
Abengourou
Bondoukou
Bouna
L. de Kossou
L. de Buyo
Ivory Coast
BURKINA FASO
Ouagadougou
Koudougou
Bobo-Dioulasso
Banfora
Gaoua
Tougan
Ouahigouya
Kaya
Dori
Boulsa
Fada-n-Gourma
Botou
Kandi
Gaya
Dapaong
Mango
Bawku
Bolgatanga
Tumu
Wa
Black Volta
Savelugu
Tamale
Salaga
GHANA
Wenchi
Berekum
Kumasi
Obuasi
Kade
Nkawkaw
Lake Volta
Koforidua
Nsawam
Tema
ACCRA
Winneba
Cape Coast
Asamankese
Tarkwa
Sekondi-Takoradi
C. Three Points
Axim
Gold Coast
TOGO
Sokodé
Savalou
Atakpamé
Kpalimé
Kluto
Ho
Volta
Tsévié
Lomé
Slave Coast
BENIN
Natitingou
Djougou
Parakou
Bembèrèkè
Abomey
Ouidah
Cotonou
Porto-Novo
Bight of Benin
NIGERIA
Sokoto
Rima
Gusau
Kano
Hadejia
Gumel
Azare
Bauchi
Jos
Zaria
Funtua
Kaduna
Kafanchan
Abuja
Keffi
Lafia
Shendam
Wukari
Makurdi
Benue
Oturkpo
Lokoja
Minna
Bida
Baro
Kontagora
Bena
Birnin Kebbi
Jega
Argungu
Shanga
Kainji Res.
Ilorin
Offa
Oshogbo
Ilesha
Ife
Ikare
Owo
Akure
Ogbomosho
Oyo
Iwo
IBADAN
Abeokuta
Ijebu-Ode
LAGOS
Shaki
Benin City
Enugu
Sapele
Warri
Burutu
Port Harcourt
Aba
Onitsha
Opobo
Calabar
Uyo
Bamenda
CAMEROON
Bafoussam
Nkongsamba
Kumba
Mt. Cameroun 4070
Limbe
DOUALA
Bioko
Rey Malabo
3008
West from Greenwich 0 East from Greenwich
Projection: Sanson-Flamsteed's Sinusoidal
m 4000 2000 1000 200
ft 12 000 6000 3000 600 0
COPYRIGHT PHILIPS

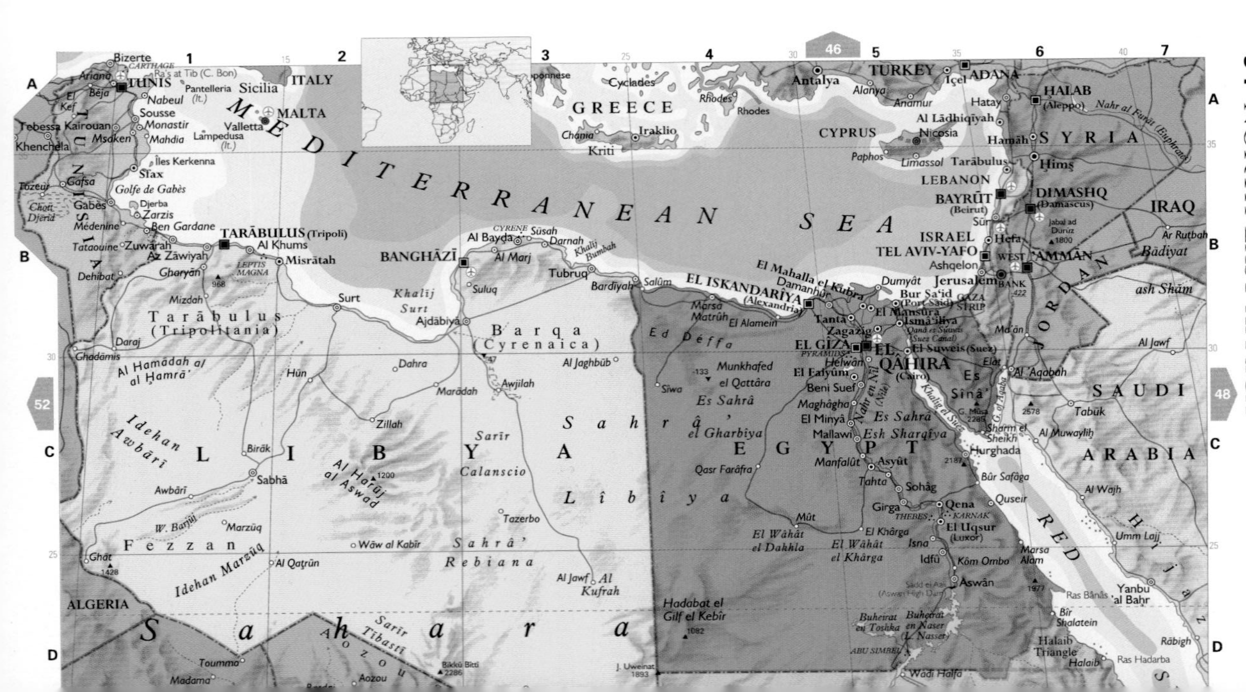

MEDITERRANEAN SEA
RED SEA
TURKEY
SYRIA
IRAQ
LEBANON
ISRAEL
CYPRUS
GREECE
ITALY
MALTA
JORDAN
SAUDI ARABIA
EGYPT
LIBYA
TUNISIA
ALGERIA
Sahara
HALAB (Aleppo)
DIMASHQ (Damascus)
BAYRŪT (Beirut)
'AMMĀN
TEL AVIV-YAFO
Jerusalem
Nicosia
EL QÂHIRA (Cairo)
EL ISKANDARÎYA (Alexandria)
EL GÎZA
Aswân
El Uqsur (Luxor)
Asyût
Bur Sa'id (Port Said)
El Suweis (Suez)
TARĀBULUS (Tripoli)
BANGHĀZĪ
Misrātah
Sabhā
TUNIS
Valletta
Sicilia
Kriti
Rhodes
Antalya
ADANA
Sînâ'
Khalig el Suez
Nahr en Nîl (Nile)
Barqa (Cyrenaica)
Tarābulus (Tripolitania)
Fezzan
Khalīj Surt
Al Harūj al Aswad
Es Sahrâ el Gharbîya
Sahrâ' Rebiana
Sarīr Calanscio
Aozou
Halaib Triangle
Wadi Halfa

NIGER
CHAD
SUDAN
SOUTH SUDAN
ETHIOPIA
ERITREA
NIGERIA
CAMEROON
CENTRAL AFRICAN REPUBLIC
CONGO
S a h a r a
B o r k o u
E n n e d i
Z a g a o u a
D a r f û r
K o r d o f â n
B a h r e l G h a z a l
S u d d
E q u a t o r i a
Grand Erg de Bilma
Erg du Djourab
Dépression du Bodéle
Dépression du Mourdi
Lac Tchad
Massif des Bongos
Massif de l'Adamaoua
Bahr el Ghazal
Nahr en Nil (Nile)
Nahr 'Atbara
Nil el Azraq (Blue Nile)
Nil el Abyad (White Nile)
Bahr el Jebel (Nile)
Bahr el 'Arab
Abay (Blue Nile)
W. Howar (Shau)
Chari
Logone
Oubangi
Bomu
Uele
Kotto
Chinko
Ouarra
Sobat
Jur
L. Tana
L. Abaya
L. Shamo
Chew Bahir
L. Turkana
Roseires Res.
Elemi Triangle
Ouninga Kébir
Bilma
Fachi
Faya-Largeau
Fada
Oum Chalouba
Biltine
Abéché
Ndjamena
Omdurmân
EL KHARTÛM (Khartoum)
El Khartûm Bahrî
Kassalâ
Wad Medanî
Gedaref
El Obeid
Kôstî
El Fâsher
Nyâlâ
Ed Da'ein
En Nahud
Malakal
Juba
Wau
Bangui
YAOUNDÉ
Maiduguri
Garoua
Ngaoundéré
Moundou
Sarh
Bir 'Atrun
Ed Debba
Kareima
Atbara
Berber
Ed Dâmer
Shendî
Sinkat
Suakin
Haiya
Trinkitat
Karora
Nakfa
Akordat
Metema
Gonder
Bahir Dar
Debre Markos
Nekemte
Metu
Gore
Jima
Arba Minch
Dembidolo
Pibor Post
Kapoeta
Torit
Kajo Kaji
Lokitaung
Mongalla
Bôr
Tali Post
Amâdi
Yei
Rumbêk
Tonj
Gogriâl
Abyei
Râgâ
Sa'id Bundas
Birao
Ndélé
Bria
Ippy
Bakouma
Yalinga
Bambari
Sibut
Kaga Bandoro
Batangafo
Bangassou
Mobaye
Gbadolite
Bondo
Ango
Dungu
Faradje
Yambiô
Obo
Zongo
Bosobolo
Libenge
Bimbo
Mbaïki
Berbérati
Carnot
Bossembélé
Bozoum
Bossangoa
Bouar
Baboua
Batouri
Bertoua
Nanga-Eboko
Abong-Mbang
Foumban
Yoko
Tibati
Bétaré Oya
Meiganga
Banyo
Gashaka
Jalingo
Jimeta
Numan
Gombe
Kumo
Biu
Mubi
Maroua
Guider
Bama
Kousseri
Dikwa
Goniri
Chibuk
Bajoga
Duku
Damatura
Nguru
Gashua
Geidam
Kumaganum
Titiwa
Bosso
Nguigmi
Boultoum
Mao
Ziguéy
Moussoro
Massakory
Ati
Oum Hadjer
Mongo
Bokoro
Bitkine
Massenya
Abou-Deïa
Am Timan
Goz Beïda
Bousso
Bongor
Kélo
Laï
Pala
Doba
Koumra
Goré
Baïbokoum
Paoua
Harazé
Al Junaynah
Zalingei
Kutum
Malha
Umm Keddada
El Odaiya
Abû Zabad
Kâdugli
Er Rahad
Umm Ruwaba
Jibalan Nubah
Ed Damazin
Singa
Ed Dueim
El Gezira
Sodiri
El Wuz
Wad Hamid
Khashm el Girba
Adarama
Merowe Dam
5th Cataract
6th Cataract
J. Marrah 3088
Mt. Toussoro 1330
1310
1954
1325
3202
3688
3187
2780
2042
1960
2419
346
1830
375
Lac de Lagdo
Lac de Mbakaou
Gibe II
Gibe III
Omo
Projection : Sanson-Flamsteed's Sinusoidal
East from Greenwich
COPYRIGHT PHILIPS
m 4000 2000 1000 200
ft 12 000 6000 3000 600 0
100 0 100 200 300 400 500 600 km
100 0 100 200 300 400 miles
53
56
57
49
E F G H
1 2 3 4 5 6
15 10 5
15 20 25 30

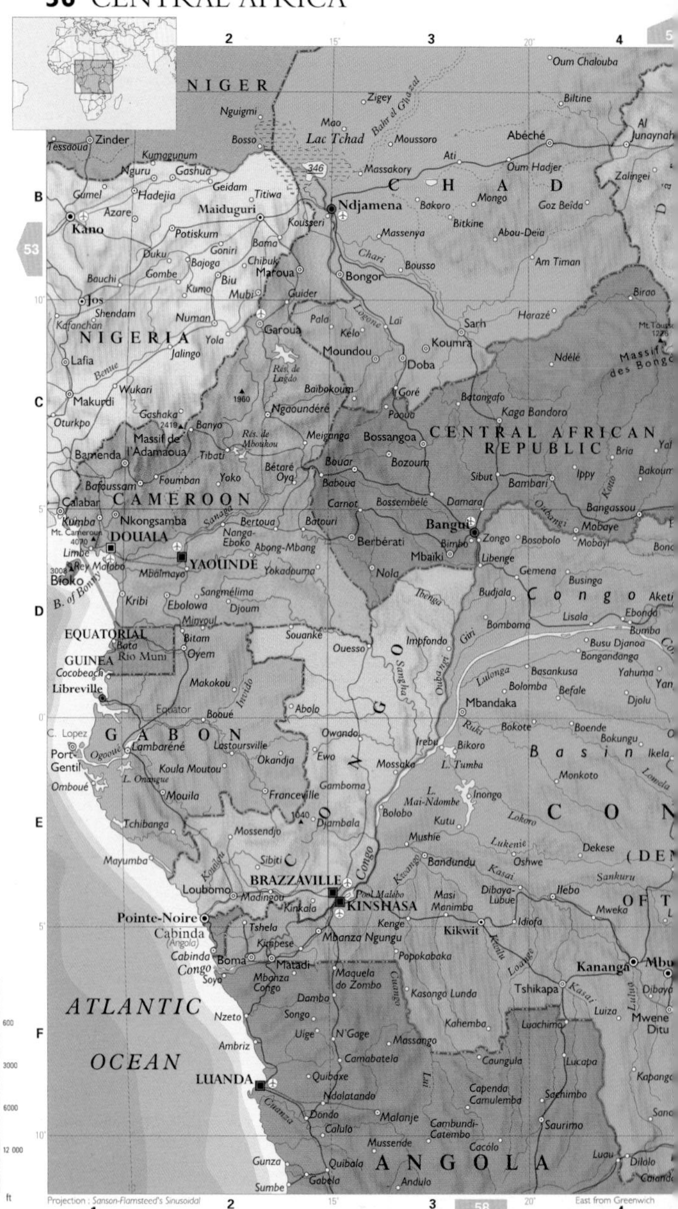
NIGER
Nguigmi
Bosso
Zinder
Tessaoua
Kumagunum
Nguru
Gashua
Geidam
Titiwa
Gumel
Hadejia
Azare
Kano
Maiduguri
Potiskum
Goniri
Bama
Kousseri
Ndjamena
Lac Tchad
Mao
Zigey
Bahr el Ghazal
Moussoro
Massakory
346
CHAD
Bokoro
Mongo
Ati
Abéché
Oum Hadjer
Biltine
Oum Chalouba
Al Junaynah
Zalingei
Goz Beïda
Bitkine
Abou-Deia
Massenya
Chari
Bousso
Am Timan
Bongor
Birao
Duku
Bajoga
Gombe
Chibuk
Maroua
Bauchi
Biu
Kumo
Mubi
Guider
Jos
Shendam
Numan
Kafanchan
NIGERIA
Yola
Jalingo
Garoua
Pala
Kelo
Logone
Laï
Sarh
Harazé
Mt. Toussoro 1275
Lafia
Benue
Moundou
Koumra
Doba
Ndélé
Massif des Bongo
Rés. de Lagdo
1960
Baibokoum
Wukari
Makurdi
Goré
Batangafo
Kaga Bandoro
Gashaka
Oturkpo
2419
Banyo
Ngaoundéré
Rés. de Mbakaou
Meiganga
Bossangoa
Paoua
CENTRAL AFRICAN REPUBLIC
Bria
Massif de l'Adamaoua
Bamenda
Tibati
Bouar
Bozoum
Bétaré Oya
Sibut
Bambari
Ippy
Bakouma
Bafoussam
Foumban
Yoko
Baboua
Kotto
CAMEROON
Calabar
Carnot
Bossembélé
Damara
Ouaka
Bangassou
Kumba
Nkongsamba
Sanaga
Bertoua
Batouri
Bangui
Mobaye
Mt. Cameroun 4070
DOUALA
Nanga-Eboko
Abong-Mbang
Berbérati
Bimbo
Zongo
Bosobolo
Mobayi
Limbe
YAOUNDE
Mbaïki
Libenge
3008
Rey Malabo
Bioko
Mbalmayo
Yokadouma
Nola
Gemena
Businga
B. of Bonny
Sangmélima
Ibenga
Budjala
Kribi
Ebolowa
Djoum
Congo
Aketi
Minvoul
Lisala
Ebonda
Bomboma
Bumba
EQUATORIAL GUINEA
Bata
Rio Muni
Bitam
Oyem
Souanké
Ouesso
Impfondo
Giri
Busu Djanoa
Bongandanga
Cocobeach
Sangha
Oubangui
Lulonga
Basankusa
Yahuma
Libreville
Makokou
Ivindo
Bolomba
Befale
Mbandaka
Djolu
Equator
Abolo
Booué
Ruki
Bokote
Boende
C. Lopez
GABON
Owando
Bikoro
Bokungu
Lambaréné
Lastoursville
Irebu
Basin
Ikela
Port-Gentil
Ogooué
Okandja
Ewo
Mossaka
L. Tumba
Lomela
Koula Moutou
Monkoto
Omboué
L. Onangue
Mouila
Gamboma
Franceville
L. Mai-Ndombe
Inongo
CONGO
Bolobo
Lokoro
Tchibanga
1040
Djambala
Kutu
Mossendjo
Mushie
Lukenie
Dekese
Mayumba
Sibiti
Bandundu
Kwango
Oshwe
Kasai
(DEM
Kouilou
BRAZZAVILLE
Sankuru
Loubomo
Madingou
Pool Malebo
KINSHASA
Masi Manimba
Dibaya-Lubue
Ilebo
OF T
Mweka
Pointe-Noire
Kinkala
Kenge
Kikwit
Idiofa
Cabinda (Angola)
Tshela
Kimpese
Mbanza Ngungu
Kwilu
Cabinda
Boma
Matadi
Popokabaka
Loange
Kananga
Mbu
Congo
Soyo
Mbanza Congo
Maquela do Zombo
Cuango
Kasongo Lunda
Tshikapa
Dibaya
ATLANTIC OCEAN
Damba
Lulua
Nzeto
Songo
Kahemba
Luachimo
Luiza
Mwene Ditu
Uíge
N'Gage
Massango
Ambriz
Camabatela
Caungula
Lucapa
Kapanga
LUANDA
Quibaxe
Lui
Ndalatando
Capenda Camulemba
Saurimo
Cuanza
Dondo
Malanje
Cambundi-Catembo
Calulo
Mussende
Cacólo
Gunza
Quibala
ANGOLA
Luau
Dilolo
Sumbe
Gabela
Andulo
Caianda
10°
5°
0°
15°
20°
1
2
3
4
B
C
D
E
F
53
0
200
600
1000
3000
2000
6000
4000
12 000
m
ft

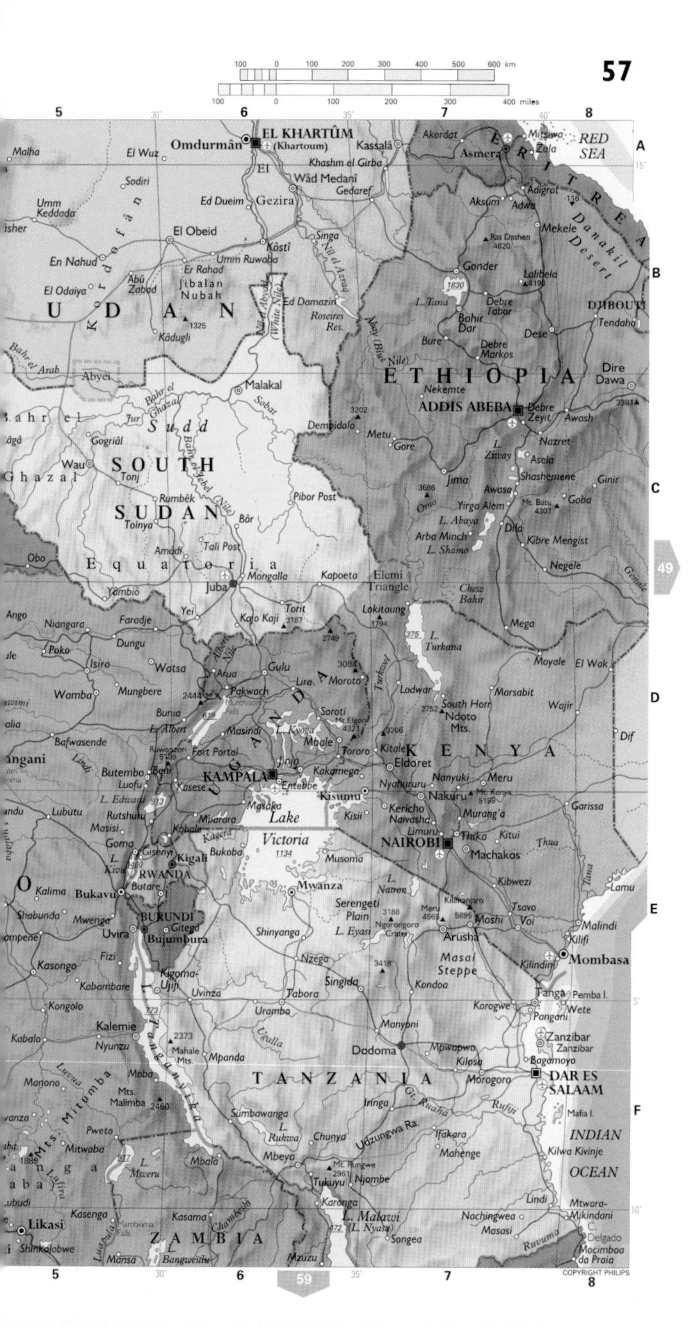

100 0 100 200 300 400 500 600 km
100 0 100 200 300 400 miles
5
6
7
8
A
B
C
D
E
F
RED SEA
E R I T R E A
EL KHARTÛM (Khartoum)
Omdurmân
El Wuz
Malha
Kassalâ
Akordat
Asmera
Mitsiwa
Zula
Khashm el Girba
Wâd Medanî
Gedaref
Gezira
Ed Dueim
Sodiri
Umm Keddada
El Obeid
Kôstî
Singa
Umm Ruwaba
Er Rahad
En Nahud
El Odaiya
Abû Zabad
Jibalan Nubah
Kordofân
Kâdugli
1325
SUDAN
Nîl el Abyad (White Nile)
Nîl el Azraq
Ed Damazin
Roseires Res.
Abay (Blue Nile)
Adigrat
Aksum
Adwa
Mekele
Danakil Desert
Ras Dashen 4620
Gonder
Lalibela 4190
1830
L. Tana
Debre Tabor
Bahir Dar
Bure
Debre Markos
DJIBOUTI
Tendaho
Dese
ETHIOPIA
Dire Dawa
Nekemte
ADDIS ABEBA
Debre Zeyit
Awash
3381
Bahr el Arab
Abyei
Malakal
Sobat
Bahr el Ghazal
Jur
Sudd
Bahr el Jebel (Nile)
3202
Dembidolo
Metu
Gore
Nazret
L. Ziway
Asela
Gogriâl
Wau
SOUTH SUDAN
Tonj
Rumbêk
Toinya
Bôr
Pibor Post
Jima
Shashemene
Ginir
3686
Omo
Awasa
Mt. Batu 4307
Goba
Yirga Alem
L. Abaya
Dila
Arba Minch
Kibre Mengist
L. Shamo
Negele
Genale
Tali Post
Amâdi
Obo
Equatoria
Mongalla
Kapoeta
Elemi Triangle
Juba
Yambio
Chew Bahir
Yei
Torit
Kajo Kaji
3187
Lokitaung
1794
Mega
Ango
Niangara
Faradje
Dungu
2749
375
L. Turkana
Poko
Isiro
Watsa
Albert Nile
Arua
Gulu
3084
Moroto
Lira
UGANDA
Turkwel
Moyale
El Wak
Wamba
Mungbere
2444
Pakwach
Murchison Falls
Lodwar
Marsabit
Wajir
Bunia
619
L. Albert
Masindi
Soroti
L. Kyoga
Mt. Elgon 4321
South Horr
2752
Ndoto Mts.
3206
Bafwasende
Mbale
Tororo
Kitale
Dif
Ruwenzori 5109
Fort Portal
Jinja
Eldoret
KENYA
Lindi
Butembo
Beni
KAMPALA
Kakamega
Luofu
Kasese
Entebbe
Kisumu
Nyahururu
Nanyuki
Meru
L. Edward
913
Masaka
Kisii
Nakuru
Mt. Kenya 5199
Kericho
Naivasha
Garissa
Lubutu
Rutshuru
Mbarara
Lake Victoria
1134
Murang'a
Masisi
Kabale
Kagera
Limuru
Thika
Kitui
Goma
Gisenyi
Bukoba
NAIROBI
Thua
L. Kivu
1460
Kigali
RWANDA
Musoma
Machakos
Tana
Kalima
Bukavu
Butare
Mwanza
L. Natron
Kibwezi
Lamu
Shabunda
Mwenga
BURUNDI
Gitega
Bujumbura
Uvira
Serengeti Plain
3188
Ngorongoro Crater
Kilimanjaro
Meru 4565
5895
Moshi
Tsavo
Voi
Malindi
Kilifi
Shinyanga
L. Eyasi
Arusha
Fizi
Kasongo
Nzega
3418
Masai Steppe
Kilindini
Mombasa
Kabambare
Kigoma-Ujiji
Singida
Kondoa
Kongolo
Uvinza
Tabora
Tanga
Pemba I.
Wete
Korogwe
Pangani
773
Urambo
Manyoni
Kalemie
Nyunzu
2373
Mahale Mts.
Mpanda
Ugalla
Zanzibar
Kabalo
Dodoma
Mpwapwa
Kilosa
Bagamoyo
Luvua
Moba
TANZANIA
Morogoro
DAR ES SALAAM
Manono
Mts. Malimba
2460
Lake Tanganyika
Gt. Ruaha
Iringa
Rufiji
Mafia I.
Mts. Mitumba
Sumbawanga
L. Rukwa
Chunya
Udzungwa Ra.
Ifakara
INDIAN OCEAN
Pweto
Mahenge
Mitwaba
917
L. Mweru
Mbala
Mbeya
Kilwa Kivinje
1889
Mt. Rungwe 2961
Tukuyu
Njombe
Lufira
Karonga
Lindi
Mtwara-Mikindani
Kasenga
Kasama
Chambeshi
L. Malawi (L. Nyasa)
472
Nachingwea
C. Delgado
Likasi
Mambilima Falls
Songea
Masasi
Ruvuma
Shinkolobwe
Luapula
ZAMBIA
L. Bangweulu
Mansa
Mzuzu
Mocimboa da Praia
15°
5°
10°
30°
35°
40°

49
59

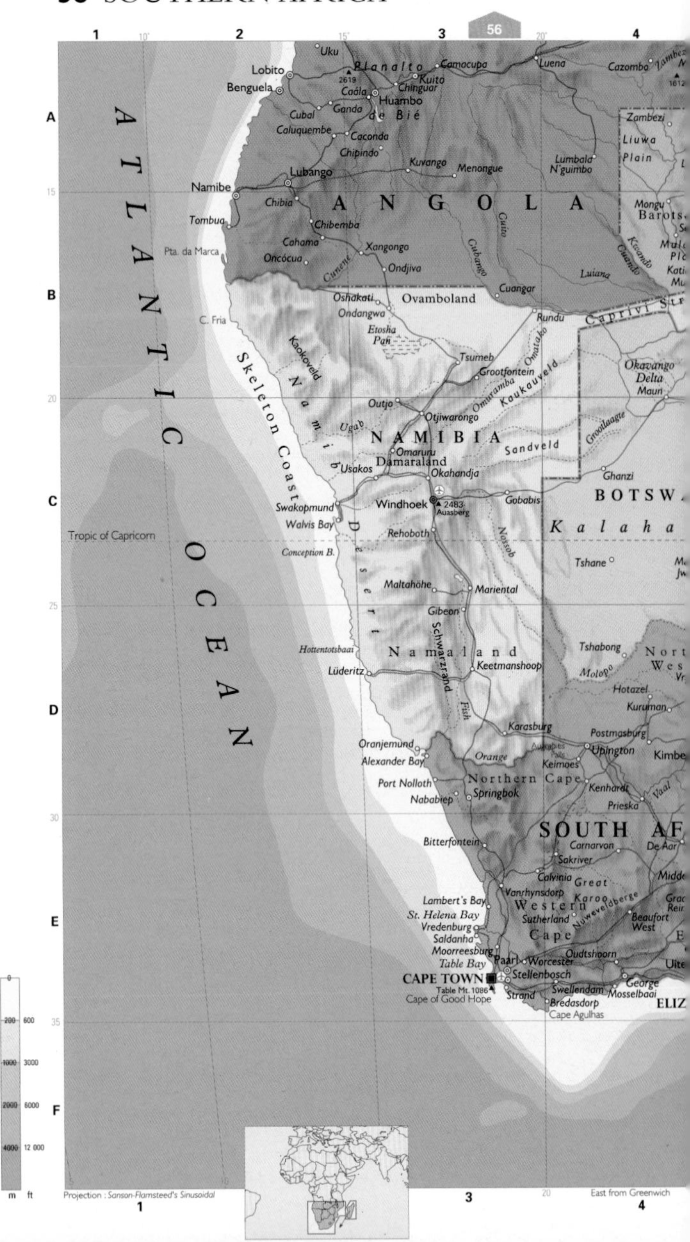
ATLANTIC OCEAN
Tropic of Capricorn
ANGOLA
NAMIBIA
BOTSWANA
SOUTH AFRICA
Lobito
Benguela
Huambo
Kuito
Namibe
Lubango
Tombua
Menongue
Ondjiva
Oshakati
Ovamboland
Etosha Pan
Skeleton Coast
Namib Desert
Kaokoveld
Tsumeb
Grootfontein
Outjo
Otjiwarongo
Omaruru
Damaraland
Okahandja
Usakos
Swakopmund
Walvis Bay
Windhoek
Gobabis
Rehoboth
Kalahari
Mariental
Gibeon
Namaland
Keetmanshoop
Lüderitz
Karasburg
Oranjemund
Alexander Bay
Port Nolloth
Springbok
Upington
Northern Cape
Western Cape
Great Karoo
CAPE TOWN
Table Mt. 1086
Cape of Good Hope
Stellenbosch
Paarl
Worcester
Oudtshoorn
George
Mosselbaai
Cape Agulhas
Rundu
Maun
Okavango Delta
Ghanzi
Tshabong
Projection : Sanson-Flamsteed's Sinusoidal
East from Greenwich

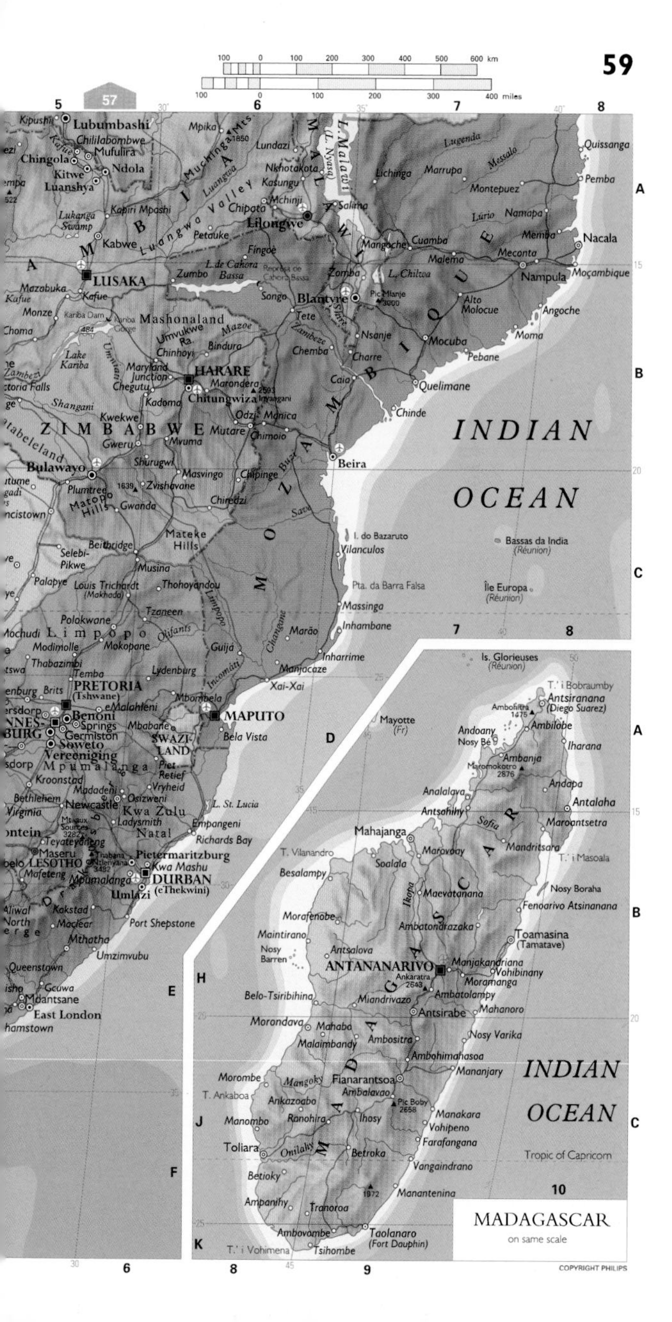
57
100 0 100 200 300 400 500 600 km
100 0 100 200 300 400 miles
Lubumbashi
Kipushi
Chililabombwe
Mufulira
Chingola
Kitwe
Ndola
Luanshya
Muchinga Mts.
Mpika
1850
Lundazi
Nkhotakota
Kasungu
Mchinji
Lilongwe
Salima
L. Malawi
(L. Nyasa)
MALAWI
Lichinga
Marrupa
Lugenda
Messalo
Quissanga
Pemba
Montepuez
Lúrio
Namapa
Memba
Nacala
Lukanga Swamp
Kapiri Mposhi
Luangwa Valley
Luangwa
Chipata
Petauke
Kabwe
Fíngoè
Mangoche
Cuamba
Malema
Meconta
Nampula
Moçambique
LUSAKA
Zumbo
L. de Cahora Bassa
Zomba
L. Chilwa
Mazabuka
Kafue
Songo
Blantyre
Pic Mlanje
3000
Alto Molocue
Angoche
Monze
Kariba Dam
Mashonaland
Tete
Zambeze
Choma
Umvukwe Ra.
Mazoe
Bindura
Nsanje
Mocuba
Moma
Lake Kariba
Chinhoyi
Chemba
Charre
Pebane
Maryland Junction
HARARE
Marondera
Chegutu
Chitungwiza
Caia
Quelimane
Victoria Falls
Kadoma
Inyangani
2593
Shangani
Kwekwe
Odzi
Manica
Chinde
ZIMBABWE
Mutare
Chimoio
INDIAN
Gweru
Mvuma
Matabeleland
Bulawayo
Shurugwi
Beira
Masvingo
Chipinge
Buzi
Plumtree
1639
Zvishavane
OCEAN
Matopo Hills
Gwanda
Chiredzi
Francistown
Save
MOZAMBIQUE
Mateke Hills
I. do Bazaruto
Bassas da India
(Réunion)
Beitbridge
Vilanculos
Selebi-Pikwe
Musina
Palapye
Louis Trichardt
(Makhado)
Thohoyandou
Pta. da Barra Falsa
Île Europa
(Réunion)
Limpopo
Massinga
Tzaneen
Polokwane
Inhambane
Olifants
Mochudi
Limpopo
Changane
Marão
Modimolle
Mokopane
Guijá
Inharrime
Thabazimbi
Lydenburg
Manjacaze
Temba
Incomáti
PRETORIA
(Tshwane)
Xai-Xai
Brits
Mbombela
eMalahleni
MAPUTO
Benoni
Springs
Mbabane
Germiston
SWAZILAND
Bela Vista
Soweto
Vereeniging
Mpumalanga
Piet Retief
Kroonstad
Vryheid
Madadeni
Osizweni
L. St. Lucia
Bethlehem
Newcastle
Virginia
Kwa Zulu
Ladysmith
Empangeni
Natal
Richards Bay
Teyateyaneng
Maseru
LESOTHO
Thabana Ntlenyana
3482
Pietermaritzburg
Kwa Mashu
Mafeteng
Mpumalanga
DURBAN
(eThekwini)
Umlazi
Aliwal North
Kakstad
Maclear
Port Shepstone
Mthatha
Umzimvubu
Queenstown
Gcuwa
Mdantsane
East London
Is. Glorieuses
(Réunion)
T.' i Bobraumby
Antsiranana
(Diego Suarez)
Ambohitra
1475
Ambilobe
Mayotte
(Fr)
Andoany
Nosy Bé
Iharana
Ambanja
Maromokotro
2876
Andapa
Analalava
Antalaha
Antsohihy
Sofia
Maroantsetra
Mahajanga
Mandritsara
T. Vilanandro
Marovoay
T.' i Masoala
Soalala
Besalampy
Ikopa
Maevatanana
Nosy Boraha
Fenoarivo Atsinanana
Morafenobe
Ambatondrazaka
Maintirano
Toamasina
(Tamatave)
Nosy Barren
Antsalova
ANTANANARIVO
Manjakandriana
Vohibinany
Ankaratra
2643
Moramanga
Belo-Tsiribihina
Miandrivazo
Ambatolampy
Antsirabe
Mahanoro
Morondava
Mahabo
Malaimbandy
Ambositra
Nosy Varika
Ambohimahasoa
INDIAN
Mananjary
Morombe
Mangoky
Fianarantsoa
T. Ankaboa
Ambalavao
Ankazoabo
Pic Boby
2658
OCEAN
Manakara
Manombo
Ranohira
Ihosy
Vohipeno
Farafangana
Toliara
Onilahy
Betroka
Tropic of Capricorn
Vangaindrano
Betioky
1972
Manantenina
Ampanihy
Tranoroa
MADAGASCAR
on same scale
Ambovombe
Taolanaro
(Fort Dauphin)
T.' i Vohimena
Tsihombe
COPYRIGHT PHILIPS

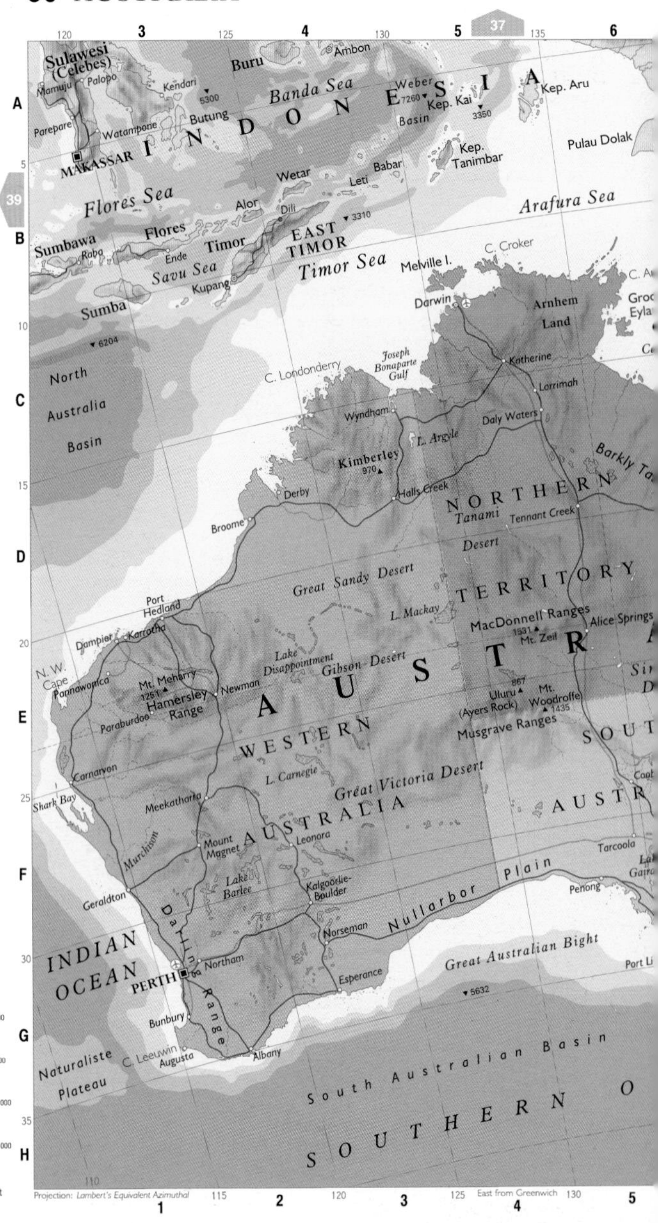
Sulawesi (Celebes)
Buru
Ambon
Banda Sea
INDONESIA
Kendari
Butung
Watampone
Parepare
Mamuju
Palopo
MAKASSAR
Weber Basin
Kep. Kai
Kep. Aru
Pulau Dolak
Kep. Tanimbar
Babar
Leti
Wetar
Flores Sea
Alor
Dili
Arafura Sea
Sumbawa
Flores
Timor
EAST TIMOR
Raba
Ende
Savu Sea
Kupang
Timor Sea
Melville I.
C. Croker
Sumba
Darwin
Arnhem Land
North Australia Basin
C. Londonderry
Joseph Bonaparte Gulf
Katherine
Larrimah
Wyndham
Daly Waters
L. Argyle
Kimberley
Barkly Tableland
Derby
Halls Creek
NORTHERN TERRITORY
Broome
Tanami Desert
Tennant Creek
Great Sandy Desert
Port Hedland
L. Mackay
MacDonnell Ranges
Alice Springs
Mt. Zeil
Dampier
Karratha
N. W. Cape
Pannawonica
Mt. Meharry
Hamersley Range
Newman
Lake Disappointment
Gibson Desert
Uluru (Ayers Rock)
Mt. Woodroffe
Musgrave Ranges
Paraburdoo
WESTERN AUSTRALIA
AUSTRALIA
Carnarvon
L. Carnegie
Great Victoria Desert
SOUTH AUSTRALIA
Shark Bay
Meekatharra
Mount Magnet
Leonora
Murchison
Lake Barlee
Kalgoorlie-Boulder
Tarcoola
Nullarbor Plain
Penong
Geraldton
Darling Range
Norseman
INDIAN OCEAN
PERTH
Northam
Esperance
Great Australian Bight
Bunbury
Albany
Augusta
C. Leeuwin
Naturaliste Plateau
South Australian Basin
SOUTHERN OCEAN
Projection: Lambert's Equivalent Azimuthal
East from Greenwich
m
ft

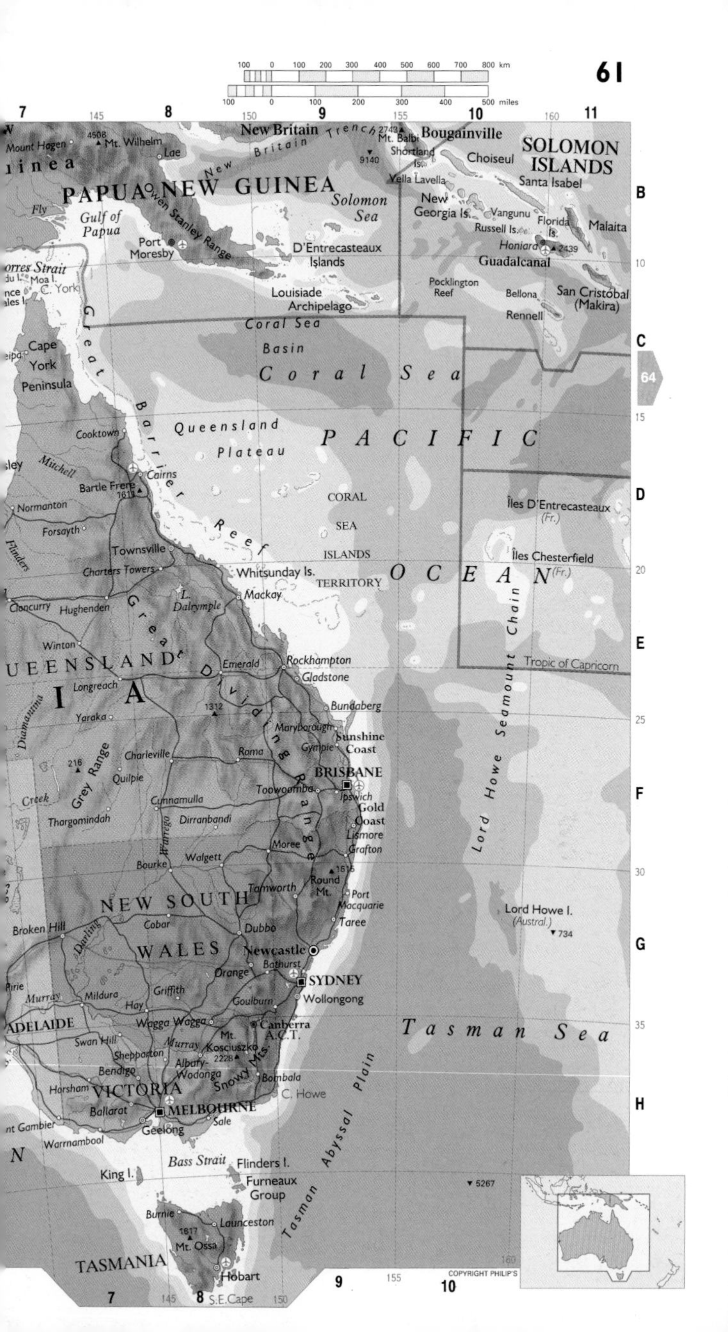

100 0 100 200 300 400 500 600 700 800 km
100 0 100 200 300 400 500 miles
New Britain
Trench
Britain
New
Bougainville
2743 Mt. Balbi
9140
Shortland Is.
SOLOMON ISLANDS
Choiseul
Mount Hagen
4508 Mt. Wilhelm
Lae
Vella Lavella
Santa Isabel
PAPUA NEW GUINEA
Solomon Sea
New Georgia Is.
Vangunu
Florida Is.
Malaita
Russell Is.
Fly
Gulf of Papua
Owen Stanley Range
Port Moresby
D'Entrecasteaux Islands
Honiara
2439
Guadalcanal
Torres Strait
Moa I.
C. York
Louisiade Archipelago
Pocklington Reef
Bellona
San Cristobal (Makira)
Rennell
Coral Sea Basin
Cape York Peninsula
Coral Sea
64
Great Barrier Reef
Queensland Plateau
PACIFIC OCEAN
Cooktown
Mitchell
Cairns
Bartle Frere
Normanton
Forsayth
CORAL SEA ISLANDS TERRITORY
Îles D'Entrecasteaux (Fr.)
Îles Chesterfield (Fr.)
Flinders
Townsville
Charters Towers
Whitsunday Is.
L. Dalrymple
Mackay
Cloncurry
Hughenden
Great Dividing Range
Winton
Lord Howe Seamount Chain
QUEENSLAND
Emerald
Rockhampton
Gladstone
Tropic of Capricorn
Longreach
1312
Bundaberg
Diamantina
Yaraka
Maryborough
Gympie
Sunshine Coast
216
Grey Range
Charleville
Quilpie
Roma
BRISBANE
Toowoomba
Ipswich
Gold Coast
Creek
Cunnamulla
Thargomindah
Dirranbandi
Lismore
Warrego
Moree
Grafton
Walgett
1615
Bourke
Tamworth
Round Mt.
Port Macquarie
NEW SOUTH WALES
Cobar
Taree
Lord Howe I. (Austral.)
734
Broken Hill
Darling
Dubbo
Newcastle
Bathurst
Orange
SYDNEY
Murray
Mildura
Griffith
Wollongong
Hay
Goulburn
ADELAIDE
Wagga Wagga
Canberra A.C.T.
Tasman Sea
Swan Hill
Murray
Mt. Kosciuszko 2228
Shepparton
Albury-Wodonga
Snowy Mts.
Bendigo
Bombala
Horsham
VICTORIA
C. Howe
Tasman Abyssal Plain
Ballarat
MELBOURNE
Geelong
Sale
Warrnambool
Bass Strait
Flinders I.
King I.
Furneaux Group
5267
Burnie
Launceston
1617 Mt. Ossa
TASMANIA
Hobart
S.E.Cape
COPYRIGHT PHILIP'S

SOUTH AUSTRALIA
Lake Eyre (North)
LAKE EYRE
Lake Eyre (South)
Sturt Stony Desert
Strzelecki Desert
LAKE TORRENS
Lake Torrens
Lake Gairdner
LAKE GAIRDNER
Lake Frome
Flinders Ranges
Port Augusta
Whyalla
Port Pirie
Eyre Peninsula
Port Lincoln
Spencer Gulf
Gulf St. Vincent
ADELAIDE
Elizabeth
Salisbury
Gawler
Brighton
Murray Bridge
Kangaroo I.
Mount Gambier
Broken Hill
Mildura
Horsham
Warrnambool
Portland
Bass Strait
King Island
Flinders Island
Furneaux Group
Cape Barren I.
Devonport
Launceston
Hobart
Glenorchy
TASMANIA
SOUTHERN OCEAN
on same scale
Projection: Bonne
East from Greenwich
m ft

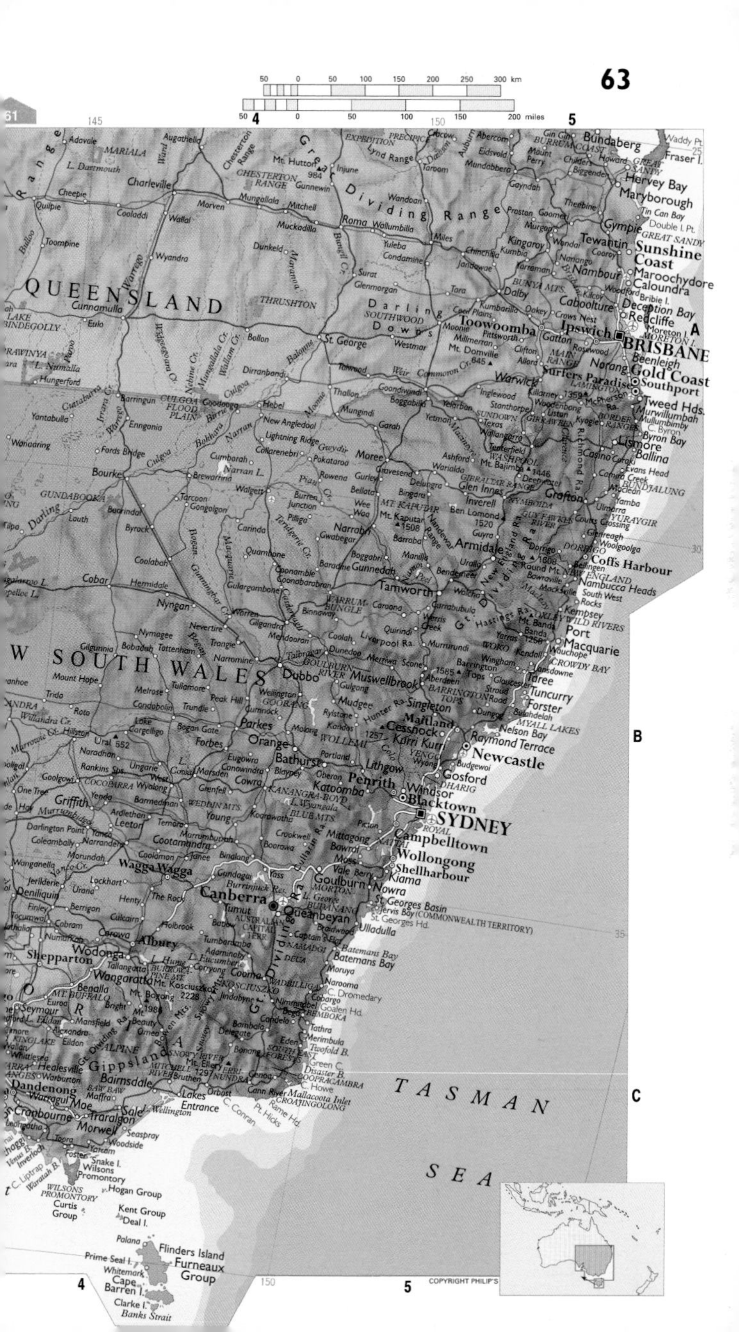

50 0 50 100 150 200 250 300 km
50 0 50 100 150 200 miles
61
145
4
150
5
QUEENSLAND
NEW SOUTH WALES
Great Dividing Range
Darling Downs
TASMAN SEA
Bundaberg
Fraser I.
Hervey Bay
Maryborough
Gympie
Tewantin
Sunshine Coast
Nambour
Maroochydore
Caloundra
Caboolture
Deception Bay
Redcliffe
Moreton I.
Ipswich
BRISBANE
Beenleigh
Surfers Paradise
Gold Coast
Southport
Tweed Hds.
Murwillumbah
Lismore
Ballina
Byron Bay
Casino
Grafton
Yamba
Coffs Harbour
Nambucca Heads
Kempsey
Port Macquarie
Taree
Tuncurry
Forster
Charleville
Augathella
Adavale
Quilpie
Cunnamulla
Morven
Mitchell
Roma
Wallumbilla
Miles
Dalby
Kingaroy
Toowoomba
Gatton
Warwick
Goondiwindi
St. George
Dirranbandi
Hebel
Mungindi
Moree
Bourke
Cobar
Nyngan
Brewarrina
Walgett
Narrabri
Gunnedah
Tamworth
Armidale
Inverell
Glen Innes
Tenterfield
Dubbo
Mudgee
Muswellbrook
Singleton
Maitland
Cessnock
Kurri Kurri
Raymond Terrace
Newcastle
Gosford
Windsor
Blacktown
SYDNEY
Penrith
Katoomba
Lithgow
Bathurst
Orange
Parkes
Forbes
Cowra
Young
Griffith
Leeton
Narrandera
Wagga Wagga
Cootamundra
Goulburn
Campbelltown
Wollongong
Shellharbour
Kiama
Nowra
Canberra
Queanbeyan
Ulladulla
Batemans Bay
Moruya
Narooma
Bega
Eden
Cooma
Albury
Wodonga
Shepparton
Wangaratta
Mt. Kosciuszko 2228
Bairnsdale
Sale
Traralgon
Morwell
Moe
Dandenong
Cranbourne
Lakes Entrance
Wilsons Promontory
Flinders Island
Furneaux Group
Cape Barren I.
Banks Strait
A
B
C
COPYRIGHT PHILIP'S

# NEW ZEALAND, CENTRAL AND SOUTH-WEST PACIFIC

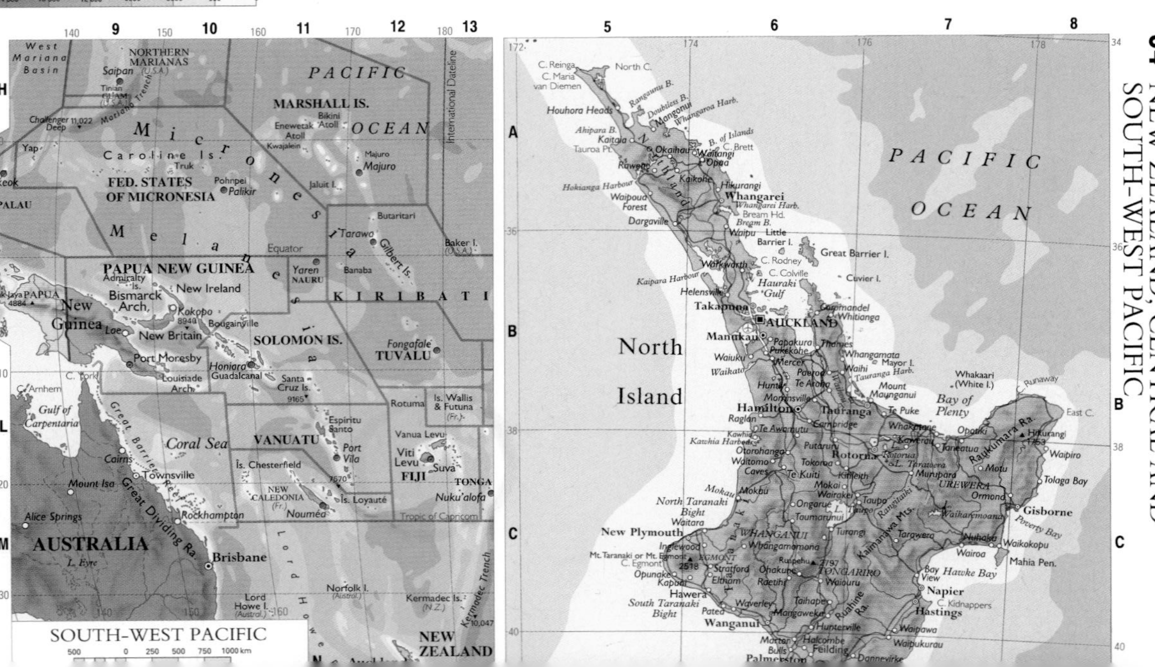

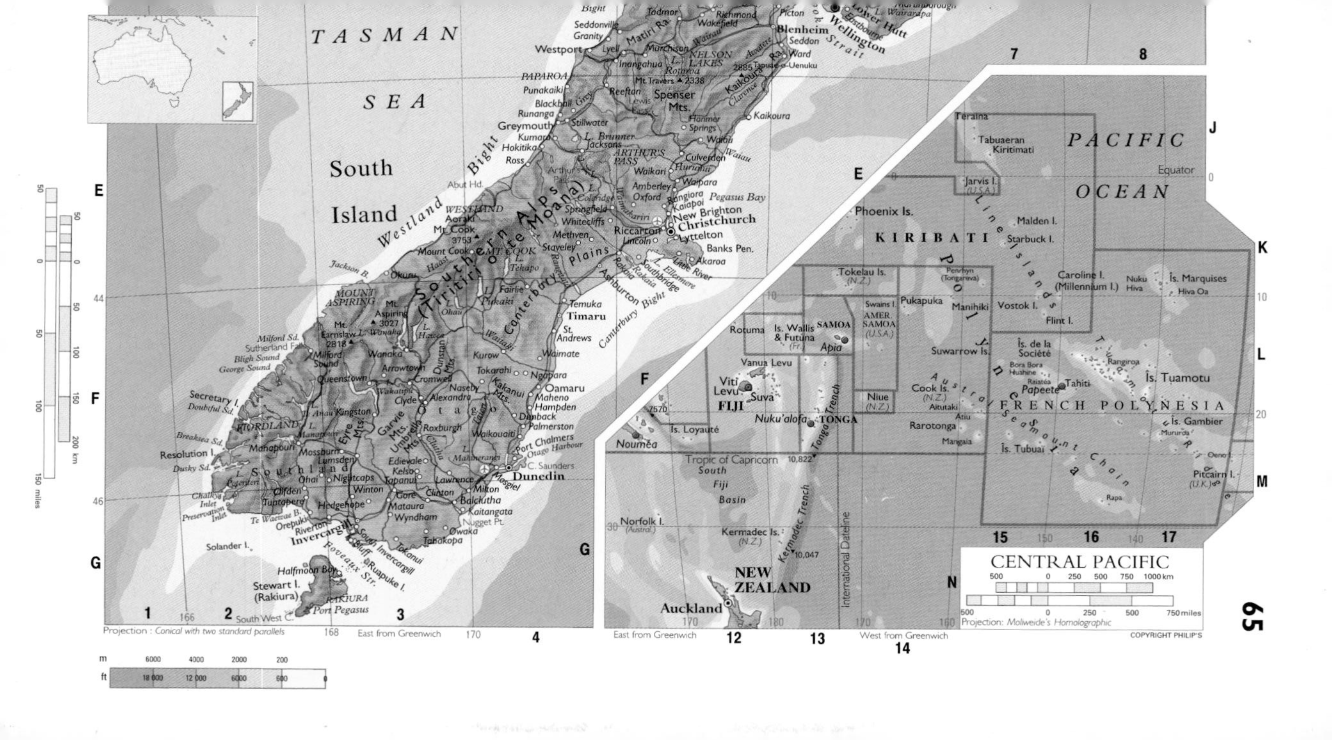

TASMAN SEA
South Island
Westland Bight
Southern Alps (Tiritiri o te Moana)
Canterbury Plains
Canterbury Bight
Pegasus Bay
Otago
Southland
FIORDLAND
Foveaux Str.
Stewart I. (Rakiura)
Westport
Greymouth
Hokitika
Blenheim
Kaikoura
Christchurch
Lyttelton
Timaru
Oamaru
Dunedin
Invercargill
Queenstown
Wanaka
Mt. Cook 3753
Mt. Aspiring 3027
Spenser Mts.
Wellington
Lower Hutt
Cook Strait
Projection : Conical with two standard parallels
East from Greenwich
m 6000 4000 2000 200
ft 18 000 12 000 6000 600 0
CENTRAL PACIFIC
PACIFIC OCEAN
KIRIBATI
Phoenix Is.
Line Islands
Tabuaeran
Kiritimati
Jarvis I. (U.S.A.)
Malden I.
Starbuck I.
Caroline I. (Millennium I.)
Vostok I.
Flint I.
Tokelau Is. (N.Z.)
SAMOA
Apia
AMER. SAMOA (U.S.A.)
Is. Wallis & Futuna (Fr.)
Rotuma
FIJI
Vanua Levu
Viti Levu
Suva
TONGA
Nuku'alofa
Tonga Trench
Kermadec Trench
Niue (N.Z.)
Cook Is. (N.Z.)
Rarotonga
POLYNESIA
FRENCH POLYNESIA
Îs. de la Société
Papeete
Tahiti
Îs. Tuamotu
Îs. Marquises
Îs. Gambier
Îs. Tubuai
Austral Seamount Chain
Pitcairn I. (U.K.)
Is. Loyauté
Nouméa
Norfolk I. (Austral.)
Kermadec Is. (N.Z.)
NEW ZEALAND
Auckland
South Fiji Basin
Tropic of Capricorn
Equator
International Dateline
Projection: Mollweide's Homolographic
COPYRIGHT PHILIP'S

ARCTIC OCEAN
Beaufort Sea
Bering Sea
Bering Strait
Gulf of Alaska
Hudson Bay
Hudson Strait
Baffin Bay
Davis Strait
Denmark Strait
GREENLAND
(Denmark)
Nuuk
ICELAND
Reykjavik
Ellesmere I.
Queen Elizabeth Is.
Victoria I.
Baffin Island
NUNAVUT
NORTHWEST TERRITORIES
YUKON TERRITORY
BRITISH COLUMBIA
ALBERTA
SASKATCHEWAN
MANITOBA
ONTARIO
QUÉBEC
NEWFOUNDLAND & LABRADOR
SCOTIA
PRINCE EDWARD I.
NEW BRUNSWICK
CANADA
ALASKA
(USA)
RUSSIA
Asia
St. Lawrence I.
Kodiak I.
Mt. McKinley 6194
Anchorage
Fairbanks
Juneau
Whitehorse
Yellowknife
Edmonton
Calgary
Vancouver
Victoria
Halifax
Charlottetown
St. John's
St.-Pierre et Miquelon (Fr.)
Great Bear L.
Great Slave L.
L. Athabasca
L. Winnipeg
Yukon
Porcupine
Mackenzie
Peace
Athabasca
Saskatchewan
Churchill
Nelson
Back
Dubawnt
Fraser
Skeena
Liard
Eastmain
St. Lawrence
Arctic Circle
International Date Line
A
B
C
D
E
50
60
70
80

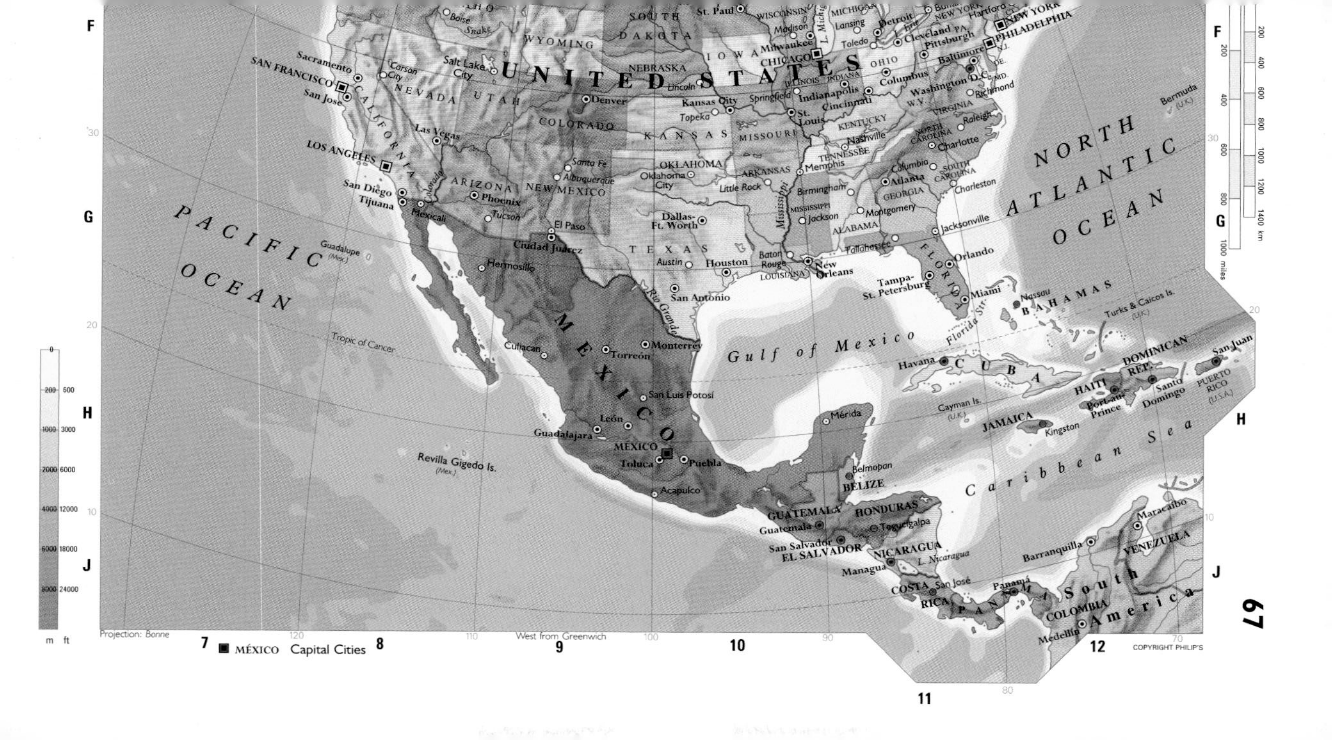

UNITED STATES
NORTH ATLANTIC OCEAN
PACIFIC OCEAN
Gulf of Mexico
Caribbean Sea
South America
MEXICO
CUBA
BAHAMAS
JAMAICA
HAITI
DOMINICAN REP.
PUERTO RICO (U.S.A.)
BELIZE
GUATEMALA
HONDURAS
EL SALVADOR
NICARAGUA
COSTA RICA
PANAMA
COLOMBIA
VENEZUELA
WYOMING
SOUTH DAKOTA
NEBRASKA
IOWA
WISCONSIN
MICHIGAN
NEW YORK
PA.
N.J.
DE.
MD.
OHIO
INDIANA
ILLINOIS
W.V.
VIRGINIA
KENTUCKY
TENNESSEE
NORTH CAROLINA
SOUTH CAROLINA
GEORGIA
ALABAMA
MISSISSIPPI
LOUISIANA
ARKANSAS
MISSOURI
KANSAS
OKLAHOMA
TEXAS
NEW MEXICO
COLORADO
ARIZONA
UTAH
NEVADA
CALIFORNIA
FLORIDA
SAN FRANCISCO
Sacramento
San Jose
Carson City
Salt Lake City
Boise
Snake
Las Vegas
LOS ANGELES
San Diego
Tijuana
Mexicali
Colorado
Phoenix
Tucson
Santa Fe
Albuquerque
El Paso
Ciudad Juárez
Denver
Lincoln
Kansas City
Topeka
St. Paul
Madison
Milwaukee
CHICAGO
L. Michigan
Lansing
Detroit
L. Erie
Toledo
Cleveland
Pittsburgh
Buffalo
Hartford
NEW YORK
PHILADELPHIA
Baltimore
Washington D.C.
Richmond
Raleigh
Charlotte
Columbia
Charleston
Columbus
Indianapolis
Cincinnati
Springfield
St. Louis
Nashville
Memphis
Little Rock
Oklahoma City
Dallas-Ft. Worth
Austin
San Antonio
Houston
Baton Rouge
New Orleans
Jackson
Birmingham
Montgomery
Atlanta
Tallahassee
Jacksonville
Orlando
Tampa-St. Petersburg
Miami
Mississippi
Rio Grande
Florida Str.
Nassau
Turks & Caicos Is. (U.K.)
Bermuda (U.K.)
Havana
Cayman Is. (U.K.)
Kingston
Port-au-Prince
Santo Domingo
San Juan
Hermosillo
Culiacán
Torreón
Monterrey
San Luis Potosí
León
Guadalajara
MÉXICO
Toluca
Puebla
Acapulco
Mérida
Belmopan
Guatemala
San Salvador
Tegucigalpa
Managua
L. Nicaragua
San José
Panamá
Barranquilla
Maracaibo
Medellín
Guadalupe (Mex.)
Revilla Gigedo Is. (Mex.)
Tropic of Cancer
Projection: Bonne
West from Greenwich
■ MÉXICO Capital Cities
COPYRIGHT PHILIP'S
0 200 400 600 800 1000 1200 1400 km
0 200 400 600 800 1000 miles
m ft
0
200 600
1000 3000
2000 6000
4000 12000
6000 18000
8000 24000
F
G
H
J
7
8
9
10
11
12
30
20
10
120
110
100
90
80
70

PACIFIC
Hudson Bay
NUNAVUT
NORTHWEST TERRITORIES
YUKON TERRITORY
ALASKA (USA)
BRITISH
Victoria Island
Banks Island
Prince Albert Pen.
Wollaston Pen.
Prince of Wales I.
Somerset Island
Boothia Peninsula
King William I.
Adelaide Pen.
Viscount Melville Sound
M'Clintock Channel
Amundsen Gulf
Coronation Gulf
Queen Maud Gulf
Great Bear L.
Great Slave L.
Lake Athabasca
Mackenzie Mountains
Selwyn Mts.
Franklin Mts.
Cassiar Mountains
Rocky
Coast
Wrangell Mts.
St. Elias Mts.
Caribou Mts.
Alexander Archipelago
Haida Gwaii (Queen Charlotte Is.)
Arctic Circle
Anchorage
Fairbanks
Whitehorse
Yellowknife
Juneau
Dawson
Inuvik
Tuktoyaktuk
Baker Lake
Rankin Inlet
Whale Cove
Arviat
Uranium City
Fort Smith
Hay River
Fort Nelson
Fort Simpson
Norman Wells
Watson Lake
Prince Rupert
Sitka
Ketchikan
Valdez
Cordova
Yakutat
Skagway
Kugluktuk
Holman
Paulatuk
Cambridge Bay
Gjoa Haven
Déline
Mt. Logan 5959
Mt. St. Elias 5489
Mt. Lucania 5226
Mt. Sanford 4940
Mt. Fairweather 4663

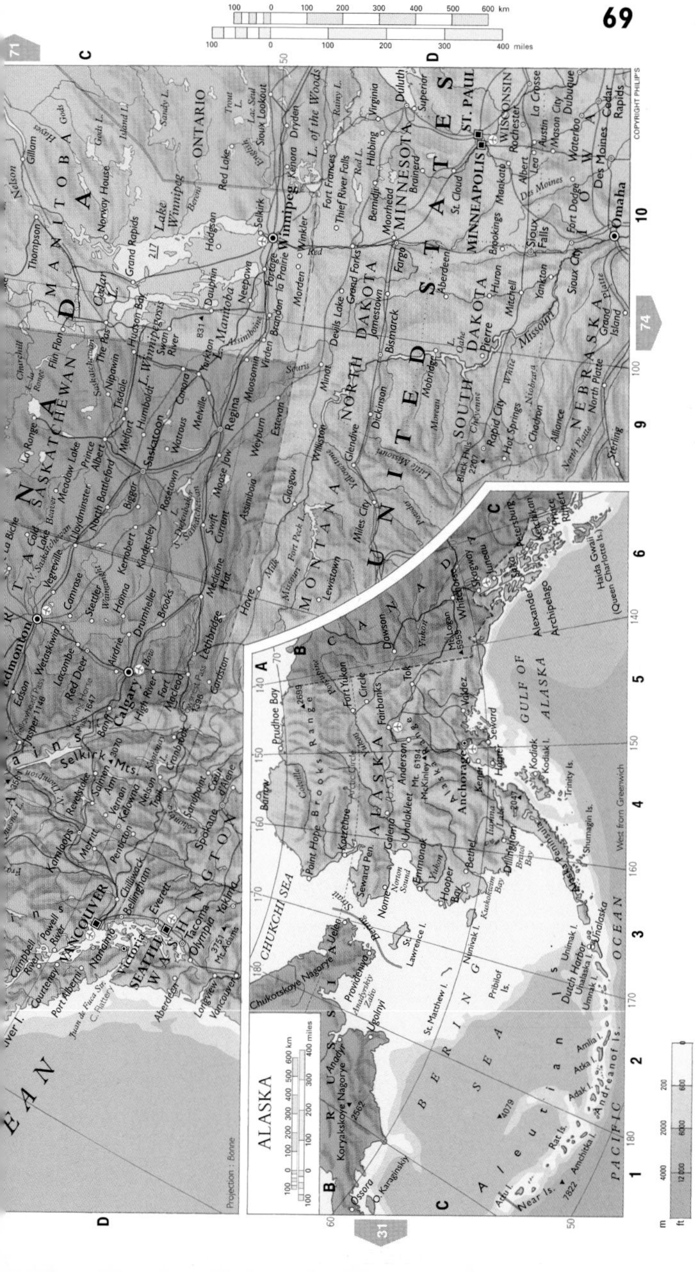

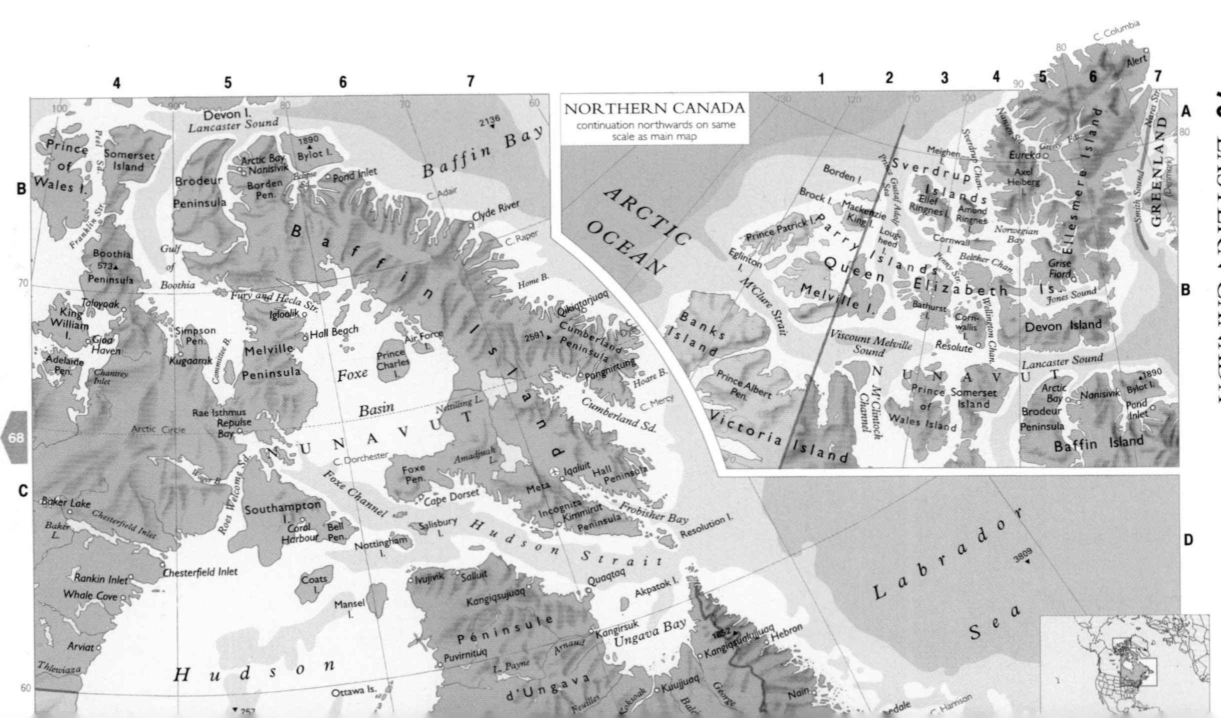
NORTHERN CANADA
continuation northwards on same scale as main map
ARCTIC OCEAN
GREENLAND
(Denmark)
Nares Str.
Smith Sound
C. Columbia
Alert
Ellesmere Island
Greely Fd.
Eureka
Nansen Sd.
Axel Heiberg I.
Sverdrup Chan.
Sverdrup Islands
Meighen I.
Ellef Ringnes I.
Amund Ringnes I.
Norwegian Bay
Cornwall I.
Belcher Chan.
Grise Fiord
Jones Sound
Devon Island
Lancaster Sound
Penny Str.
Wellington Chan.
Queen Elizabeth Is.
Cornwallis I.
Bathurst I.
Resolute
Prince Gustaf Adolf Sea
Borden I.
Mackenzie King I.
Lougheed I.
Parry Islands
Brock I.
Prince Patrick I.
Melville I.
Viscount Melville Sound
M'Clintock Channel
M'Clure Strait
Eglinton I.
Banks Island
Prince Albert Pen.
Victoria Island
NUNAVUT
Prince of Wales Island
Somerset Island
Arctic Bay
Brodeur Peninsula
Nanisivik
Pond Inlet
Bylot I.
1890
Baffin Island
Labrador Sea
3809
Baffin Bay
2136
Clyde River
C. Adair
C. Raper
Home B.
Qikiqtarjuaq
Cumberland Peninsula
2591
Pangnirtung
Hoare B.
C. Mercy
Cumberland Sd.
Iqaluit
Hall Peninsula
Frobisher Bay
Resolution I.
Meta Incognita Peninsula
Kimmirut
Hudson Strait
Akpatok I.
Quaqtaq
Kangirsuk
Ungava Bay
Kangiqsualujjuaq
1652
Hebron
Nain
C. Harrison
George
Kuujjuaq
Koksoak
Feuilles
Baffin Island
Nettilling L.
Amadjuak L.
Air Force I.
Prince Charles I.
Foxe Basin
Foxe Pen.
Cape Dorset
Salisbury I.
Nottingham I.
C. Dorchester
Foxe Channel
Hall Beach
Igloolik
Fury and Hecla Str.
Melville Peninsula
Devon I.
Lancaster Sound
Arctic Bay
Nanisivik
Borden Pen.
Eclipse Sd.
Bylot I.
1890
Pond Inlet
Brodeur Peninsula
Gulf of Boothia
Simpson Pen.
Kugaaruk
Committee B.
Rae Isthmus
Repulse Bay
Arctic Circle
NUNAVUT
Southampton I.
Coral Harbour
Bell Pen.
Roes Welcome Sd.
Wager B.
Coats I.
Mansel I.
Ottawa Is.
257
Ivujivik
Salluit
Kangiqsujuaq
Péninsule d'Ungava
Puvirnituq
L. Payne
Arnaud
Hudson
Somerset Island
Peel Sd.
Prince of Wales I.
Franklin Str.
Boothia Peninsula
573
Taloyoak
King William I.
Gjoa Haven
Chantrey Inlet
Adelaide Pen.
Baker Lake
Baker L.
Chesterfield Inlet
Chesterfield Inlet
Rankin Inlet
Whale Cove
Arviat
Thlewiaza

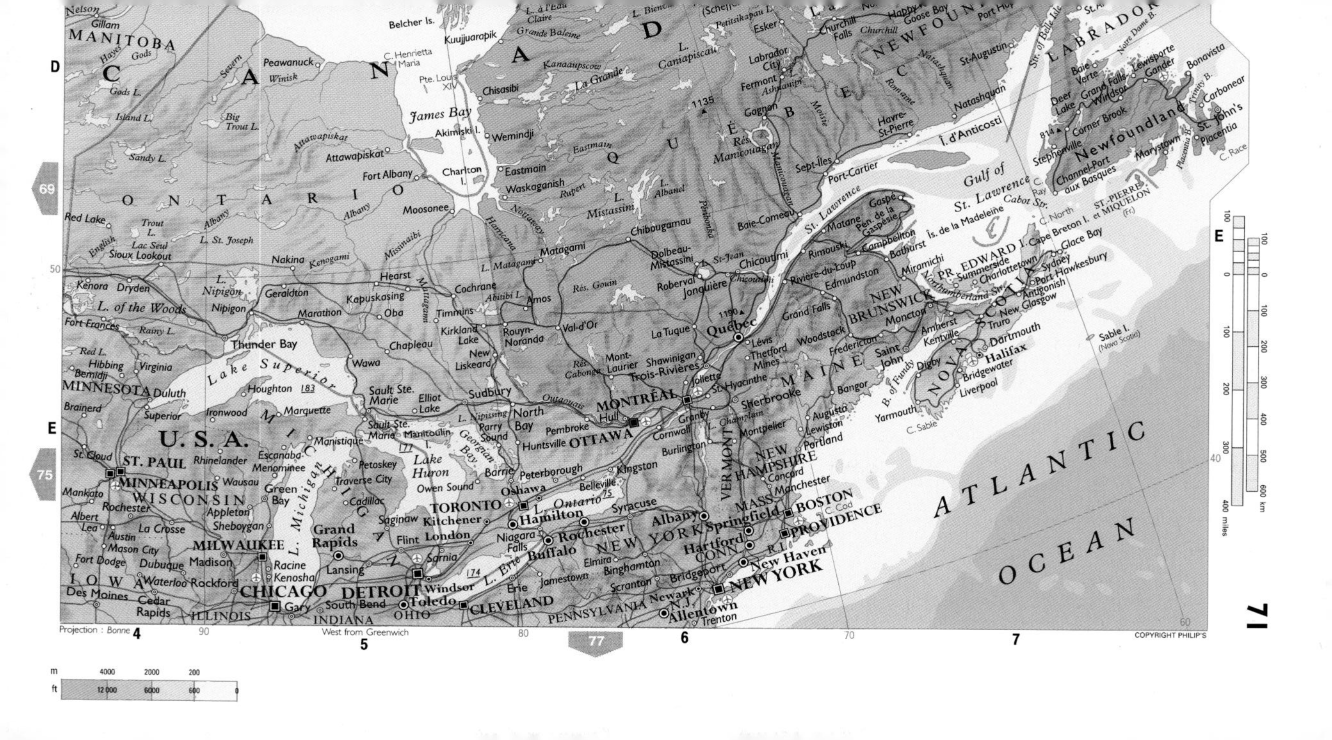
CANADA
ONTARIO
QUÉBEC
NEWFOUNDLAND
LABRADOR
MANITOBA
NEW BRUNSWICK
NOVA SCOTIA
PR. EDWARD I.
U.S.A.
MINNESOTA
WISCONSIN
MICHIGAN
IOWA
ILLINOIS
INDIANA
OHIO
PENNSYLVANIA
NEW YORK
VERMONT
NEW HAMPSHIRE
MAINE
MASS.
CONN.
R.I.
N.J.
ATLANTIC OCEAN
Gulf of St. Lawrence
James Bay
Lake Superior
L. Michigan
Lake Huron
Georgian Bay
L. Erie
L. Ontario
L. of the Woods
L. Nipigon
L. Mistassini
Rés. Manicouagan
Rés. Gouin
Î. d'Anticosti
Îs. de la Madeleine
Cape Breton I.
Sable I. (Nova Scotia)
ST.-PIERRE et MIQUELON (Fr.)
Cabot Str.
Str. of Belle Isle
Northumberland Str.
B. of Fundy
C. Race
C. Sable
C. Cod
Belcher Is.
Akimiski I.
C. Henrietta Maria
Pte. Louis XIV
MONTRÉAL
OTTAWA
TORONTO
Québec
Hamilton
Kitchener
London
Windsor
Sudbury
North Bay
Thunder Bay
Sault Ste. Marie
Timmins
Kingston
Sherbrooke
Trois-Rivières
Chicoutimi
Halifax
Dartmouth
Saint John
Moncton
Fredericton
St. John's
Corner Brook
Gander
Sept-Îles
Baie-Comeau
Labrador City
Goose Bay
CHICAGO
DETROIT
CLEVELAND
NEW YORK
BOSTON
PROVIDENCE
MILWAUKEE
ST. PAUL
MINNEAPOLIS
Buffalo
Rochester
Toledo
Albany
Springfield
Hartford
New Haven
Allentown
Duluth
Grand Rapids
Projection : Bonne
West from Greenwich
4
5
6
7
D
E
90
80
70
60
50
40
69
75
77
0 100 200 300 400 500 600 km
0 100 200 300 400 miles
m 4000 2000 200
ft 12 000 6000 600 0
COPYRIGHT PHILIP'S

Projection: Albers' Equal Area with two standard parallels
State Capitals

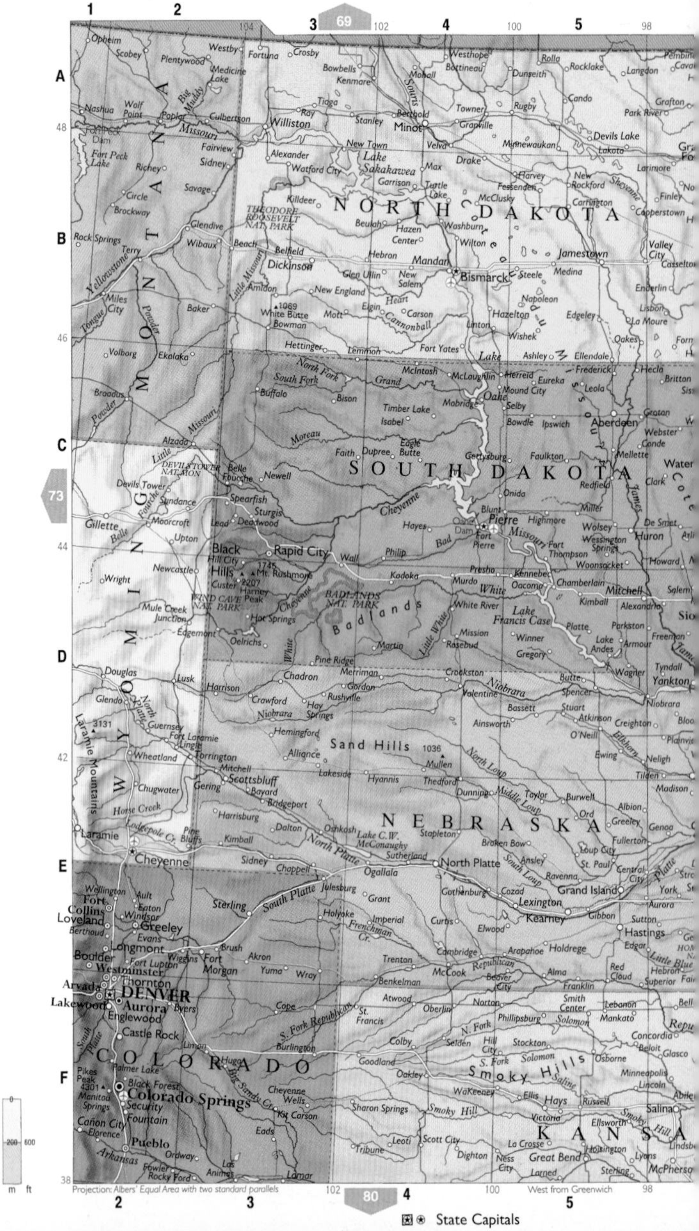

69

73

Projection: Albers' Equal Area with two standard parallels

West from Greenwich

80

State Capitals

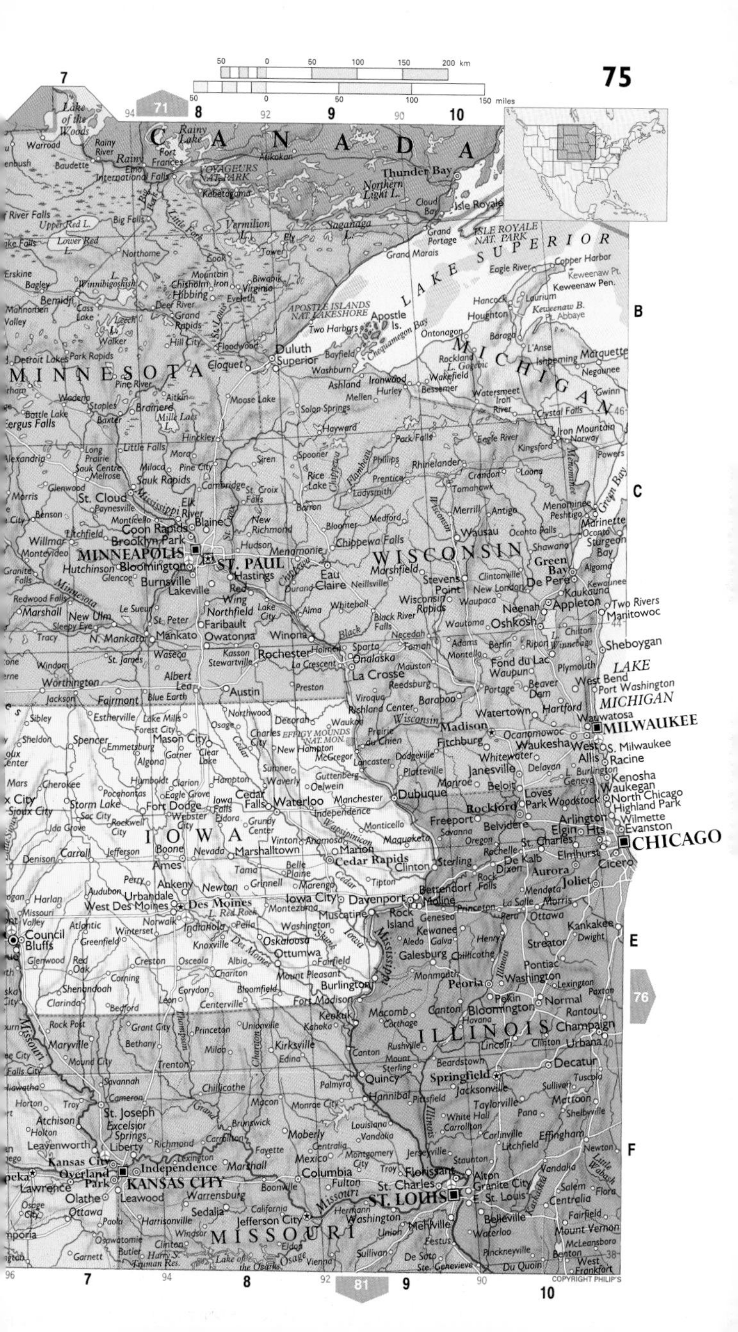

50 0 50 100 150 200 km
50 0 50 100 150 miles
7
71
8
9
10
94
92
90
CANADA
Lake of the Woods
Rainy Lake
Warroad
Rainy River
Baudette
Rainy
Fort Frances
Emo
International Falls
Atikokan
VOYAGEURS NAT. PARK
Kabetogama
Thunder Bay
Northern Light L.
Cloud Bay
Isle Royale
River Falls
Upper Red L.
Lower Red L.
Big Falls
Big Fork
Little Fork
Vermilion L.
Saganaga L.
Ely
Tower
Grand Portage
Grand Marais
ISLE ROYALE NAT. PARK
LAKE SUPERIOR
Northome
Cook
Erskine
Bagley
Winnibigoshish L.
Chisholm
Mountain Iron
Biwabik
Virginia
Hibbing
Eveleth
Bemidji
Deer River
Cass Lake
Leech L.
Grand Rapids
St. Louis
Walker
Hill City
Floodwood
APOSTLE ISLANDS NAT. LAKESHORE
Apostle Is.
Two Harbors
Chequamegon Bay
Eagle River
Copper Harbor
Keweenaw Pt.
Keweenaw Pen.
Hancock
Laurium
Houghton
Keweenaw B.
Pt. Abbaye
Ontonagon
Baraga
L'Anse
Duluth
Superior
Bayfield
Park Rapids
Detroit Lakes
Cloquet
MINNESOTA
Washburn
Ashland
Ironwood
Hurley
Bessemer
Wakefield
Rockland
L. Gogebic
MICHIGAN
Ishpeming
Marquette
Negaunee
Pine River
Wadena
Aitkin
Moose Lake
Mellen
Watersmeet
Iron River
Gwinn
Staples
Brainerd
Mille Lacs L.
Solon Springs
Battle Lake
Baxter
Fergus Falls
Hayward
Crystal Falls
Iron Mountain
Norway
Hinckley
Park Falls
Eagle River
Kingsford
Long Prairie
Little Falls
Mora
Pine City
Siren
Spooner
Phillips
Rhinelander
Powers
Menominee
Alexandria
Sauk Centre
Melrose
Milaca
Sauk Rapids
Cambridge
St. Croix Falls
Rice Lake
Chippewa
Flambeau
Prentice
Crandon
Laona
Tomahawk
Glenwood
Mississippi
Ladysmith
Wisconsin
Green Bay
Morris
St. Cloud
Paynesville
Elk River
Barron
Merrill
Antigo
Menominee
Peshtigo
Marinette
Benson
Monticello
Blaine
New Richmond
Bloomer
Medford
Oconto
Litchfield
Coon Rapids
Brooklyn Park
Wausau
Oconto Falls
Sturgeon Bay
Willmar
Chippewa Falls
Shawano
Montevideo
MINNEAPOLIS
ST. PAUL
Hudson
Menomonie
WISCONSIN
Green Bay
Algoma
Granite Falls
Hutchinson
Bloomington
Hastings
Eau Claire
Marshfield
Stevens Point
Clintonville
Glencoe
Burnsville
Lakeville
Durand
Neillsville
New London
De Pere
Kaukauna
Kewaunee
Redwood Falls
Red Wing
Whitehall
Wisconsin Rapids
Waupaca
Neenah
Appleton
Two Rivers
Marshall
New Ulm
Le Sueur
Northfield
Lake City
Alma
Black River Falls
Manitowoc
Sleepy Eye
St. Peter
Faribault
Wautoma
Oshkosh
Chilton
Tracy
N. Mankato
Mankato
Owatonna
Winona
Black
Necedah
Tomah
L. Winnebago
Adams
Berlin
Ripon
Sheboygan
Windom
St. James
Waseca
Kasson
Stewartville
Rochester
Holmen
Sparta
Onalaska
La Crescent
Mauston
Montello
Fond du Lac
Waupun
Plymouth
LAKE MICHIGAN
Worthington
Albert Lea
Austin
Preston
La Crosse
Reedsburg
Portage
Beaver Dam
West Bend
Port Washington
Jackson
Fairmont
Blue Earth
Viroqua
Richland Center
Baraboo
Watertown
Hartford
Sibley
Estherville
Lake Mills
Northwood
Decorah
Waukon
Wisconsin
Madison
Wauwatosa
MILWAUKEE
Sheldon
Spencer
Forest City
Mason City
Osage
Charles City
EFFIGY MOUNDS NAT. MON.
Prairie du Chien
Fitchburg
Oconomowoc
Waukesha
West Allis
S. Milwaukee
Racine
Emmetsburg
Algona
Garner
Clear Lake
Cedar
New Hampton
McGregor
Lancaster
Dodgeville
Whitewater
Delavan
Mars
Cherokee
Humboldt
Clarion
Hampton
Sumner
Waverly
Guttenberg
Oelwein
Platteville
Monroe
Janesville
Beloit
Lake Geneva
Burlington
Kenosha
Waukegan
North Chicago
Highland Park
Sioux City
Storm Lake
Pocahontas
Eagle Grove
Fort Dodge
Iowa Falls
Cedar Falls
Waterloo
Manchester
Independence
Dubuque
Rockford
Loves Park
Woodstock
Sac City
Webster City
Rockwell City
Eldora
Grundy Center
Wapsipinicon
Monticello
Freeport
Belvidere
Arlington Hts.
Wilmette
Evanston
Ida Grove
IOWA
Vinton
Anamosa
Maquoketa
Savanna
Oregon
Elgin
St. Charles
CHICAGO
Denison
Carroll
Jefferson
Boone
Nevada
Marshalltown
Marion
Cedar Rapids
Clinton
Sterling
Rochelle
De Kalb
Elmhurst
Cicero
Ames
Tama
Belle Plaine
Dixon
Aurora
Perry
Ankeny
Grinnell
Marengo
Cedar
Tipton
Rock Falls
Joliet
Harlan
Audubon
Urbandale
Newton
Iowa City
Davenport
Bettendorf
Moline
Mendota
Missouri Valley
West Des Moines
Des Moines
L. Red Rock
Montezuma
Rock Island
Princeton
La Salle
Peru
Morris
Ottawa
Council Bluffs
Atlantic
Greenfield
Winterset
Norwalk
Indianola
Pella
Muscatine
Washington
Geneseo
Kewanee
Kankakee
Dwight
Knoxville
Oskaloosa
Skunk
Iowa
Aledo
Galva
Henry
Streator
Ottumwa
Des Moines
Galesburg
Chillicothe
Glenwood
Red Oak
Creston
Osceola
Albia
Fairfield
Mississippi
Illinois
Pontiac
Chariton
Mount Pleasant
Monmouth
Peoria
Washington
Lexington
Corning
Burlington
Pekin
Normal
Paxton
Shenandoah
Corydon
Bloomfield
Fort Madison
Clarinda
Bedford
Leon
Centerville
Keokuk
Macomb
Canton
Bloomington
Rantoul
Havana
Carthage
ILLINOIS
Champaign
Urbana
Lincoln
Clinton
Rock Port
Grant City
Princeton
Unionville
Kahoka
Rushville
Thompson
Chariton
Maryville
Bethany
Milan
Kirksville
Edina
Canton
Mount Sterling
Beardstown
Decatur
Mound City
Trenton
Missouri
Quincy
Springfield
Tuscola
Falls City
Savannah
Chillicothe
Palmyra
Sullivan
Hiawatha
Macon
Hannibal
Pittsfield
Jacksonville
Mattoon
Cameron
Grand
Monroe City
Taylorville
Pana
Shelbyville
Horton
Troy
St. Joseph
Illinois
White Hall
Atchison
Excelsior Springs
Brunswick
Louisiana
Carrollton
Holton
Moberly
Vandalia
Carlinville
Effingham
Leavenworth
Richmond
Carrollton
Centralia
Litchfield
Liberty
Lexington
Fayette
Mexico
Montgomery City
Jerseyville
Staunton
Newton
Little Wabash
Kansas City
Independence
Marshall
Columbia
Troy
Florissant
Alton
Vandalia
Topeka
Overland Park
KANSAS CITY
Fulton
St. Charles
Granite City
Kaskaskia
Salem
Flora
Lawrence
Warrensburg
Boonville
Missouri
ST. LOUIS
E. St. Louis
Centralia
Olathe
Leawood
Sedalia
California
Jefferson City
Hermann
Washington
Mehlville
Belleville
Fairfield
Osage City
Ottawa
Paola
Harrisonville
Union
Festus
Waterloo
Mount Vernon
Emporia
Osawatomie
Windsor
MISSOURI
Eldon
McLeansboro
Clinton
Butler
Harry S. Truman Res.
Lake of the Ozarks
Osage
Vienna
Sullivan
De Soto
Ste. Genevieve
Pinckneyville
Du Quoin
Benton
West Frankfort
Garnett
76
81
B
C
E
F
46
44
40
38
96
COPYRIGHT PHILIP'S

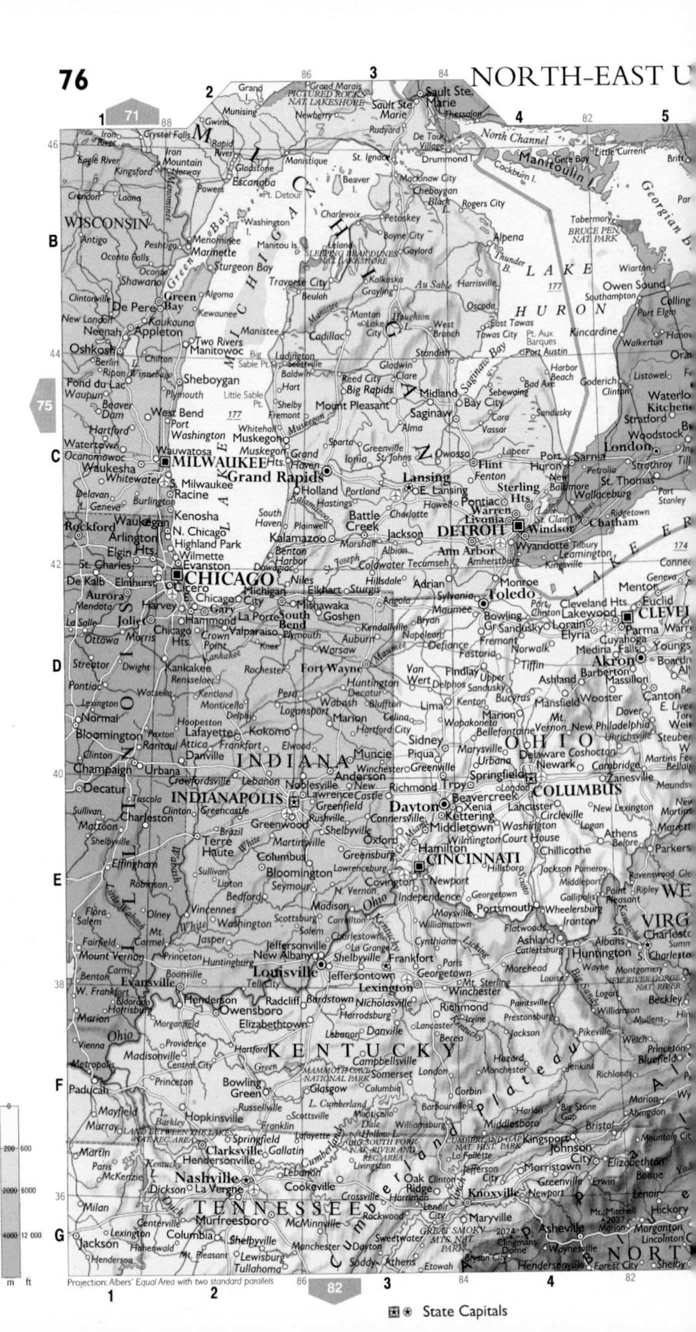

WISCONSIN
MICHIGAN
LAKE MICHIGAN
LAKE HURON
LAKE ERIE
INDIANA
OHIO
KENTUCKY
TENNESSEE
ILLINOIS
Cumberland Plateau
MILWAUKEE
CHICAGO
DETROIT
Grand Rapids
INDIANAPOLIS
COLUMBUS
CINCINNATI
Louisville
Nashville
Lansing
Toledo
Dayton
Lexington
Frankfort
Knoxville
Windsor
London
Akron
Green Bay
Sault Ste. Marie
Manitoulin I.
North Channel
Georgian Bay
Saginaw Bay
PICTURED ROCKS NAT. LAKESHORE
SLEEPING BEAR DUNES NAT. LAKESHORE
MAMMOTH CAVE NATIONAL PARK
GREAT SMOKY MTS. NAT. PARK
Projection: Albers' Equal Area with two standard parallels
State Capitals
m ft

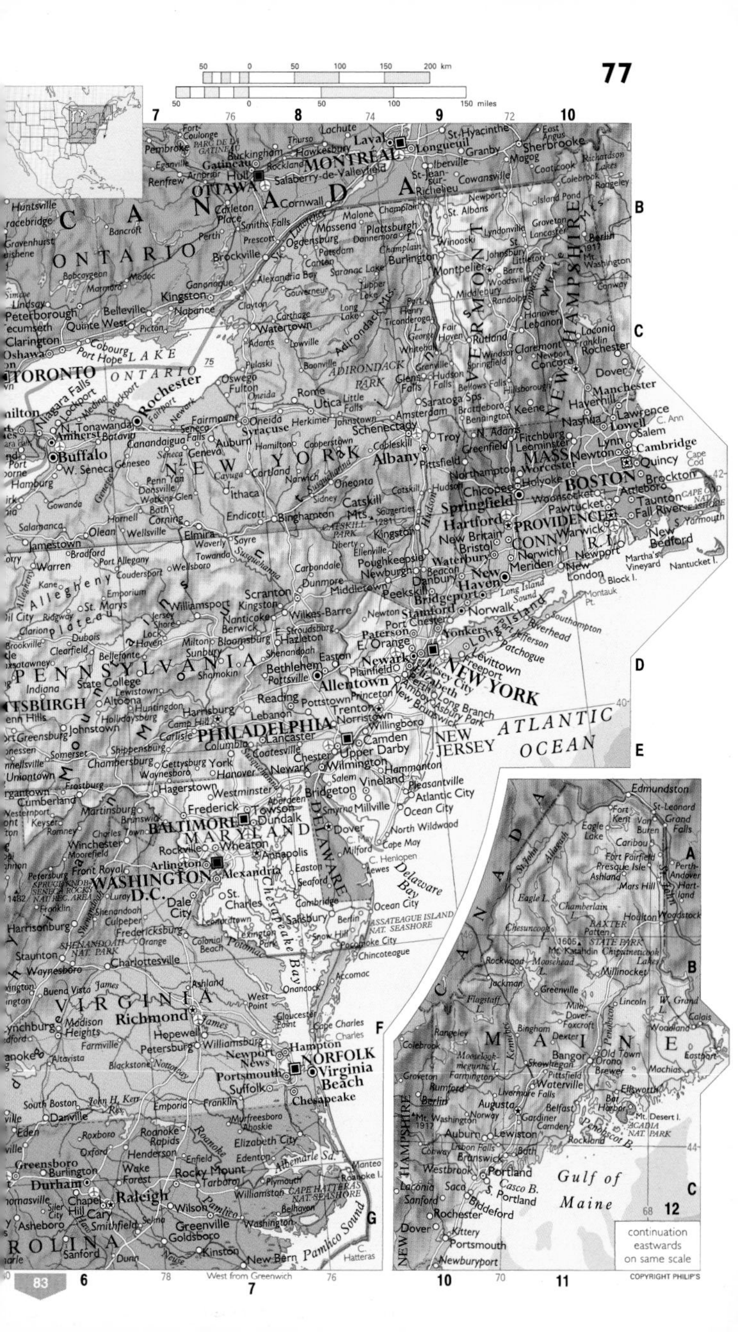

50 0 50 100 150 200 km
50 0 50 100 150 miles
CANADA
ONTARIO
Pembroke
Renfrew
Arnprior
Gatineau
Hull
OTTAWA
Buckingham
Hawkesbury
Lachute
Laval
MONTRÉAL
Longueuil
St-Hyacinthe
Granby
Sherbrooke
Magog
Coaticook
East Angus
Salaberry-de-Valleyfield
Cornwall
Carleton Place
Smiths Falls
Perth
Bancroft
Huntsville
Gravenhurst
Brockville
Prescott
Ogdensburg
Gananoque
Kingston
Napanee
Belleville
Quinte West
Picton
Peterborough
Lindsay
Clarington
Oshawa
Cobourg
Port Hope
TORONTO
LAKE ONTARIO
Niagara Falls
Lockport
Rochester
Buffalo
Amherst
N. Tonawanda
W. Seneca
Hamburg
Batavia
Canandaigua
Geneseo
Geneva
Seneca Falls
Auburn
Fairmount
Oneida
Syracuse
Herkimer
Utica
Rome
Oswego
Fulton
Pulaski
Watertown
Carthage
Lowville
Boonville
Adams
Clayton
Alexandria Bay
Massena
Malone
Potsdam
Canton
Plattsburgh
Champlain
Saranac Lake
Tupper Lake
Long Lake
Adirondack Mts.
ADIRONDACK PARK
Glens Falls
Hudson Falls
Saratoga Sps.
Amsterdam
Schenectady
Albany
Troy
Cobleskill
Cooperstown
Oneonta
Norwich
Cortland
Ithaca
Penn Yan
Dansville
Watkins Glen
Bath
Corning
Hornell
Wellsville
Olean
Salamanca
Jamestown
Elmira
Binghamton
Endicott
Sidney
Catskill Mts.
CATSKILL PARK
Kingston
Poughkeepsie
Newburgh
Middletown
Peekskill
Liberty
Ellenville
NEW YORK
Burlington
Montpelier
Barre
St. Albans
Winooski
Middlebury
Rutland
VERMONT
St. Johnsbury
Lyndonville
Newport
Bennington
Brattleboro
NEW HAMPSHIRE
Berlin
Mt. Washington
Conway
Laconia
Concord
Manchester
Nashua
Keene
Lebanon
Hanover
Claremont
Dover
Rochester
Haverhill
Lawrence
Lowell
Salem
Lynn
Cambridge
Newton
Quincy
BOSTON
Brockton
Worcester
Fitchburg
Leominster
Pittsfield
Springfield
Holyoke
Chicopee
Northampton
Greenfield
MASS.
Woonsocket
Pawtucket
PROVIDENCE
Warwick
Attleboro
Taunton
Fall River
New Bedford
Newport
R.I.
Cape Cod
Martha's Vineyard
Nantucket I.
Block I.
Hartford
New Britain
Bristol
Waterbury
Meriden
Norwich
New London
CONN.
New Haven
Bridgeport
Danbury
Stamford
Norwalk
Long Island Sound
Long Island
Montauk Pt.
Southampton
Riverhead
Port Jefferson
Patchogue
Levittown
Freeport
Yonkers
Port Chester
NEW YORK
Jersey City
Newark
Paterson
E. Orange
Plainfield
Elizabeth
Perth Amboy
New Brunswick
Long Branch
Asbury Park
Princeton
Trenton
NEW JERSEY
ATLANTIC OCEAN
PENNSYLVANIA
Allegheny Plateau
Appalachian Mountains
Erie
Warren
Bradford
Kane
St. Marys
Emporium
Coudersport
Wellsboro
Towanda
Sayre
Waverly
Williamsport
Jersey Shore
Lock Haven
Bellefonte
State College
Clearfield
Dubois
Clarion
Oil City
Ridgway
Brookville
Indiana
Altoona
Huntingdon
Lewistown
Hollidaysburg
Johnstown
PITTSBURGH
Greensburg
Somerset
Scranton
Wilkes-Barre
Hazleton
Kingston
Nanticoke
Berwick
Bloomsburg
Milton
Sunbury
Shamokin
Carbondale
Dunmore
E. Stroudsburg
Pottsville
Bethlehem
Allentown
Easton
Reading
Pottstown
Lebanon
Harrisburg
Camp Hill
Carlisle
Lancaster
Columbia
Coatesville
PHILADELPHIA
Norristown
Camden
Upper Darby
Chester
Willingboro
Chambersburg
Shippensburg
Gettysburg
York
Hanover
Waynesboro
Uniontown
Morgantown
Cumberland
Frostburg
Hagerstown
Westminster
Aberdeen
Frederick
Towson
BALTIMORE
Dundalk
MARYLAND
Martinsburg
Brunswick
Charles Town
Winchester
Moorefield
Keyser
Romney
Front Royal
Rockville
Wheaton
Annapolis
Arlington
Alexandria
WASHINGTON D.C.
Dale City
St. Charles
Chesapeake Bay
Wilmington
Newark
Salem
Bridgeton
Vineland
Millville
Hammonton
Pleasantville
Atlantic City
Ocean City
North Wildwood
Cape May
C. May
Smyrna
Dover
Milford
Lewes
C. Henlopen
DELAWARE
Delaware Bay
Easton
Seaford
Cambridge
Salisbury
Berlin
Ocean City
ASSATEAGUE ISLAND NAT. SEASHORE
Snow Hill
Pocomoke City
Chincoteague
Accomac
Onancock
Leonardtown
Lexington Park
Colonial Beach
Potomac
Fredericksburg
Culpeper
Orange
Luray
Shenandoah
SHENANDOAH NAT. PARK
Harrisonburg
Staunton
Waynesboro
Charlottesville
Ashland
Richmond
VIRGINIA
Hopewell
Petersburg
Williamsburg
West Point
Gloucester Point
Cape Charles
C. Charles
Hampton
Newport News
NORFOLK
Virginia Beach
Portsmouth
Suffolk
Chesapeake
Franklin
Emporia
Blackstone
Farmville
Lynchburg
Madison Heights
Buena Vista
Altavista
South Boston
John H. Kerr Res.
Danville
Eden
Roxboro
Oxford
Henderson
Roanoke Rapids
Murfreesboro
Ahoskie
Elizabeth City
Edenton
Albemarle Sd.
Manteo
Roanoke I.
Plymouth
Williamston
CAPE HATTERAS NAT. SEASHORE
Greensboro
Burlington
Durham
Chapel Hill
Cary
Raleigh
Wake Forest
Rocky Mount
Tarboro
Enfield
Wilson
Smithfield
Selma
Greenville
Goldsboro
Kinston
Washington
Belhaven
Pamlico Sound
New Bern
C. Hatteras
Asheboro
Sanford
Dunn
CAROLINA
Edmundston
St-Leonard
Grand Falls
Fort Kent
Van Buren
Eagle Lake
Caribou
Fort Fairfield
Presque Isle
Ashland
Perth-Andover
Mars Hill
Hartland
Houlton
Woodstock
Chamberlain L.
Eagle L.
BAXTER STATE PARK
Mt. Katahdin
Chesuncook L.
Moosehead L.
Rockwood
Millinocket
Jackman
Greenville
Flagstaff L.
Milo
Dover-Foxcroft
Lincoln
Calais
Woodland
MAINE
Rangeley
Colebrook
Bingham
Dexter
Bangor
Old Town
Orono
Brewer
Eastport
Machias
Skowhegan
Pittsfield
Waterville
Farmington
Rumford
Livermore Falls
Ellsworth
Bar Harbor
Mt. Desert I.
ACADIA NAT. PARK
Augusta
Gardiner
Belfast
Camden
Rockland
Penobscot B.
Norway
Auburn
Lewiston
Lisbon Falls
Brunswick
Bath
Westbrook
Portland
Casco B.
S. Portland
Saco
Biddeford
Sanford
Kittery
Portsmouth
Newburyport
Gulf of Maine
continuation eastwards on same scale
West from Greenwich


83

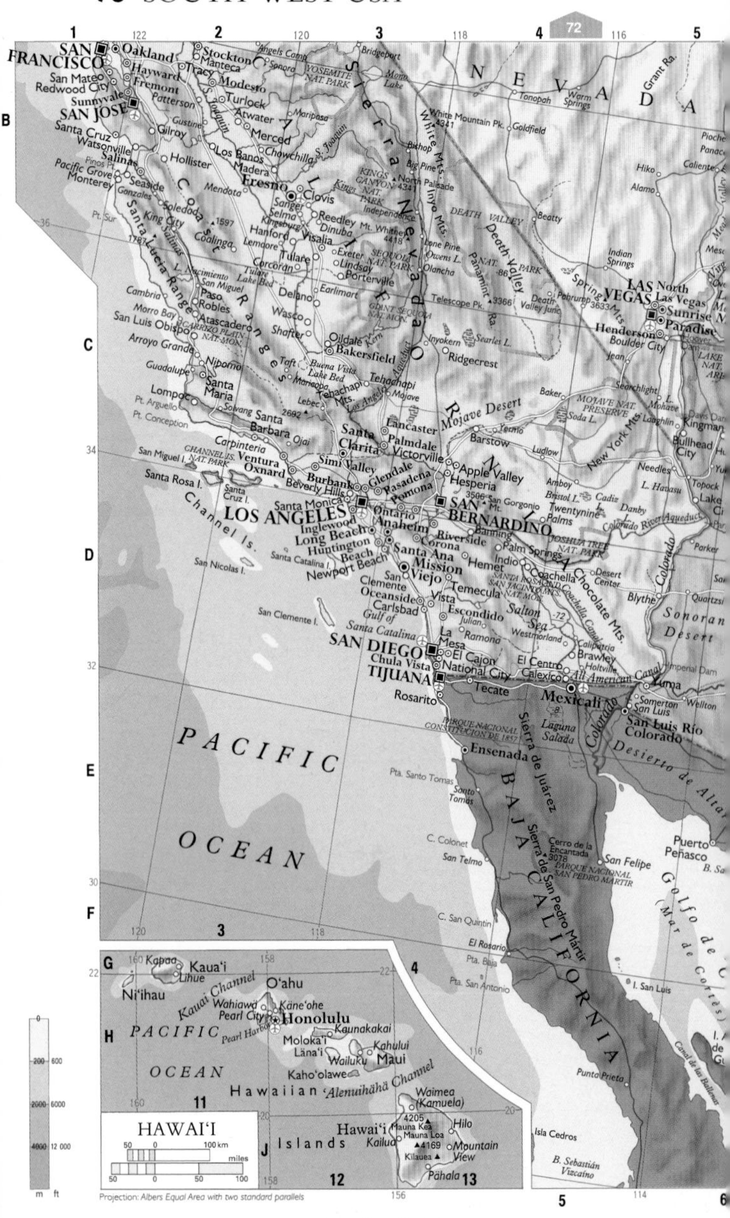
72
NEVADA
CALIFORNIA
BAJA CALIFORNIA
PACIFIC OCEAN
SAN FRANCISCO
Oakland
San Mateo
Redwood City
Hayward
Fremont
Sunnyvale
SAN JOSE
Stockton
Manteca
Tracy
Modesto
Turlock
Patterson
Atwater
Merced
Gilroy
Santa Cruz
Watsonville
Salinas
Pacific Grove
Monterey
Seaside
Hollister
Los Banos
Chowchilla
Madera
Fresno
Clovis
Sanger
Selma
Reedley
Kingsburg
Dinuba
Hanford
Visalia
Lemoore
Coalinga
Exeter
Lindsay
Tulare
Corcoran
Porterville
Delano
Earlimart
Wasco
Shafter
Oildale
Bakersfield
Tehachapi
Mojave
Lancaster
Palmdale
Santa Clarita
Victorville
Apple Valley
Hesperia
Barstow
Ridgecrest
Bishop
Big Pine
Lone Pine
Olancha
Independence
Mt. Whitney 4418
White Mountain Pk. 4341
Tonopah
Goldfield
Beatty
Pahrump
Indian Springs
LAS VEGAS
North Las Vegas
Sunrise
Paradise
Henderson
Boulder City
Searchlight
Kingman
Bullhead City
Needles
Laughlin
Lake Havasu
Parker
Blythe
Yuma
Somerton
San Luis
San Luis Río Colorado
Mexicali
Calexico
El Centro
Brawley
Calipatria
Westmorland
Indio
Coachella
Palm Springs
Banning
Hemet
Temecula
Riverside
Corona
SAN BERNARDINO
Twentynine Palms
Ontario
Pomona
Pasadena
Glendale
Burbank
Beverly Hills
Santa Monica
LOS ANGELES
Inglewood
Long Beach
Huntington Beach
Anaheim
Santa Ana
Newport Beach
Mission Viejo
San Clemente
Oceanside
Carlsbad
Vista
Escondido
Ramona
Julian
La Mesa
El Cajon
SAN DIEGO
Chula Vista
National City
TIJUANA
Tecate
Rosarito
Ensenada
San Felipe
Puerto Peñasco
Santo Tomas
San Telmo
El Rosario
Punta Prieta
Isla Cedros
Simi Valley
Ventura
Oxnard
Carpinteria
Santa Barbara
Ojai
Solvang
Lompoc
Santa Maria
Nipomo
Guadalupe
Arroyo Grande
San Luis Obispo
Morro Bay
Atascadero
Paso Robles
Cambria
King City
Soledad
Gonzales
Pt. Sur
Pt. Arguello
Pt. Conception
San Miguel I.
Santa Rosa I.
Santa Cruz I.
Santa Catalina I.
San Nicolas I.
San Clemente I.
Channel Is.
Gulf of Santa Catalina
Sierra Nevada
Coast Ranges
Santa Lucia Range
White Mts.
Inyo Mts.
Death Valley
Mojave Desert
Salton Sea
Chocolate Mts.
Sonoran Desert
Desierto de Altar
Golfo de California (Mar de Cortés)
Sierra de Juárez
Sierra de San Pedro Mártir
Colorado
San Joaquin
Mono Lake
YOSEMITE NAT. PARK
KINGS CANYON NAT. PARK
SEQUOIA NAT. PARK
DEATH VALLEY NAT. PARK
JOSHUA TREE NAT. PARK
MOJAVE NAT. PRESERVE
CHANNEL IS. NAT. PARK
All American Canal
Colorado River Aqueduct
HAWAI'I
Kaua'i
Ni'ihau
Kapaa
Lihue
O'ahu
Wahiawā
Kāne'ohe
Pearl City
Honolulu
Pearl Harbor
Moloka'i
Kaunakakai
Lāna'i
Maui
Kahului
Wailuku
Kaho'olawe
Hawai'i
Hilo
Kailua
Waimea (Kamuela)
Mauna Kea 4205
Mauna Loa 4169
Kilauea
Mountain View
Pāhala
Kauai Channel
'Alenuihāhā Channel
Hawaiian Islands
PACIFIC OCEAN
Projection: Albers Equal Area with two standard parallels
State Capitals

50 0 50 100 150 200 km
50 0 50 100 150 miles
6
73
112
7
110
8
108
9
106
10
A
B
C
D
E
F
80
COLORADO
Sawatch Range
Sangre de Cristo Mts.
Grand Junction
Clifton
Aspen
Leadville
Fairplay
Mt. Elbert 4399
Buena Vista
Mt. Antero
Orchard City
Paonia
Hotchkiss
Delta
BLACK CANYON OF THE GUNNISON NAT. PARK
Gunnison
Montrose
Blue Mesa Res.
Uncompahgre Plateau
Gunnison
Dolores
Uncompahgre Peak 4359
Ouray
Telluride
Lake City
Saguache
GREAT SAND DUNES NAT. MON.
Silverton
Creede
Rio Grande
Del Norte
Monte Vista
Alamosa
Blanca Pk. 4378
Ft. Garland
San Juan Mts.
Pagosa Springs
4045
Summit Peak
Durango
Cortez
Dolores
Dove Creek
CANYON OF THE ANCIENTS NAT. MON.
MESAVERDE NAT. PARK
Animas
San Luis
Manassa
Dulce
Chama
Navajo Res.
Aztec
Bloomfield
Farmington
Kirtland
Shiprock
Tierra Amarilla
Questa
Wheeler Pk. 4011
Eagle Nest
Taos
Fillmore
Sevier
Salina
Richfield
Ferron
Green River
Green
Sevier
Monroe
Milford
Delano Peak 3710
Beaver
Loa
Junction
Torrey
Fremont
Muddy Cr.
Hanksville
ARCHES NAT. PARK
Thompson Springs
Moab
Mt. Peale 3877
UTAH
CAPITOL REEF NAT. PARK
CANYONLANDS NATIONAL PARK
Parowan
Panguitch
Cedar City
BRYCE CANYON NAT. PARK
Escalante
Tropic
Escalante
Glen Canyon
Lake Powell
Monticello
NATURAL BRIDGES NAT. MON.
Blanding
HOVENWEEP NAT. MON.
Bluff
San Juan
Orderville
GLEN CANYON NAT. REC. AREA
GRAND STAIRCASE-ESCALANTE NAT. MON.
Kanab
Fredonia
Paria
RAINBOW BRIDGE NAT. MON.
Glen Canyon Dam
Page
Mexican Water
Chuska Mts.
Jacob Lake
GRAND CANYON NAT. PARK
Supai
Grand Canyon
Grand Canyon
Colorado Plateau
Kayenta
Roof Butte 2989
Chinle
CANYON DE CHELLY NAT. MON.
Tuba City
Painted Desert
Little Colorado
Cameron
Polacca
WUPATKI NAT. MON.
Humphreys Peak 3851
Williams
Flagstaff
Ganado
Ft. Defiance
Window Rock
Chaco
CHACO CULTURE NAT. HIST. PARK
Crownpoint
Cuba
Espanola
Chimayo
Truchas Pk. 3993
Los Alamos
White Rock
Mora
Santo Domingo Pueblo
Santa Fe
Pecos
Las Vegas
Lamy
Rio Grande
NEW MEXICO
Gallup
Mt. Taylor
Grants 3445
Rio Rancho
Bernalillo
Alameda
Albuquerque
Villanueva
Zuni Pueblo
San Rafael
San Jose
Laguna
South Valley
Moriarty
Los Lunas
Bosque Farms
Valencia
Estancia
Belen
EL MALPAIS NAT. MON.
Manzano Mts.
Encino
Vaughn
Mountainair
SALINAS PUEBLO MISSIONS NAT. MON.
Corona
Sanders
Chambers
Puerco
PETRIFIED FOREST NAT. PARK
TUZIGOOT NAT. MON.
WALNUT CANYON NAT. MON.
Winslow
Holbrook
Clarkdale
Sedona
Cottonwood
Camp Verde
MONTEZUMA CASTLE NAT. MON.
Mayer
Mogollon Rim
Snowflake
Concho
St. Johns
Quemado
AGUA FRIA NAT. MON.
Payson
Show Low
Pinetop-Lakeside
ARIZONA
Wickenburg
Cave Creek
Theodore Roosevelt L.
TONTO NAT. MON.
Eagar
Springerville
Magdalena
South Baldy 3287
Socorro
San Antonio
Peoria
Glendale
Scottsdale
Tempe
Mesa
Apache Junction
Chandler
Sun Lakes
Maricopa
Salt
Black
Baldy Peak 3476
Whiteriver
Alpine
Reserve
San Francisco
Black Range
Elephant Butte Res.
Claypool
Globe
Superior
San Carlos
San Carlos L.
Coolidge Dam
Gila
Coolidge
Florence
Kearny
Bylas
Whitewater Baldy 3321
GILA CLIFF DWELLINGS NAT. MON.
Truth or Consequences
Casa Grande
Eloy
Pima
Thatcher
Safford
Clifton
Gila
San Pedro
Galiuro Mts.
Mammoth
Oracle
Catalina
San Manuel
Mt. Graham 3267
Duncan
Silver City
Santa Rita
Bayard
Hurley
Hatch
Rio Grande
San Andres Mts.
Carrizozo
Capitan
Sierra Blanca Peak 3659
Lincoln
Ruidoso
Tularosa
Cloudcroft
Mayhill
Alamogordo
Sacramento Mts.
WHITE SANDS NAT. MON.
IRONWOOD FOREST NAT. MON.
Marana
SAGUARO NAT. PARK
Oro Valley
Willcox
Bowie
San Simon
Lordsburg
Tucson
SAGUARO NAT. PARK
ORGAN PIPE CACTUS NAT. MON.
Sells
Sahuarita
Green Valley
Benson
CHIRICAHUA NAT. MON.
Deming
Mesilla
Las Cruces
University Park
Mt. Wrightson 2881
2986
Chiricahua Peak
TUMACACORI NAT. HIST. PARK
Patagonia
Tombstone
Sierra Vista
Bisbee
Nogales
Nogales
Douglas
Agua Prieta
Columbus
Sunland Park
Anthony
Canutillo
GUADALUPE MTS. NAT. PARK
Dell City
2667
Guadalupe Peak
El Paso
General Rodrigo M. Quevedo
CIUDAD JUÁREZ
Socorro
Clint
Fabens
TEXAS
Guadalupe Bravos
Fort Hancock
Sierra Blanca
Van Horn
El Porvenir
Rio Grande
Rio Bravo del Norte
L. de Guzmán
L. de Sta. María
Janos
Villa Ahumada
MEXICO
Altar
Magdalena de Kino
Imuris
Cananea
Magdalena
Santa Ana
Nacozari de García
Arizpe
Nuevo Casas Grandes
Benjamín Hill
Sonora
Bavispe
Villa Hidalgo
Cumpas
Moctezuma
Santa María
Galeana
Carmen
Buenaventura
Moctezuma
El Sueco
SONORA
CHIHUAHUA
Ures
Hermosillo
Nicolás Bravo
Madera
Namiquipa
Mazatán
Sonora
Sahuaripa
Bacanora
Papigochic
Yaqui
Temósachic
PARQUE NACIONAL CUMBRES DE MAJALCA
West from Greenwich
COPYRIGHT PHILIP'S
84

COLORADO
KANSAS
NEW MEXICO
TEXAS
OKL
MEXICO
COAHUILA
CHIHUAHUA
Sangre de Cristo Mts.
Llano Estacado
Edwards Plateau
Stockton Plateau
Balcones Escarpment
Bolsón de Mapimí
La Junta
Granada
Syracuse
Garden City
Jetmore
Hutchinson
Wichita
Dodge City
Liberal
Guymon
Amarillo
Lubbock
Midland
Odessa
Abilene
San Angelo
Oklahoma City
Wichita Falls
Roswell
Carlsbad
Hobbs
Clovis
Tucumcari
Raton
Trinidad
Walsenburg
Las Vegas
Santa Rosa
Pecos
Del Rio
Ciudad Acuña
Piedras Negras
Eagle Pass
Nuevo Laredo
Laredo
SAN ANTONIO
Kerrville
San Marcos
New Braunfels
Seguin
Georgetown
Killeen
Lawton
Altus
Enid
Woodward
Plainview
Big Spring
Sweetwater
Snyder
Brownwood
Fort Stockton
Alpine
Marfa
Presidio
Ojinaga
Big Bend Nat. Park
Chisos Mts.
Guadalupe Peak
Carlsbad Caverns Nat. Park
Davis Mts.
Melchor Múzquiz
Nueva Rosita
Sabinas
Allende
Nava
Zaragoza
Alice
Kingsville
Robstown
Corpus Christi
Rio Grande
Pecos
Canadian
Colorado
Brazos
Red
Cimarron
Arkansas
Nueces
Rio Bravo del Norte
Projection: Albers' Equal Area with two standard parallels
West from Greenwich
104
102
100
98
36
34
32
28
1
2
3
4
A
B
C
D
E
F
74
79
84
m
ft
200
600
0

81
50 0 50 100 150 200 km
50 0 50 100 150 miles
75
82
MISSOURI
ARKANSAS
LOUISIANA
MISSISSIPPI
TENNESSEE
TEXAS
MEXICO
GULF OF MEXICO
Boston Mts.
Ouachita Mts.
Rolla
Springfield
Joplin
Carthage
Farmington
Cape Girardeau
Sikeston
Poplar Bluff
West Plains
Carbondale
Marion
Paducah
Mayfield
Union City
Dyersburg
Jackson
Tulsa
Broken Arrow
Muskogee
Okmulgee
Fayetteville
Springdale
Rogers
Bentonville
Harrison
Jonesboro
Paragould
Blytheville
Memphis
Germantown
Collierville
Southaven
Olive Branch
Fort Smith
Van Buren
Russellville
Conway
Searcy
North Little Rock
Little Rock
Jacksonville
Benton
Hot Springs
Pine Bluff
Arkadelphia
Texarkana
Magnolia
El Dorado
Camden
Tupelo
Oxford
Clarksdale
Greenville
Greenwood
Columbus
Starkville
Meridian
Jackson
Vicksburg
Hattiesburg
Laurel
Natchez
McComb
Gulfport
Biloxi
Pascagoula
Shreveport
Bossier City
Monroe
West Monroe
Ruston
Alexandria
Pineville
Natchitoches
Lake Charles
Lafayette
Baton Rouge
Hammond
Slidell
New Orleans
Metairie
Kenner
Houma
Thibodaux
New Iberia
Abbeville
Opelousas
Houston
Pasadena
Baytown
Galveston
Beaumont
Port Arthur
Orange
Conroe
The Woodlands
Huntsville
College Station
Lufkin
Nacogdoches
Tyler
Longview
Marshall
Paris
Kingsville
Falfurrias
Rio Grande City
McAllen
Edinburg
Mission
Harlingen
Brownsville
PADRE ISLAND NAT. SEASHORE
continuation southwards on same scale
Mississippi
Arkansas
Red
White
Ouachita
Pearl
Mississippi River Delta
Chandeleur Is.
COPYRIGHT PHILIP'S
State Capitals

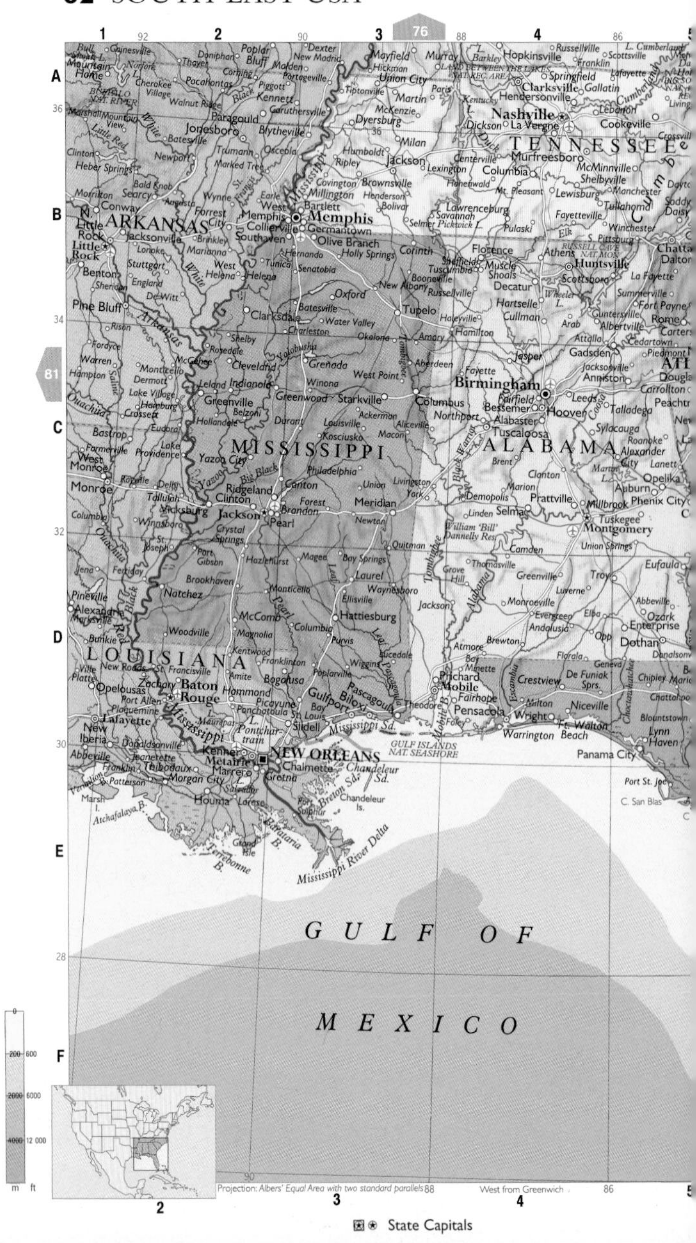
76
81
TENNESSEE
ARKANSAS
MISSISSIPPI
ALABAMA
LOUISIANA
GULF OF MEXICO
Nashville
Memphis
Little Rock
Jackson
Birmingham
Montgomery
Baton Rouge
NEW ORLEANS
Mobile
Huntsville
Clarksville
Murfreesboro
Jonesboro
Pine Bluff
Tupelo
Hattiesburg
Gulfport
Biloxi
Pensacola
Tuscaloosa
Hoover
Meridian
Vicksburg
Natchez
Lafayette
Monroe
Dothan
Panama City
Mississippi River Delta
GULF ISLANDS NAT. SEASHORE
Projection: Albers' Equal Area with two standard parallels
West from Greenwich
State Capitals
m ft
200 600
2000 6000
4000 12 000

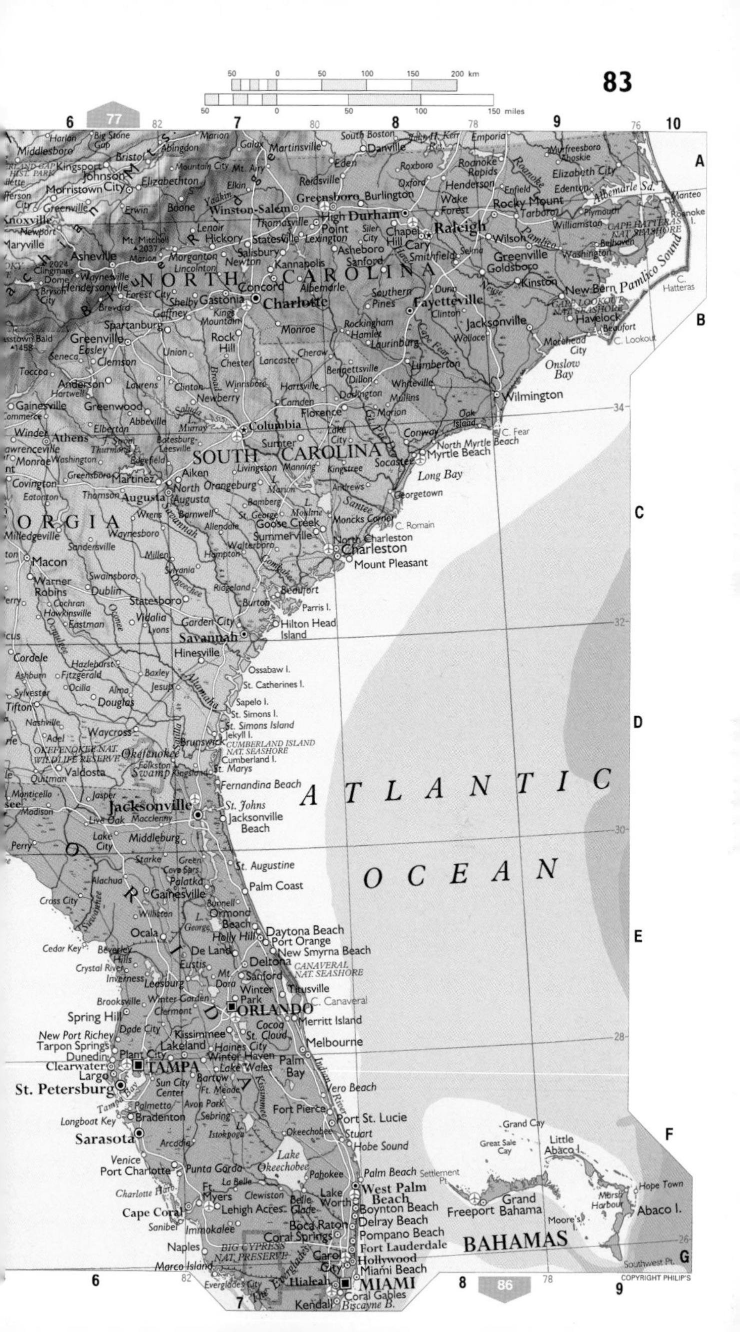
50 0 50 100 150 200 km
50 0 50 100 150 miles
6
77
82
7
80
8
78
9
76
10
A
B
C
D
E
F
G
NORTH CAROLINA
SOUTH CAROLINA
ORGIA
BAHAMAS
ATLANTIC
OCEAN
Albemarle Sd.
Pamlico Sound
Onslow Bay
Long Bay
Harlan
Big Stone Gap
Marion
Galax
Martinsville
South Boston
Danville
Emporia
Murfreesboro
Ahoskie
Middlesboro
Bristol
Abingdon
Kingsport
Johnson City
Mountain City
Mt. Airy
Eden
Roxboro
Roanoke Rapids
Elizabeth City
Morristown
Elizabethton
Reidsville
Oxford
Henderson
Enfield
Edenton
Manteo
Greeneville
Erwin
Boone
Winston-Salem
Greensboro
Burlington
Wake Forest
Rocky Mount
Tarboro
Plymouth
Knoxville
Newport
Thomasville
High Point
Durham
Chapel Hill
Raleigh
Williamston
CAPE HATTERAS NAT. SEASHORE
Maryville
Lenoir
Hickory
Statesville
Lexington
Siler City
Cary
Wilson
Belhaven
Mt. Mitchell 2037
Salisbury
Asheboro
Smithfield
Greenville
Washington
Asheville
Morganton
Newton
Kannapolis
Sanford
Selma
Goldsboro
Clingmans Dome 2024
Waynesville
Hendersonville
Lincolnton
Concord
Albemarle
Kinston
Bryson City
Forest City
Shelby
Gastonia
Charlotte
Southern Pines
Dunn
Fayetteville
New Bern
C. Hatteras
Brevard
Gaffney
Kings Mountain
Clinton
CAPE LOOKOUT NAT. SEASHORE
Spartanburg
Monroe
Rockingham
Hamlet
Jacksonville
Havelock
Greenville
Easley
Rock Hill
Laurinburg
Wallace
Beaufort
C. Lookout
Seneca
Clemson
Union
Chester
Lancaster
Cheraw
Morehead City
Toccoa
Bennettsville
Lumberton
Anderson
Laurens
Clinton
Winnsboro
Dillon
Hartsville
Whiteville
Hartwell
Newberry
Camden
Darlington
Mullins
Wilmington
Gainesville
Greenwood
Abbeville
Florence
Marion
Commerce
Elberton
Columbia
Lake City
Oak Island
C. Fear
Conway
Winder
Athens
Batesburg-Leesville
Sumter
North Myrtle Beach
Myrtle Beach
Lawrenceville
Monroe
Washington
Edgefield
Socastee
Livingston
Manning
Kingstree
Greensboro
Martinez
Aiken
Covington
North Augusta
Orangeburg
Andrews
Augusta
Eatonton
Thomson
Georgetown
Wrens
Barnwell
Bamberg
St. George
Moncks Corner
C. Romain
Milledgeville
Waynesboro
Allendale
Goose Creek
Summerville
North Charleston
Sandersville
Charleston
Walterboro
Macon
Millen
Hampton
Mount Pleasant
Sylvania
Warner Robins
Swainsboro
Dublin
Ridgeland
Beaufort
Cochran
Parris I.
Hawkinsville
Statesboro
Burton
Vidalia
Eastman
Lyons
Garden City
Hilton Head Island
Savannah
Cordele
Hinesville
Hazlehurst
Ashburn
Fitzgerald
Baxley
Ossabaw I.
Jesup
St. Catherines I.
Sylvester
Ocilla
Alma
Douglas
Tifton
Sapelo I.
St. Simons I.
Nashville
St. Simons Island
Waycross
Jekyll I.
Adel
Brunswick
CUMBERLAND ISLAND NAT. SEASHORE
OKEFENOKEE NAT. WILDLIFE RESERVE
Okefenokee Swamp
Folkston
Cumberland I.
Valdosta
Kingsland
St. Marys
Quitman
Fernandina Beach
Monticello
Jasper
Jacksonville
St. Johns
Madison
Live Oak
Macclenny
Jacksonville Beach
Lake City
Middleburg
Perry
Starke
Green Cove Springs
St. Augustine
Palatka
Alachua
Gainesville
Palm Coast
Cross City
Bunnell
Williston
Ormond Beach
Daytona Beach
Ocala
Holly Hill
Port Orange
Cedar Key
Beverley Hills
De Land
New Smyrna Beach
Crystal River
Eustis
Deltona
CANAVERAL NAT. SEASHORE
Inverness
Mt. Dora
Sanford
Leesburg
Winter Park
Titusville
Brooksville
Winter Garden
C. Canaveral
Clermont
ORLANDO
Spring Hill
Cocoa
Merritt Island
Dade City
Kissimmee
St. Cloud
New Port Richey
Melbourne
Tarpon Springs
Lakeland
Haines City
Dunedin
Plant City
Winter Haven
Palm Bay
Clearwater
TAMPA
Lake Wales
Largo
Bartow
Sun City Center
Ft. Meade
St. Petersburg
Vero Beach
Tampa Bay
Palmetto
Avon Park
Fort Pierce
Longboat Key
Bradenton
Sebring
Port St. Lucie
Sarasota
Arcadia
Istokpoga
Okeechobee
Stuart
Grand Cay
Hobe Sound
Great Sale Cay
Little Abaco I.
Venice
Lake Okeechobee
Port Charlotte
Punta Gorda
Pahokee
Palm Beach
Settlement Pt.
La Belle
West Palm Beach
Hope Town
Charlotte Harb.
Ft. Myers
Clewiston
Lake Worth
Marsh Harbour
Cape Coral
Lehigh Acres
Belle Glade
Boynton Beach
Freeport
Grand Bahama
Abaco I.
Sanibel
Immokalee
Boca Raton
Delray Beach
Moore's I.
Coral Springs
Pompano Beach
Naples
BIG CYPRESS NAT. PRESERVE
Fort Lauderdale
Hollywood
Carol City
Miami Beach
Southwest Pt.
Marco Island
Everglades City
The Everglades
Hialeah
MIAMI
Kendall
Coral Gables
Biscayne B.
34
32
30
28
26
86
COPYRIGHT PHILIP'S

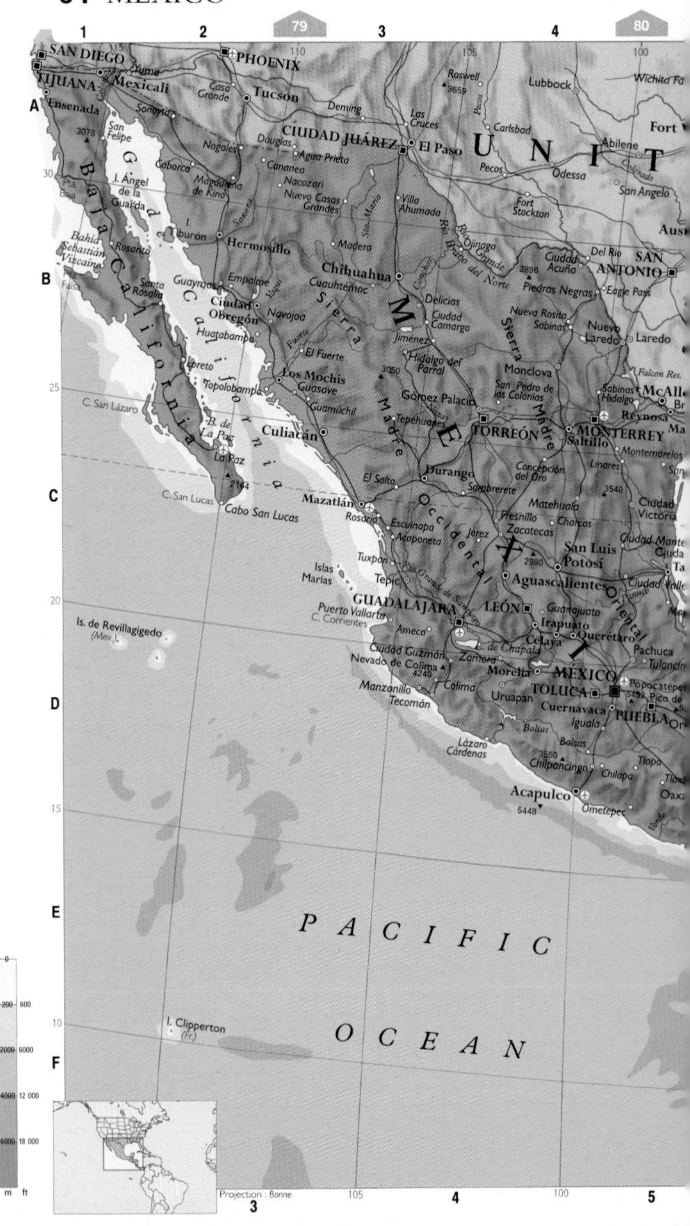
SAN DIEGO
TIJUANA
Mexicali
PHOENIX
Tucson
Ensenada
CIUDAD JUÁREZ
El Paso
Roswell
Lubbock
Carlsbad
Odessa
Abilene
San Angelo
Baja California
Golfo de California
Hermosillo
Chihuahua
Ciudad Obregón
Los Mochis
Culiacán
La Paz
Cabo San Lucas
Mazatlán
Durango
TORREÓN
MONTERREY
Saltillo
Nuevo Laredo
Laredo
SAN ANTONIO
Piedras Negras
Sierra Madre Occidental
Sierra Madre Oriental
Zacatecas
San Luis Potosí
Aguascalientes
GUADALAJARA
LEÓN
Guanajuato
Irapuato
Querétaro
Celaya
Morelia
MÉXICO
TOLUCA
PUEBLA
Cuernavaca
Acapulco
Chilpancingo
Puerto Vallarta
Manzanillo
Colima
Tepic
Islas Marías
Is. de Revillagigedo (Mex.)
I. Clipperton (Fr.)
PACIFIC OCEAN
Projection : Bonne

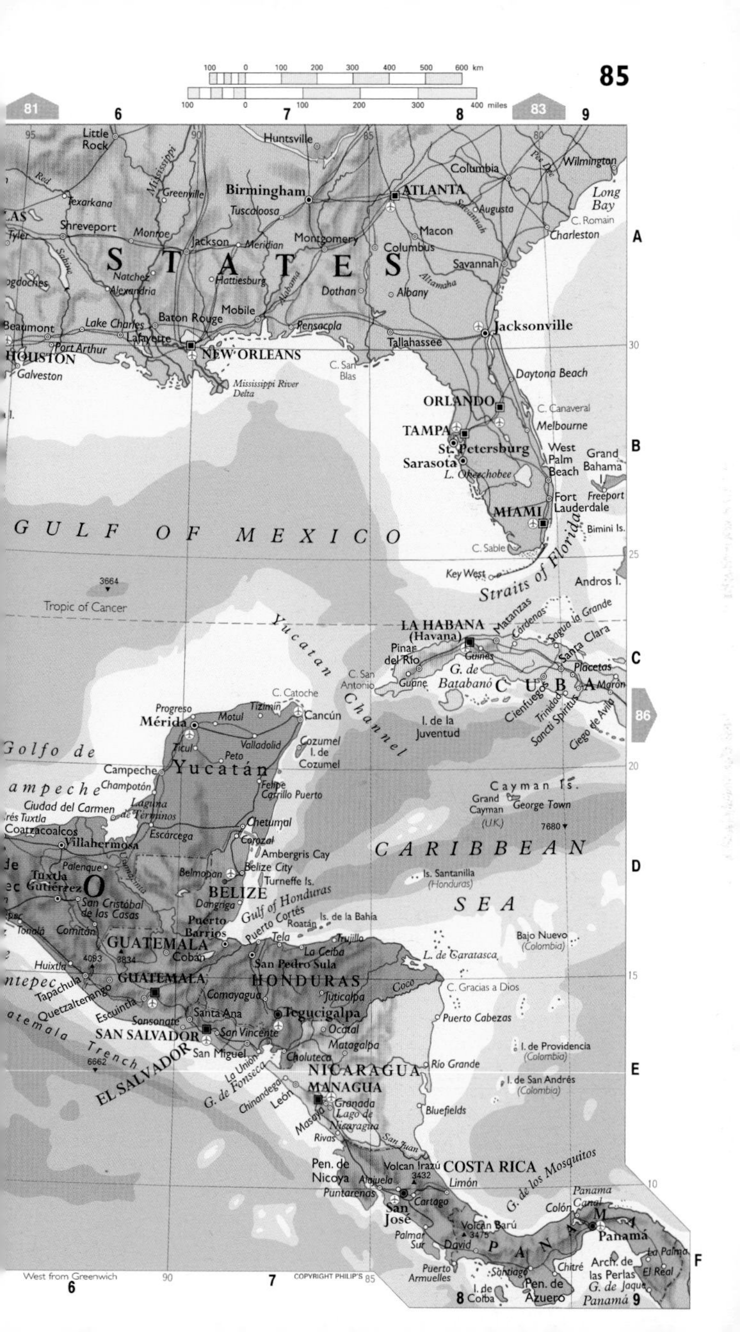

81
83
86
6
7
8
9
A
B
C
D
E
F
100 0 100 200 300 400 500 600 km
100 0 100 200 300 400 miles
Little Rock
Huntsville
Columbia
Wilmington
Long Bay
C. Romain
Birmingham
ATLANTA
Augusta
Charleston
Texarkana
Shreveport
Tyler
Monroe
Jackson
Meridian
Montgomery
Columbus
Macon
Savannah
S T A T E S
Natchez
Alexandria
Hattiesburg
Dothan
Albany
Mobile
Baton Rouge
Lake Charles
Lafayette
Beaumont
Port Arthur
HOUSTON
Galveston
Pensacola
Tallahassee
Jacksonville
NEW ORLEANS
Mississippi River Delta
C. San Blas
Daytona Beach
ORLANDO
C. Canaveral
Melbourne
TAMPA
St. Petersburg
Sarasota
L. Okeechobee
West Palm Beach
Grand Bahama I.
Freeport
Fort Lauderdale
MIAMI
Bimini Is.
C. Sable
GULF OF MEXICO
3664
Tropic of Cancer
Key West
Straits of Florida
Andros I.
LA HABANA (Havana)
Matanzas
Cárdenas
Sagua la Grande
Santa Clara
Pinar del Río
Güines
G. de Batabanó
C U B A
Placetas
Morón
Guane
C. San Antonio
C. Catoche
Cienfuegos
Trinidad
Sancti Spíritus
Ciego de Avila
Yucatan Channel
I. de la Juventud
Progreso
Mérida
Motul
Tizimín
Cancún
Cozumel
I. de Cozumel
Valladolid
Ticul
Peto
Golfo de Campeche
Campeche
Champotón
Yucatán
Felipe Carrillo Puerto
Ciudad del Carmen
Laguna de Términos
Coatzacoalcos
Villahermosa
Escárcega
Chetumal
Corozal
Ambergris Cay
Cayman Is.
Grand Cayman (U.K.)
George Town
7680
CARIBBEAN SEA
Palenque
Tuxtla Gutiérrez
Belmopan
Belize City
Turneffe Is.
Is. Santanilla (Honduras)
BELIZE
Dangriga
Gulf of Honduras
San Cristóbal de las Casas
Puerto Barrios
Puerto Cortés
Roatán
Is. de la Bahía
Tonalá
Comitán
GUATEMALA
Cobán
Tela
Trujillo
La Ceiba
Bajo Nuevo (Colombia)
L. de Caratasca
4093
3834
Huixtla
Tapachula
Quetzaltenango
GUATEMALA
San Pedro Sula
HONDURAS
Coco
C. Gracias a Dios
Comayagua
Juticalpa
Escuintla
Santa Ana
Tegucigalpa
Sonsonate
Puerto Cabezas
SAN SALVADOR
San Vincente
Ocotal
Matagalpa
I. de Providencia (Colombia)
Guatemala Trench
6662
San Miguel
EL SALVADOR
La Unión
G. de Fonseca
Choluteca
Chinandega
León
NICARAGUA
MANAGUA
Río Grande
I. de San Andrés (Colombia)
Masaya
Granada
Lago de Nicaragua
Bluefields
Rivas
San Juan
Pen. de Nicoya
Volcan Irazú
3432
COSTA RICA
G. de los Mosquitos
Alajuela
Limón
Puntarenas
Cartago
San José
Panama Canal
Colón
Volcan Barú
3475
PANAMA
Panamá
Palmar Sur
David
La Palma
Santiago
Chitré
Arch. de las Perlas
El Real
Puerto Armuelles
Pen. de Azuero
G. de Panamá
I. de Coiba
95
90
85
80
30
25
20
15
10
West from Greenwich
COPYRIGHT PHILIP'S

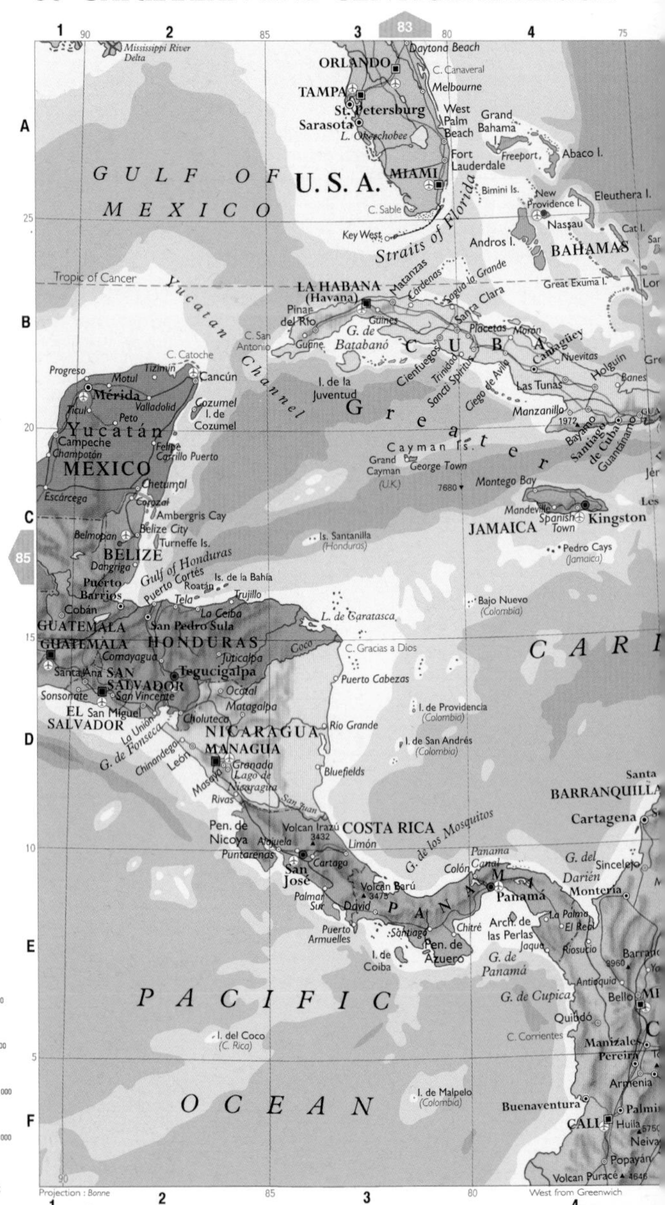
GULF OF MEXICO
U.S.A.
ORLANDO
TAMPA
St. Petersburg
Sarasota
MIAMI
Daytona Beach
C. Canaveral
Melbourne
West Palm Beach
Fort Lauderdale
L. Okeechobee
C. Sable
Key West
Straits of Florida
Grand Bahama I.
Freeport
Abaco I.
Bimini Is.
New Providence I.
Nassau
Eleuthera I.
Andros I.
Cat I.
BAHAMAS
Great Exuma I.
Tropic of Cancer
Yucatan Channel
LA HABANA (Havana)
Pinar del Río
C. San Antonio
G. de Batabanó
I. de la Juventud
CUBA
Matanzas
Cárdenas
Sagua la Grande
Santa Clara
Placetas
Morón
Camagüey
Nuevitas
Holguín
Cienfuegos
Trinidad
Sancti Spíritus
Ciego de Avila
Las Tunas
Manzanillo
Bayamo
Santiago de Cuba
Guantánamo
Greater
Cayman Is.
Grand Cayman (U.K.)
George Town
7680
Montego Bay
JAMAICA
Mandeville
Spanish Town
Kingston
Pedro Cays (Jamaica)
Bajo Nuevo (Colombia)
Is. Santanilla (Honduras)
C. Catoche
Progreso
Motul
Tizimín
Cancún
Mérida
Valladolid
Ticul
Peto
Cozumel
I. de Cozumel
Yucatán
Campeche
Champotón
Felipe Carrillo Puerto
MEXICO
Chetumal
Escárcega
Corozal
Ambergris Cay
Belmopan
Belize City
Turneffe Is.
BELIZE
Dangriga
Gulf of Honduras
Puerto Cortés
Puerto Barrios
Is. de la Bahía
Roatán
Tela
Trujillo
La Ceiba
Cobán
GUATEMALA
San Pedro Sula
HONDURAS
L. de Caratasca
C. Gracias a Dios
Coco
Comayagua
Juticalpa
Tegucigalpa
Santa Ana
SAN SALVADOR
Sonsonate
San Vincente
San Miguel
EL SALVADOR
Ocotal
Matagalpa
Choluteca
La Unión
G. de Fonseca
Chinandega
León
NICARAGUA
MANAGUA
Granada
Masaya
Lago de Nicaragua
Rivas
San Juan
Puerto Cabezas
Río Grande
Bluefields
I. de Providencia (Colombia)
I. de San Andrés (Colombia)
Pen. de Nicoya
Puntarenas
Alajuela
Volcan Irazú 3432
COSTA RICA
Limón
San José
Cartago
G. de los Mosquitos
Panama Canal
Colón
Volcan Barú 3475
PANAMA
Panamá
Palmar Sur
David
Puerto Armuelles
Santiago
Chitré
Pen. de Azuero
I. de Coiba
Arch. de las Perlas
G. de Panamá
La Palma
El Real
Jaqué
Riosucio
G. del Darién
Sincelejo
Montería
Cartagena
BARRANQUILLA
G. de Cupica
Quibdó
Antioquia
Medellín
C. Corrientes
Manizales
Pereira
Armenia
Buenaventura
CALI
Palmira
Huila
Neiva
Popayán
Volcan Puracé 4646
PACIFIC OCEAN
I. del Coco (C. Rica)
I. de Malpelo (Colombia)
CARIBBEAN
Projection: Bonne
West from Greenwich
m ft
200 600
2000 6000
4000 12 000
6000 18 000

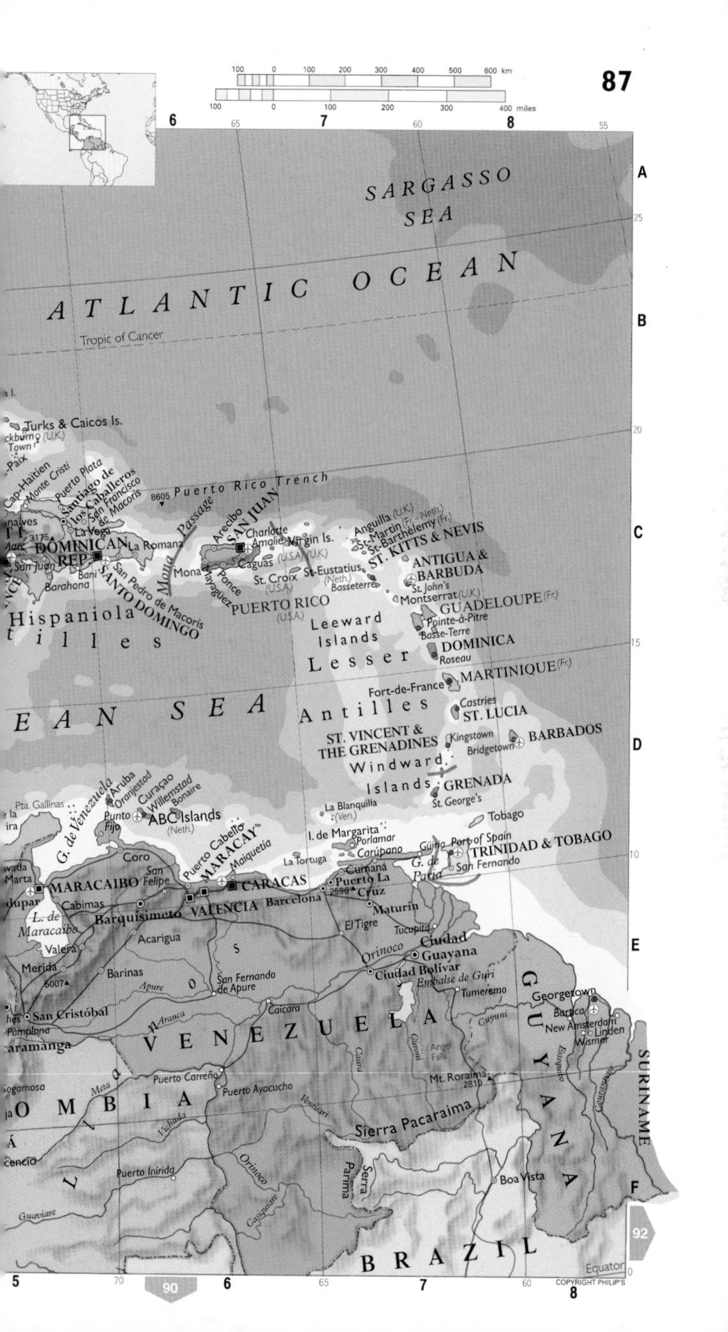
ATLANTIC OCEAN
SARGASSO SEA
Tropic of Cancer
Turks & Caicos Is. (U.K.)
Puerto Rico Trench
8605
Mona Passage
Hispaniola
DOMINICAN REP.
SANTO DOMINGO
Santiago de los Caballeros
San Francisco de Macorís
Puerto Plata
Monte Cristi
Cap-Haïtien
La Vega
La Romana
San Pedro de Macorís
Baní
Barahona
San Juan
3175
SAN JUAN
Arecibo
Mayagüez
Ponce
Caguas
Mona
PUERTO RICO (U.S.A.)
Charlotte Amalie
Virgin Is. (U.S.A.) (U.K.)
St. Croix (U.S.A.)
Anguilla (U.K.)
St-Martin (Fr. - Neth.)
St-Barthélemy (Fr.)
ST. KITTS & NEVIS
St-Eustatius (Neth.)
Basseterre
ANTIGUA & BARBUDA
St. John's
Montserrat (U.K.)
GUADELOUPE (Fr.)
Pointe-à-Pitre
Basse-Terre
DOMINICA
Roseau
MARTINIQUE (Fr.)
Fort-de-France
Castries
ST. LUCIA
ST. VINCENT & THE GRENADINES
Kingstown
Bridgetown
BARBADOS
GRENADA
St. George's
Leeward Islands
Lesser Antilles
Windward Islands
CARIBBEAN SEA
La Blanquilla (Ven.)
Tobago
TRINIDAD & TOBAGO
Port of Spain
San Fernando
Güiria
G. de Paria
I. de Margarita
Porlamar
Carúpano
La Tortuga
Cumaná
Puerto La Cruz
2596
Aruba
Oranjestad
Curaçao
Willemstad
Bonaire
ABC Islands (Neth.)
Pta. Gallinas
G. de Venezuela
Punto Fijo
Coro
Puerto Cabello
MARACAY
Maiquetía
CARACAS
San Felipe
MARACAIBO
Cabimas
L. de Maracaibo
Barquisimeto
VALENCIA
Barcelona
Maturín
El Tigre
Tucupita
Ciudad Guayana
Orinoco
Ciudad Bolívar
Embalse de Guri
Tumeremo
Acarigua
Valera
Mérida
5007
Barinas
Apure
San Fernando de Apure
San Cristóbal
Pamplona
Caicara
VENEZUELA
Arauca
Caura
Caroní
Angel Falls
Cuyuni
Georgetown
Bartica
New Amsterdam
Linden
Wismar
Essequibo
Courantyne
GUYANA
SURINAME
Mt. Roraima 2810
Puerto Carreño
Puerto Ayacucho
Meta
Vichada
Ventuari
Sierra Pacaraima
Serra Parima
Orinoco
Casiquiare
Puerto Inírida
Guaviare
Boa Vista
COLOMBIA
BRAZIL
Equator
100 0 100 200 300 400 500 600 km
100 0 100 200 300 400 miles
COPYRIGHT PHILIP'S
90
92

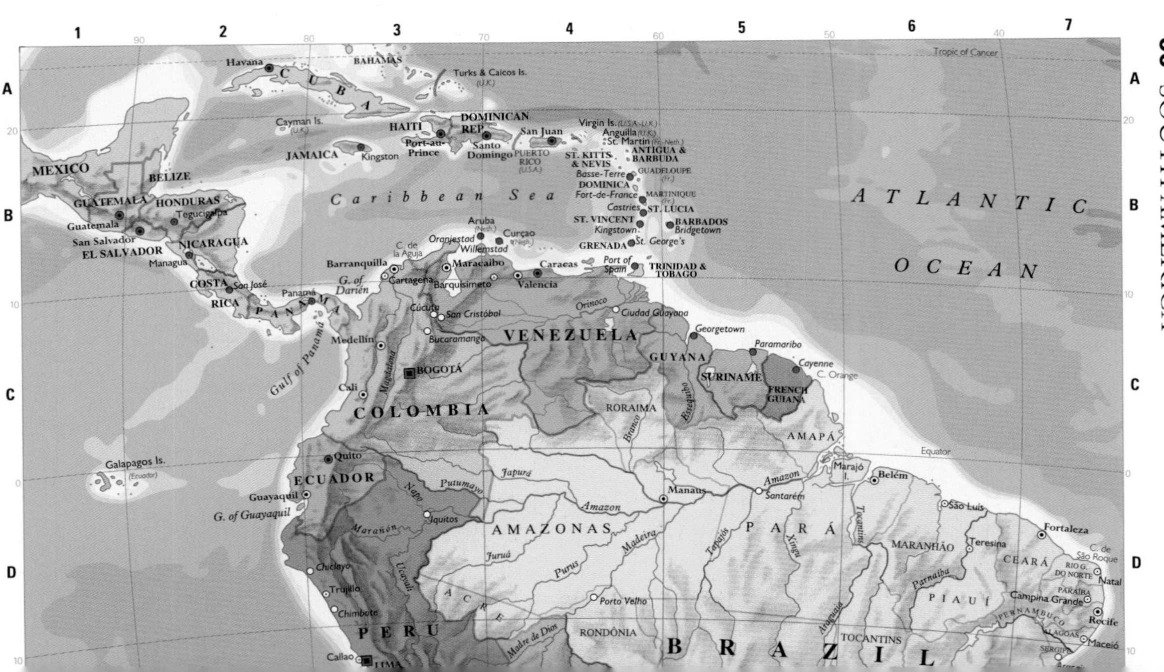
ATLANTIC
OCEAN
Caribbean Sea
Tropic of Cancer
Equator
MEXICO
BELIZE
GUATEMALA
Guatemala
HONDURAS
Tegucigalpa
San Salvador
EL SALVADOR
NICARAGUA
Managua
COSTA RICA
San José
PANAMA
Panamá
Gulf of Panama
Havana
CUBA
BAHAMAS
Turks & Caicos Is. (U.K.)
Cayman Is. (U.K.)
JAMAICA
Kingston
HAITI
Port-au-Prince
DOMINICAN REP.
Santo Domingo
San Juan
PUERTO RICO (U.S.A.)
Virgin Is. (U.S.A.-U.K.)
Anguilla (U.K.)
St. Martin (Fr.-Neth.)
ST. KITTS & NEVIS
ANTIGUA & BARBUDA
Basse-Terre
GUADELOUPE (Fr.)
DOMINICA
Fort-de-France
MARTINIQUE (Fr.)
Castries
ST. LUCIA
ST. VINCENT
Kingstown
BARBADOS
Bridgetown
GRENADA
St. George's
Port of Spain
TRINIDAD & TOBAGO
Aruba (Neth.)
Oranjestad
Curçao (Neth.)
Willemstad
C. de la Aguja
Barranquilla
Cartagena
G. of Darién
Maracaibo
Barquisimeto
Caracas
Valencia
Orinoco
Ciudad Guayana
Cúcuta
San Cristóbal
Bucaramanga
VENEZUELA
Georgetown
Paramaribo
GUYANA
Cayenne
C. Orange
SURINAME
FRENCH GUIANA
Medellín
Magdalena
BOGOTÁ
Cali
COLOMBIA
RORAIMA
Branco
Essequibo
AMAPÁ
Galapagos Is. (Ecuador)
Quito
ECUADOR
Guayaquil
G. of Guayaquil
Napo
Putumayo
Japurá
Marajó I.
Belém
Amazon
Manaus
Santarém
Iquitos
AMAZONAS
São Luís
Marañón
Madeira
Tapajós
PARÁ
Xingu
Tocantins
MARANHÃO
Teresina
Fortaleza
C. de São Roque
CEARÁ
RIO G. DO NORTE
Natal
Juruá
Purus
Chiclayo
Ucayali
Parnaíba
PIAUÍ
Campina Grande
PARAÍBA
Trujillo
ACRE
Porto Velho
Chimbote
PERNAMBUCO
Recife
Araguaia
PERU
Madre de Dios
RONDÔNIA
TOCANTINS
ALAGOAS
Maceió
Callao
LIMA
BRAZIL
SERGIPE

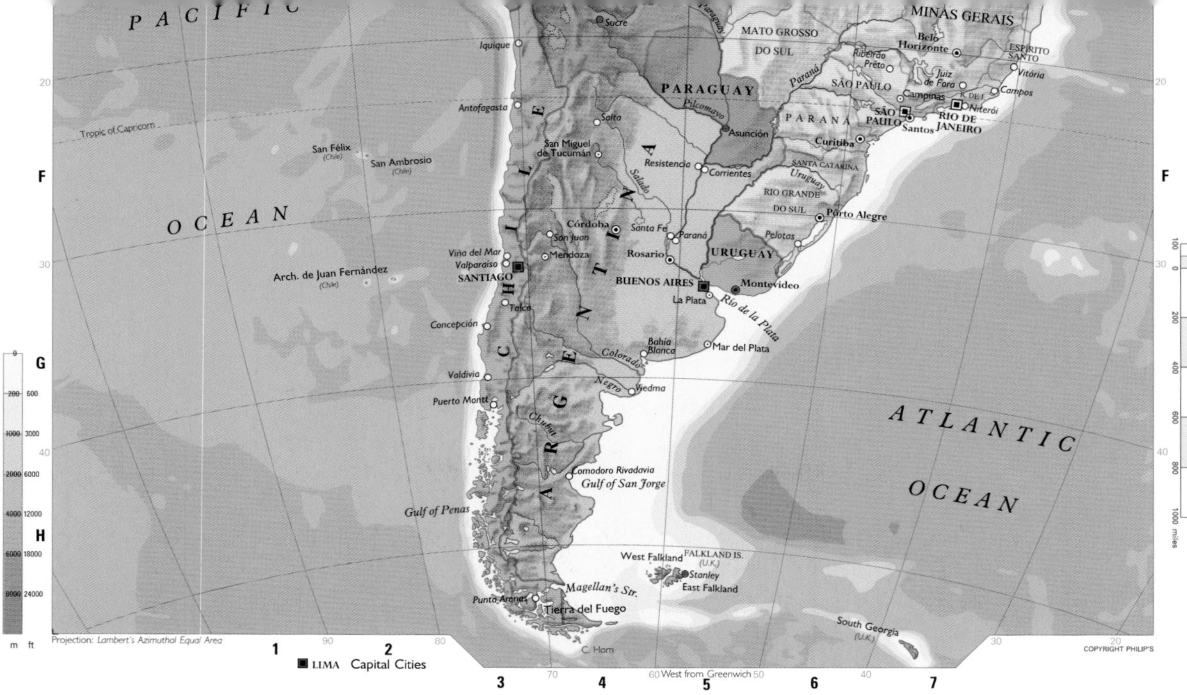

PACIFIC OCEAN

ATLANTIC OCEAN

CHILE

ARGENTINA

PARAGUAY

URUGUAY

MATO GROSSO DO SUL

MINAS GERAIS

ESPIRITO SANTO

SÃO PAULO

PARANÁ

SANTA CATARINA

RIO GRANDE DO SUL

R. DE J.

Sucre

Iquique

Antofagasta

Salta

San Miguel de Tucumán

Resistencia

Corrientes

Asunción

Pilcomayo

Paraguay

Paraná

Salado

Uruguay

Córdoba

San Juan

Mendoza

Santa Fe

Paraná

Rosario

Viña del Mar

Valparaíso

SANTIAGO

Talca

Concepción

BUENOS AIRES

La Plata

Montevideo

Río de la Plata

Mar del Plata

Bahía Blanca

Colorado

Negro

Viedma

Valdivia

Puerto Montt

Chubut

Comodoro Rivadavia

Gulf of San Jorge

Gulf of Penas

Magellan's Str.

Punta Arenas

Tierra del Fuego

C. Horn

West Falkland

FALKLAND IS. (U.K.)

Stanley

East Falkland

South Georgia (U.K.)

Belo Horizonte

Ribeirão Prêto

Juiz de Fora

Vitória

Campos

Campinas

SÃO PAULO

Santos

RIO DE JANEIRO

Niterói

Curitiba

Porto Alegre

Pelotas

Tropic of Capricorn

San Félix (Chile)

San Ambrosio (Chile)

Arch. de Juan Fernández (Chile)

F

G

H

1 2 3 4 5 6 7

20 30 40

90 80 70 60 West from Greenwich 50 40 30 20

m ft

0

200 600

1000 3000

2000 6000

4000 12000

6000 18000

8000 24000

Projection: Lambert's Azimuthal Equal Area

■ LIMA Capital Cities

100 0 200 400 600 800 1000 1200 1400 km

100 0 200 400 600 800 1000 miles

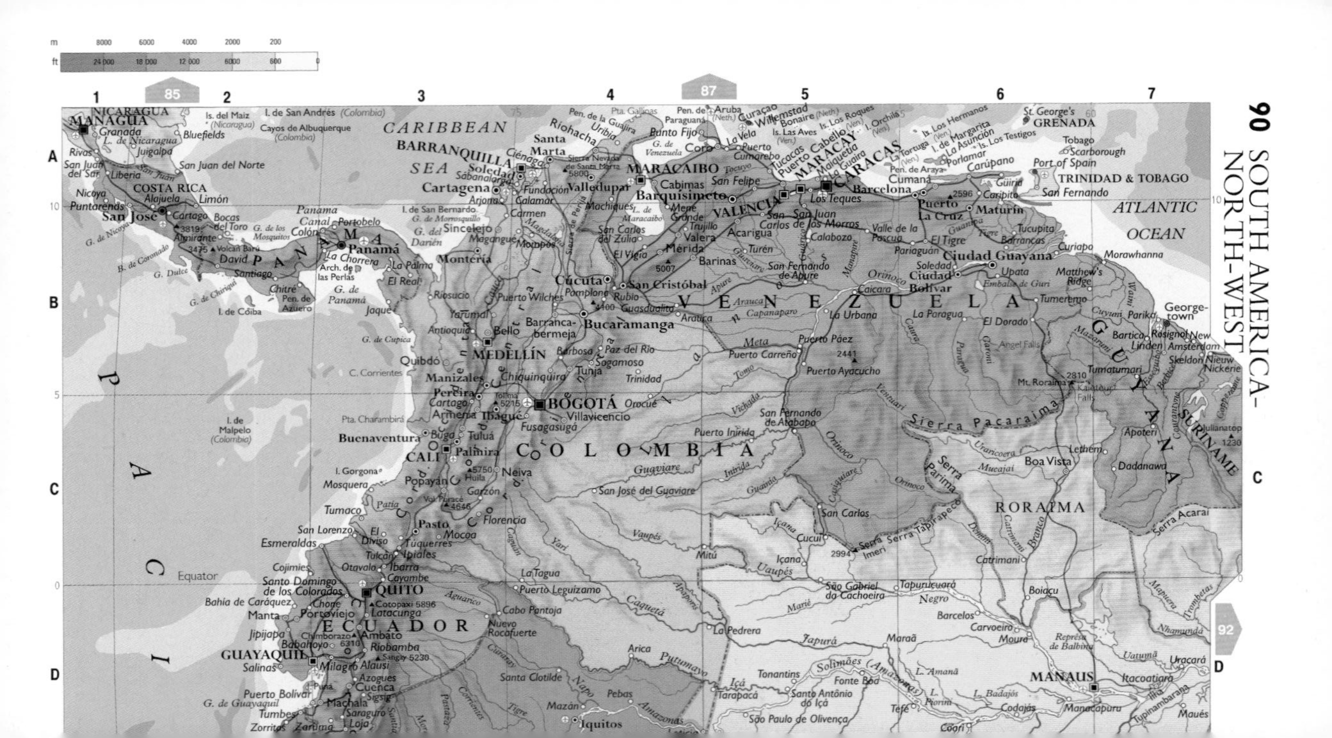

CARIBBEAN SEA
ATLANTIC OCEAN
PACIFIC
VENEZUELA
COLOMBIA
ECUADOR
GUYANA
SURINAME
PANAMA
COSTA RICA
NICARAGUA
TRINIDAD & TOBAGO
GRENADA
RORAIMA
CARACAS
BOGOTÁ
QUITO
MANAUS
MARACAIBO
BARRANQUILLA
MEDELLÍN
CALI
GUAYAQUIL
VALENCIA
MARACAY
Panamá
San José
MANAGUA
Georgetown
Port of Spain
Iquitos
Equator
85
87
92

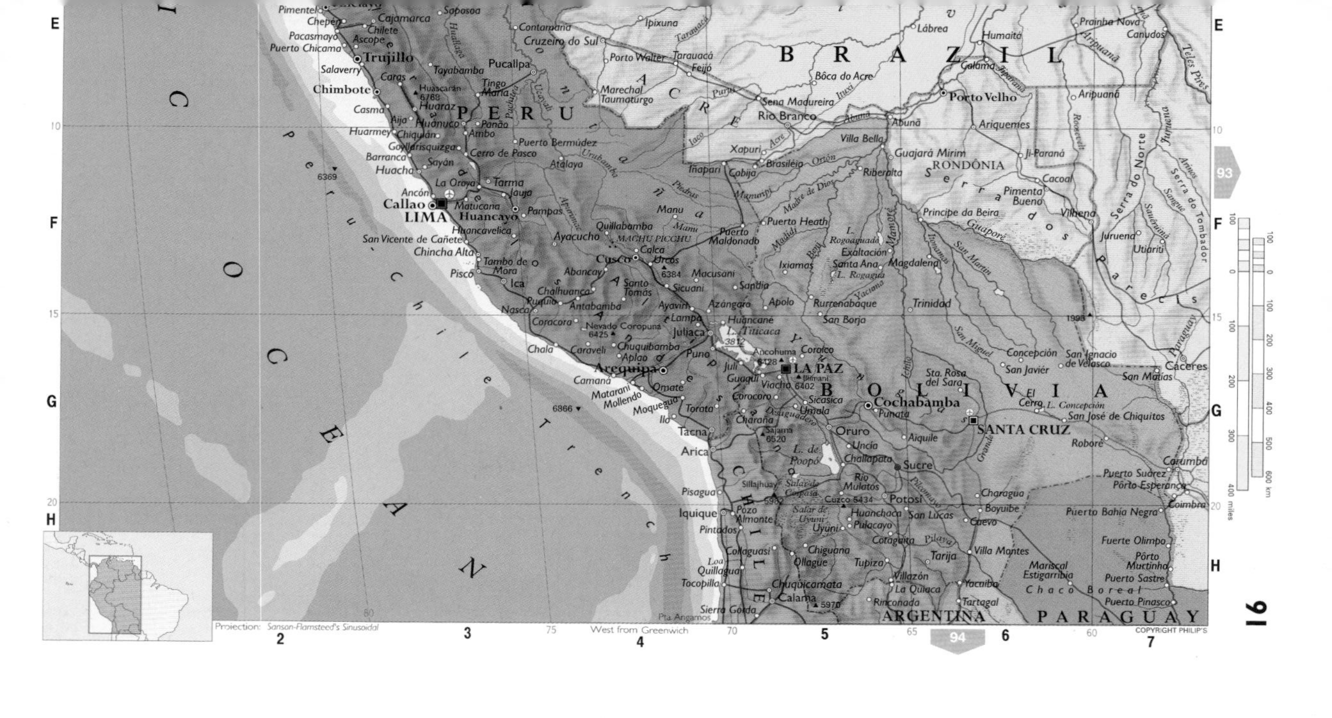

B R A Z I L
P E R U
B O L I V I A
C H I L E
P A R A G U A Y
ARGENTINA
A C R E
RONDÔNIA
O C E A N
Peru-Chile Trench
Serra dos Parecis
Serra do Norte
Serra do Tombador
Chaco Boreal
LIMA
LA PAZ
SANTA CRUZ
Sucre
Cochabamba
Arequipa
Cusco
Trujillo
Chimbote
Callao
Huancayo
Porto Velho
Rio Branco
Iquique
Arica
Tacna
Oruro
Potosí
Trinidad
Puno
Juliaca
Ica
Pisco
Huánuco
Cerro de Pasco
Pucallpa
Ayacucho
Abancay
Puerto Maldonado
Riberalta
Guajará Mirim
Cruzeiro do Sul
Cáceres
Corumbá
Tarija
Calama
Tocopilla
L. Titicaca
3812
L. de Poopó
Salar de Uyuni
Salar de Coipasa
Pimentel
Chepén
Pacasmayo
Puerto Chicama
Cajamarca
Chilete
Ascope
Salaverry
Casma
Huarmey
Barranca
Huacho
Ancón
San Vicente de Cañete
Chincha Alta
Tambo de Mora
Nasca
Chala
Camaná
Mollendo
Matarani
Moquegua
Ilo
Pisagua
Pta. Angamos
Sierra Gorda
Chuquicamata
Huascarán 6768
6369
6866
Nevado Coropuna 6425
Sajama 6520
Illimani 6402
Ancohuma 6428
Cuzco 6434
5970
5982
6384
1995
Juruena
Utiariti
Vilhena
Ariquemes
Ji-Paraná
Pimenta Bueno
Cacoal
Humaitá
Lábrea
Canutama
Prainha Nova
Aripuanã
Roosevelt
Teles Pires
Juruena
Arinos
Sangue
Sauêruiná
Guaporé
Mamoré
Madeira
Madre de Dios
Beni
Ucayali
Huallaga
Urubamba
Apurimac
Pilcomayo
Grande
Paraguay
San Ignacio de Velasco
San José de Chiquitos
Roboré
Concepción
San Javier
San Matías
Puerto Suárez
Pôrto Esperança
Coimbra
Puerto Bahía Negra
Fuerte Olimpo
Pôrto Murtinho
Puerto Sastre
Puerto Pinasco
Mariscal Estigarribia
Villa Montes
Yacuiba
Tartagal
Charagua
Boyuibe
Cuevo
Villazón
La Quiaca
Rinconada
Tupiza
Uyuni
Cotagaita
San Lucas
Huanchaca
Pulacayo
Challapata
Uncia
Río Mulatos
Aiquile
Punata
Sta. Rosa del Sara
El Cerro
L. Concepción
Magdalena
Exaltación
Santa Ana
L. Rogoaguado
L. Rogagua
Rurrenabaque
San Borja
Apolo
Ixiamas
Coroico
Viacha
Guaqui
Corocoro
Sicasica
Umala
Charaña
Puerto Heath
Cobija
Brasiléia
Xapuri
Iñapari
Sena Madureira
Tarauacá
Feijó
Bôca do Acre
Porto Walter
Marechal Taumaturgo
Ipixuna
Contamana
Puerto Bermúdez
Atalaya
Tingo María
Tarma
Jauja
La Oroya
Matucana
Huancavelica
Pampas
Quillabamba
MACHU PICCHU
Calca
Urcos
Sicuani
Ayaviri
Azángaro
Huancané
Lampa
Juli
Macusani
Sandia
Santo Tomás
Antabamba
Chalhuanca
Puquio
Coracora
Caravelí
Chuquibamba
Aplao
Omate
Torata
Pozo Almonte
Pintados
Collaguasi
Quillagua
Ollagüe
Chiguana
Sillajhuay
Manu
Tayabamba
Huaraz
Caras
Aija
Chiquián
Gollarisquizga
Sayán
Ambo
Panao
Sóposoa
Villa Bella
Abunã
Calama
Principe da Beira
Pôrto Velho
Projection: Sanson-Flamsteed's Sinusoidal
West from Greenwich
COPYRIGHT PHILIP'S
93
94
100 0 100 200 300 400 500 600 km
100 0 100 200 300 400 miles

# SOUTH AMERICA-NORTH-EAST

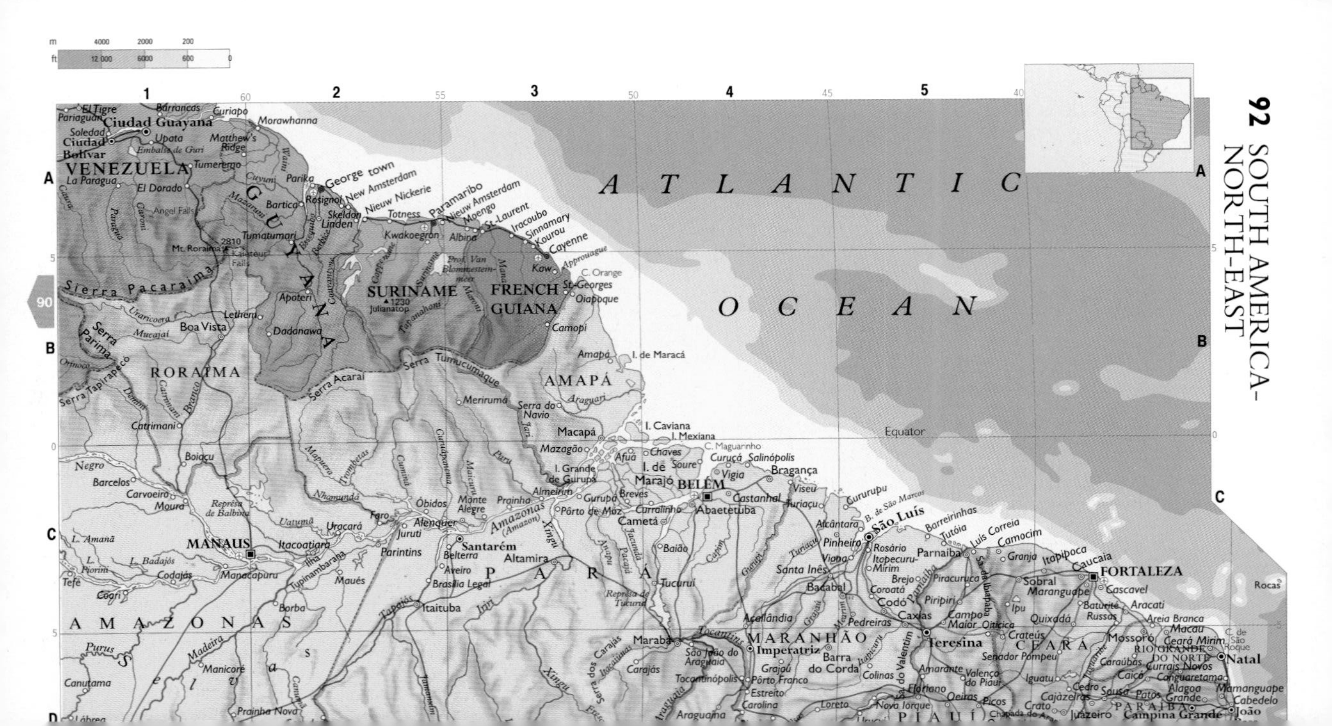

BRAZIL
RONDÔNIA
MATO GROSSO
Planalto do Mato Grosso
MATO GROSSO DO SUL
GOIÁS
TOCANTINS
BAHIA
MINAS GERAIS
SÃO PAULO
PARANÁ
RIO DE JANEIRO
ESPÍRITO SANTO
SERGIPE
BOLIVIA
PARAGUAY
ARGENTINA
BRASÍLIA
DIST. FED.
SALVADOR
BELO HORIZONTE
RIO DE JANEIRO
SÃO PAULO
CURITIBA
ASUNCIÓN
SANTA CRUZ
GOIÂNIA
CAMPINAS
SANTOS
Campo Grande
Cuiabá
Anápolis
Aracaju
Feira de Santana
Vitória
Vitória da Conquista
Montes Claros
Uberlândia
Uberaba
Juiz de Fora
Nova Iguaçu
Niterói
Petrópolis
Londrina
Maringá
Ponta Grossa
Joinville
Corrientes
Resistencia
Encarnación
Posadas
Salta
Foz do Iguaçu
Ciudad del Este
Ribeirão Prêto
São José do Rio Prêto
Guarulhos
Sorocaba
Jundiaí
Moji das Cruzes
São Bernardo do Campo
Serra dos Parecis
Serra do Roncador
Serra Formosa
Serra do Tombador
Serra do Espinhaço
Serra Geral de Goiás
Chaco Boreal
Chaco Central
Pantanal
Tropic of Capricorn
West from Greenwich
Projection: Sanson-Flamsteed's Sinusoidal
COPYRIGHT PHILIP'S
0 100 200 300 400 500 600 km
0 100 200 300 400 miles
91
94

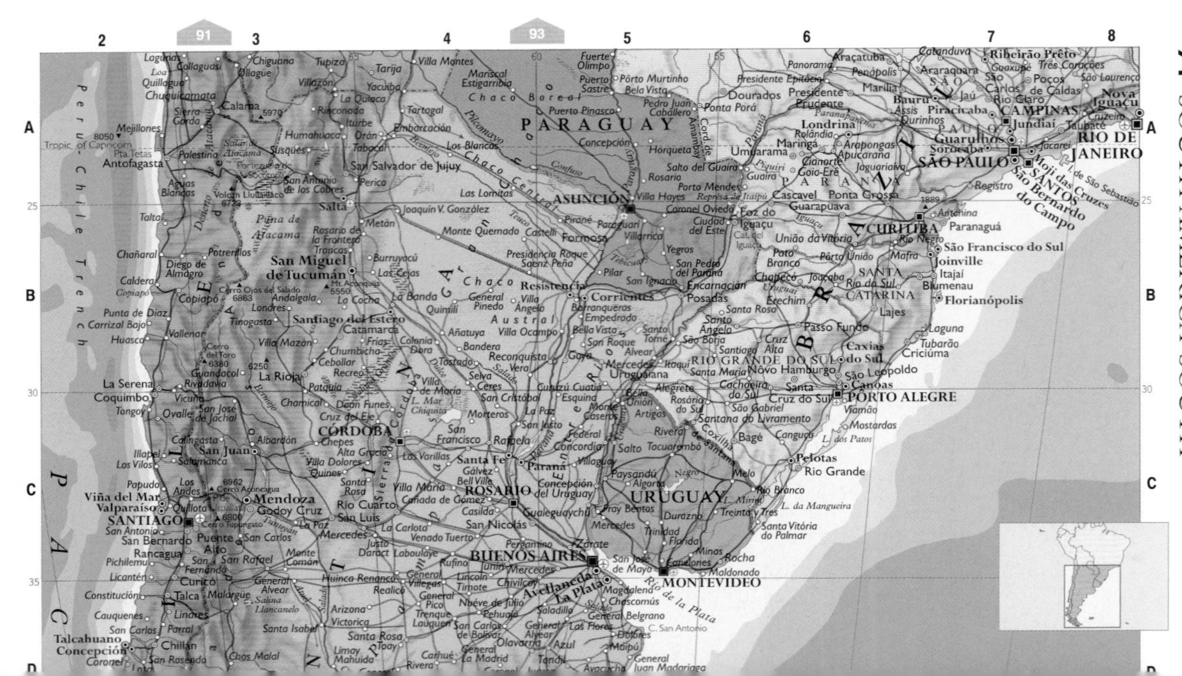
PARAGUAY
URUGUAY
ASUNCIÓN
MONTEVIDEO
BUENOS AIRES
SANTIAGO
SÃO PAULO
RIO DE JANEIRO
PORTO ALEGRE
CURITIBA
CÓRDOBA
ROSARIO
SANTOS
CAMPINAS
Mendoza
San Miguel de Tucumán
Santiago del Estero
Salta
Corrientes
Resistencia
Florianópolis
Antofagasta
Valparaíso
Concepción
Talcahuano
La Plata
Río de la Plata
Peru - Chile Trench
Tropic of Capricorn
91
93

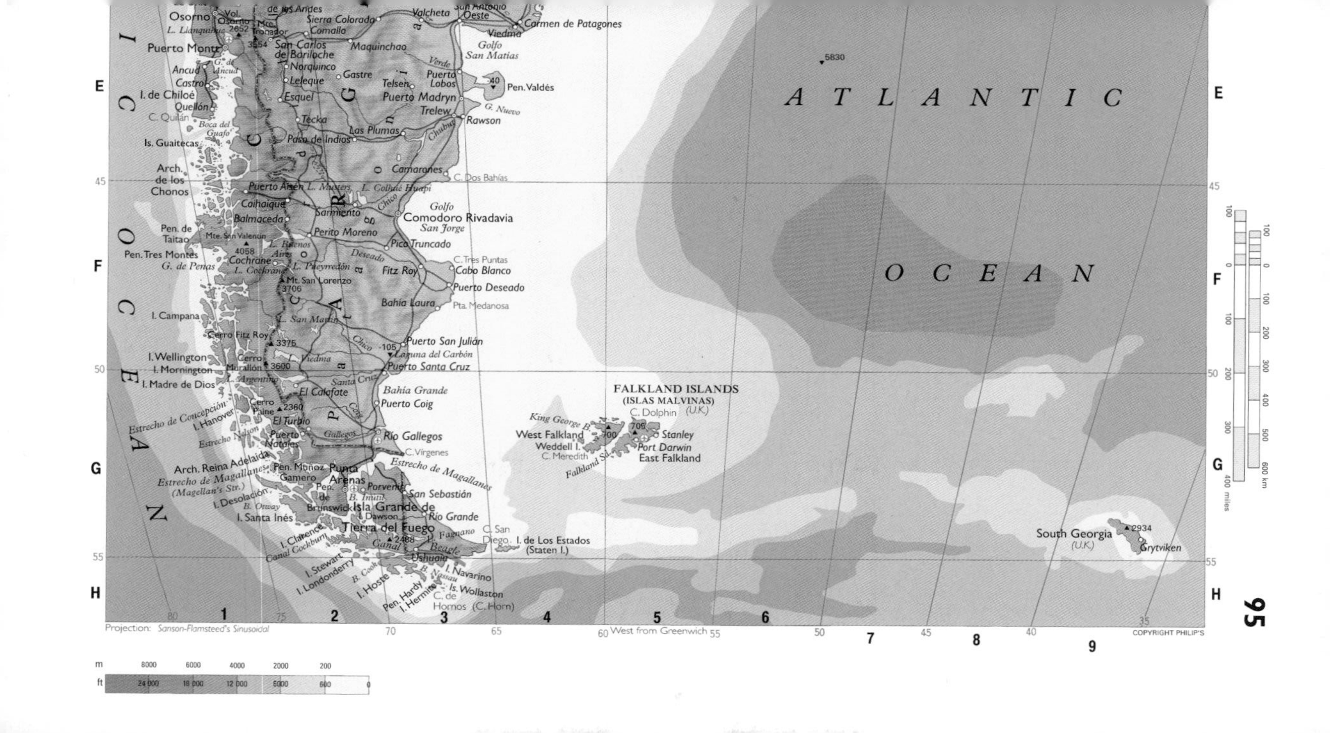
ATLANTIC OCEAN
PACIFIC OCEAN
FALKLAND ISLANDS
(ISLAS MALVINAS)
(U.K.)
C. Dolphin
King George B.
West Falkland
Weddell I.
C. Meredith
Falkland Sd.
Stanley
Port Darwin
East Falkland
South Georgia
(U.K.)
Grytviken
2934
5830
Osorno
Vol. Osorno
L. Llanquihue
Mte. Tronador
Puerto Montt
Ancud
Castro
I. de Chiloé
Quellón
C. Quilán
Boca del Guafo
Is. Guaitecas
Arch. de los Chonos
Pen. de Taitao
Mte. San Valentín
4058
Pen. Tres Montes
G. de Penas
Cochrane
L. Cochrane
I. Campana
Cerro Fitz Roy
3375
I. Wellington
I. Mornington
I. Madre de Dios
Cerro Murallón
3600
Estrecho de Concepción
I. Hanover
Estrecho Nelson
Arch. Reina Adelaida
Estrecho de Magallanes
(Magellan's Str.)
I. Desolación
B. Otway
I. Santa Inés
I. Clarence
Canal Cockburn
I. Stewart
I. Londonderry
B. Cook
I. Hoste
Pen. Hardy
I. Hermite
C. de Hornos (C. Horn)
Is. Wollaston
I. Navarino
B. Nassau
Beagle
Ushuaia
Canal
2488
Tierra del Fuego
Isla Grande de
Dawson
Pen. de Brunswick
B. Inútil
Punta Arenas
Porvenir
Pen. Muñoz Gamero
Puerto Natales
El Turbio
Cerro Paine
2360
El Calafate
L. Argentino
L. Viedma
Chico
Santa Cruz
Puerto Santa Cruz
Laguna del Carbón
-105
Puerto San Julián
Bahía Grande
Puerto Coig
Coig
Gallegos
Río Gallegos
C. Vírgenes
Estrecho de Magallanes
San Sebastián
Río Grande
L. Fagnano
C. San Diego
I. de Los Estados
(Staten I.)
L. San Martín
Mt. San Lorenzo
3706
L. Pueyrredón
L. Buenos Aires
Perito Moreno
Deseado
Fitz Roy
Pico Truncado
Bahía Laura
Pta. Medanosa
Puerto Deseado
Cabo Blanco
C. Tres Puntas
Golfo San Jorge
Comodoro Rivadavia
Balmaceda
Coihaique
Sarmiento
Puerto Aisén
L. Musters
L. Colhué Huapi
Chico
Camarones
C. Dos Bahías
Paso de Indios
Las Plumas
Chubut
Tecka
Esquel
Leleque
Norquinco
San Carlos de Bariloche
Gastre
Telsen
Puerto Madryn
Trelew
Rawson
G. Nuevo
Puerto Lobos
Pen. Valdés
40
Golfo San Matías
Verde
Maquinchao
Comallo
Sierra Colorada
Valcheta
San Antonio Oeste
Viedma
Carmen de Patagones
2652
3554
Projection: Sanson-Flamsteed's Sinusoidal
West from Greenwich
COPYRIGHT PHILIP'S
m
ft
8000
6000
4000
2000
200
24 000
18 000
12 000
6000
600
0
100
0
100
200
300
400
500
600 km
100
0
100
200
300
400 miles

# ANTARCTICA

100 0 200 400 600 800 1000 1200 1400 km

100 0 200 400 600 800 1000 miles

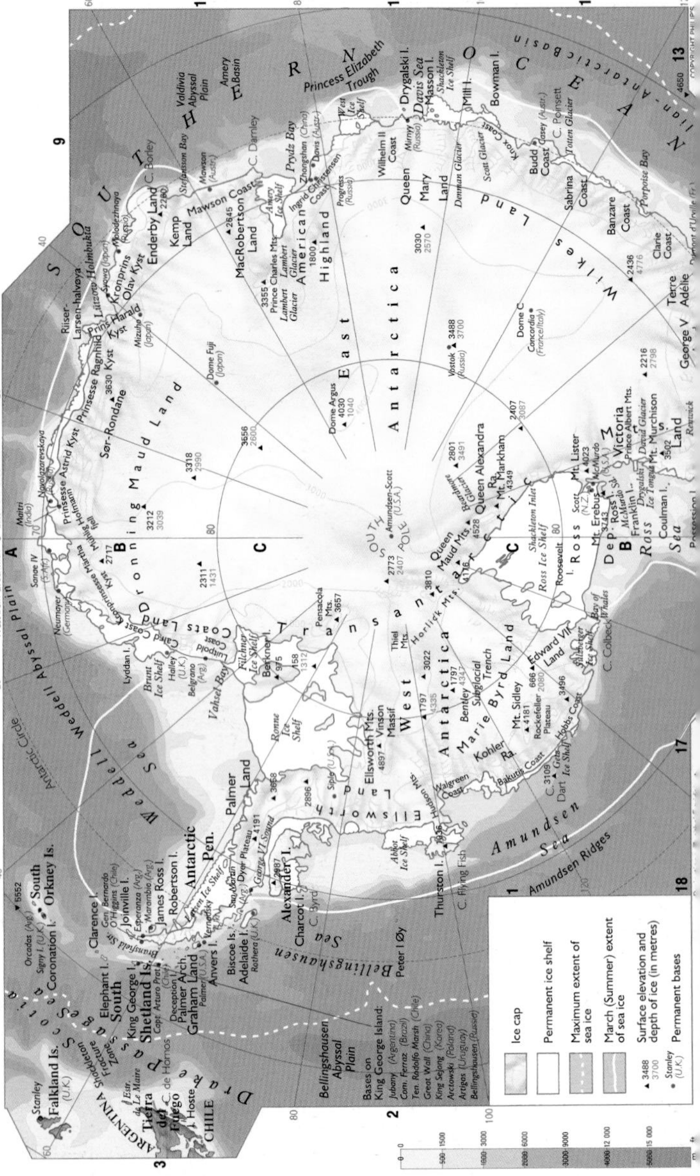

Bases on King George Island:
- Jubany (Argentina)
- Com. Ferraz (Brazil)
- Ten. Rodolfo Marsh (Chile)
- Great Wall (China)
- King Sejong (Korea)
- Arctowski (Poland)
- Artigas (Uruguay)
- Bellingshausen (Russia)

Ice cap

Permanent ice shelf

Maximum extent of sea ice

March (Summer) extent of sea ice

▲ 3488 3700 Surface elevation and depth of ice (in metres)

• Stanley (U.K.) Permanent bases

# Index to Map Pages

The index contains the names of all the principal places and features shown on the world maps. Physical features composed of a proper name (Erie) and a description (Lake) are positioned alphabetically by the proper name. The description is positioned after the proper name and is usually abbreviated:

Erie, L. **76 C5**

Where a description forms part of a settlement or administrative name, however, it is always written in full and put in its true alphabetical position:

Lake Charles **81 D7**

Names beginning St. are alphabetized under Saint, but Sankt, Sant, Santa and San are all spelt in full and are alphabetized accordingly.

The number in bold type which follows each name in the index refers to the number of the map page where that feature or place will be found. This is usually the largest scale at which the place or feature appears.

The letter and figure which are in bold type immediately after the page number give the grid square on the map page, within which the feature is situated.

Rivers are indexed to their mouths or confluences, and carry the symbol → after their names. The following symbols are also used in the index: ■ country, ▨ overseas territory or dependency, □ first order administrative area, △ national park.

## A

## B

## D

## E

## F



## G

## H

## I

## J



## K

# L

## M

## N

## O

## P

# T